Teaching and Thinking About Curriculum

Critical Inquiries

Teaching and Thinking About Curriculum

Critical Inquiries

JAMES T. SEARS
J. DAN MARSHALL

EDITORS

Foreword by Nel Noddings

Teachers College, Columbia University
New York • London

Published by Teachers College Press, 1234 Amsterdam Avenue, New York, NY 10027

Library of Congress Cataloging-in-Publication Data

Teaching and thinking about curriculum : critical inquiries / James T.
   Sears, J. Dan Marshall, editors ; foreword by Nel Noddings.
      p.   cm.
   Includes bibliographical references.
   ISBN 0-8077-2969-8. —ISBN 0-8077-2968-X (pbk.)
   1. Education—Curricula—Study and teaching.   2. Teacher
participation in curriculum planning.   I. Sears, James T.,
1951–
II. Marshall, J. Dan.
LB1570.T337   1989   89-38167
371.3'078—dc20   CIP

ISBN 0-8077-2969-8
ISBN 0-8077-2968-X (pbk.)

Printed on acid-free paper

Manufactured in the United States of America

94 93 92 91 90 89   1 2 3 4 5 6

Contents

Foreword

NEL NODDINGS

Beginning students of teaching, education, or even curriculum itself often think of curriculum as the written material to be learned in a particular subject. They already have some familiarity with curricula in school mathematics, English, and social studies, for example, and expect that their education courses will enlighten them about the construction of these materials and the ideas underlying them. Thus, students are often surprised to hear that *curriculum* is itself a field of study. Some go well beyond surprise to express skepticism and scorn for such an idea.

This book should go a long way toward removing misconceptions and negative attitudes about curriculum. The editors have gathered together a wide-ranging set of essays that challenge notions held not only by novices but also by veteran theorists whose work concentrates on describing, explaining, and refining naïve conceptions in education. The very structure of the book rejects the sharp distinction, often accepted by these theorists, between curriculum and teaching.

The book is about curriculum as a field of study and teaching. Through both explicit and implicit means, this volume suggests at once that curriculum and teaching are not easily separable and that a thinking, teaching self cannot be deftly plucked out of either teaching or curriculum and set aside. Curriculum is thoroughly mixed up in teaching, and teaching is inextricable from teachers. In some circles, such blurring of boundaries is either heresy or nonsense. Here it is a refined form of common sense and, further, its acceptance adds enormous fascination to the field of study.

Acting on the belief that curriculum, teaching, and persons are to some degree inextricable from each other, Jim Sears and Dan Marshall have asked the contributing authors to describe their own backgrounds, relationships with mentors, and special areas of interest. This autobiographical feature of the text should help students to understand that curriculum is indeed a field of study, one around which a distinctive community has grown up. As initiates in this community, students will learn something from this book about the community's history and language; they will hear some of its jokes and learn about its conceptual feuds. Further, as they read and discuss these essays, they may become aware that a special relation also exists between writer and reader. A curriculum about curriculum will be constructed by this work as teachers, students, and writers interact.

There is a post-modern flavor to this book in both its organization and the individual essays. Readers will learn that various perspectives can be taken and that each discloses something new and special about curriculum. However, readers gradually will begin to realize that it is not just a matter of perspective-taking. We do not relinquish our selves as we adopt a new standpoint, rather, we experience our existence as multiple selves. We begin to understand how the self that identifies with a particular community may come into conflict with a teacher-self or a student-self. We may, for example, resist taking on the language of one community because doing so might force us to abandon—or be abandoned by—another community. Thus we catch a glimpse of the complexity not only of curriculum making but of self-building.

Readers of this book should develop a well-grounded distrust of simple causal relations. Does community shape curriculum, or does curriculum shape community? Even at the descriptive level, the question suggests an artificial simplicity that is challenged by these essays. Clearly, curriculum and community shape each other and, further, their interaction gives continuous birth to new curricula and new communities.

Should community shape curriculum, or *should* curriculum shape community? When we understand that their mutual influence is inevitable, we can begin to ask more intelligent questions about the nature and limits of each set of influences. Although some thinkers still want to insist that we cannot derive "should" statements from "is" statements (and in a technical but almost empty sense they are right), many of us now believe that it is a far greater error to construct a set of values entirely separated from factual conditions. Such values are rather like hats that keep blowing off in the wind—they're not much use in real, hard life.

The writers of this volume continually draw to our attention the centrality of human values, desires, and encounters. What do we want or value as teachers, as students, as scholars, and as persons? Why do we want or value these things? How are our desires and needs connected to what we do, and the shaping of our work? And how does our work shape our values? These tough, sophisticated questions are handled here in a conversational and accessible manner. Indeed, the emphasis on conversation is striking throughout. The book is so constructed that each part concludes with a *conversation parmi animateurs,* in which curriculum scholars comment on the preceding chapters, their own lives as professionals in the curriculum field, and the future of curriculum. These conversations are both entertaining and enlightening.

The basic theme of this book is empowerment. There are, however, multiple understandings of what the word empowerment means. I've sometimes heard administrators say that empowering teachers means "helping them to do a better job," but often both the job and the evaluation of "better" performance are defined by someone other than teachers. For these authors, however, the word embodies notions of autonomy, reflection, and significant choice. Teachers who are *empowered* should have a greater sense of their own power to affect curriculum, students, and their own mode of working. In this book, the empowerment of teachers is taken seriously; the premise is that teachers should acquire more intellectual, personal, and professional power from studying curriculum. Ultimately, this bespeaks a radical purpose and, if successful, a revolutionary result. Teachers so empowered will not willingly play a technical role near the bottom of a semiprofessional hierarchy. However, along with a sense of professional power and pride, they should also develop a deep feeling of humility in the face of unavoidable complexity, and a steady appreciation for cooperative encounters with all those involved in the educational enterprise.

I conclude by saying that students and teachers may have fun with this book as well as learn something from it. Reading it should prove to be an encounter of the empowering kind!

Acknowledgments

Many people have played important roles in the creation of this book. We begin by thanking the many curriculum teachers who responded to our initial request for ideas and a number of our curriculum peers who assisted us along the way, especially Robert Bullough, Dick Gardiner, Paul Grant, Sue Jungck, Ken Kantor, Tom Kelly, Paul Klohr, Craig Kridel, Ethel Migra, Michael Schiro, and Jenny Wojcik.

For their commitment to this somewhat unusual project and their tolerance of our frequent intrusions, we are indebted to the writers whose chapters make up the core of this book. We also wish to acknowledge the encouragement and support of the other curriculum scholars whose voices are heard throughout the text.

Sarah Biondello, Acquisitions Editor at Teachers College Press, initiated this opportunity and has worked closely with us from start to finish. Her advocacy during those many months was a key ingredient in our pursuit of this vision.

One message embedded in this book is the importance of the collective history and mentorship within the curriculum field. Each of us owes much to our curriculum teachers, especially Norm Overly and O. L. Davis, Jr., who both modeled and encouraged reflective, interdisciplinary inquiry. Working with our own students, we strive to carry on a tradition Overly and Davis inherited from their mentors, Paul Klohr and Harold Drummond—who grew from the support and challenge of their mentors, Harold Alberty and Harold Rugg. . . .

Finally, to Bob Williamson and Tara Fulton, whose faith and emotional support have long played a major role in our lives, we remain forever grateful.

INTRODUCTION

1

Approaches to Curriculum Theory and Practice

M. FRANCES KLEIN
University of Southern California

The field of curriculum is perceived in many different ways. To many—even some who work daily with the challenges, issues, problems, and rewards of curriculum development in our schools and colleges—it is viewed as controversial, complex, fluid, and ill-defined. It is seen as even more illusive and overwhelming, or perhaps worse, as very simplistic, to those who are uninitiated in or just beginning to study curriculum. Still others may view it with great puzzlement, as did one Ph.D. candidate in English education who asked me in great sincerity, "If you don't study English, math, science, or social studies, what is it that you do study?" In recent times the field has been called moribund (Schwab, 1970), stagnant (Kliebard, 1975), and alive and well (Klein, 1986). It does not take long for a beginning student of curriculum to determine that very different perceptions exist about what one does when "doing curriculum" and how well it is done; that scholars refer to different phenomena in their work, even though all label it curriculum; and that a diversity of beliefs and value positions are expressed in the writings of many people who study the field. Our persistence in and dedication to the work of curriculum development attest to its fundamental importance regardless of how it is viewed or labeled.

In this time of school reform, the importance of curriculum—the substance of schooling—is once again reaffirmed, and attention is clearly focused on it by many groups. Those who teach and learn about curriculum are especially concerned with this timely emphasis and the implications for how our field is viewed. With great vigor, we continue our attempts to conceptualize the field, identify fundamental tasks, debate important issues, and slowly extend our knowledge and understanding of what it is we are about.

The apparent conflicts surrounding much of curriculum theory, discourse, and practice may be confusing to many educators. Our field appears to be muddled by the diversity of seemingly conflicting positions put forward by highly respected and persuasive scholars and practitioners. The work of some prestigious scholars is belittled by others; theoretical approaches of one type are strongly rejected by many; and the field seems beset by scholars and practitioners who blindly advocate one exclusive set of beliefs and practices without ever acknowledging the work of others who see the field differently.

Yet, those who diligently study curriculum come to recognize that the diversity is not as great as it first appears to be. There clearly are different ways of viewing the field, but at the same time there are groups of curriculum workers who share persistent values and belief systems, consistently address some fundamental themes and issues in education, and identify similar tasks or decisions to be made and the appropriate people to make them. There does appear to be some general structure within the field, even though the specifics are widely debated and evolve over time within a given group.

Most of the beliefs and positions within the field seem to differ primarily on a few basic areas to which scholars and practitioners consistently turn to justify, study, articulate, and implement their positions. Four fundamental sources are most readily identifiable:

1. The importance of self-development
2. The teacher as a basic source of curriculum knowledge
3. The interrelationships of the norms, values, and expectations of our society and schooling
4. An emphasis on the acquisition of knowledge and the primary role of subject matter

With some understanding of how these fundamental sources of curriculum beliefs, questions, and practices structure the field, it does not seem to be quite so diverse, confusing, argumentative, and perverse.

It is the range of the positions developed by scholars; their values, beliefs, issues, tasks, and practices; and the way in which they provide some structure to the field, which is the focus of this publication. In this chapter, I will identify some persistent beliefs and value commitments made by groups of curriculum scholars, and I will suggest their importance to our work in the study and practice of curriculum. Ultimately, it is you, the student and teacher of curriculum, who must come to terms with this range of beliefs, values, sources of knowledge, and articulated positions about curriculum. You must accept or adapt an existing view of curriculum, or create one of your own, to deal adequately (that is, clearly and consistently) with the complexity of the field.

As a beginning student of the field many years ago, I remember being intrigued by the questions raised by John Goodlad as he worked with my school faculty to improve our curriculum. His questions made me think more deeply about schooling than I ever had before—even in the daily practice of curriculum decision making in my own elementary school classroom. His questions imposed some structure on the field for me, helped me to clarify and prioritize daily practices, and identified a process that enabled me to plan more effectively for my students' education. This practical introduction led me to the curriculum field and convinced me of the importance of curriculum to American education. I became immersed in the field during doctoral studies under the expert and highly influential guidance of Goodlad and Louise Tyler at UCLA. Both introduced me to the field of formal curriculum studies, helped me examine the interrelationships of theory and practice in far more insightful ways than I previously had, and inspired me to adopt a persistent attitude of inquiry into the field. Their strong influence in my study of curriculum, teaching about it, and practice in the field, and their mentoring as I extended my work in a rich variety of ways have continued throughout my career.

As I worked in curriculum theory, research, teaching, and practice, I became increasingly aware of alternative ways of viewing curriculum and that a few scholars were writing about curriculum in very different ways from the rest. These scholars raised different questions, espoused alternative values and belief systems, proposed different purposes and practices for curriculum, and drew upon fields other than the familiar (to me) behavioral and social sciences as a basis for curriculum thought. Although advised by a well-meaning colleague at one point not to pay any attention to "that other group of people" because they had no substance, I continued to study and tried to keep abreast of the rapidly growing body of literature on alternative views of curriculum. When I had serious questions about the effort I was spending on studying ideas that were significantly different from mine, I kept in mind Tyler's admonition never to dismiss scholars' ideas, however strange and different from mine, without serious consideration, because they too had spent their lives studying curriculum.

These ideas remained largely an intellectual curiosity until I was invited to write two different encyclopedia articles, one on independent study (Klein, 1982) and the other on curriculum design (Klein, 1985). Those articles forced me to consider alternative views in an organized, conceptual fashion, and although I began to see more possibilities and desirability for them, I still retained allegiance to my roots in the more traditional view. Now I strongly believe that these alternative views deserve very serious consideration by every student and teacher of curriculum, even though you may disagree with parts of some and perhaps even reject others outright. Only by studying all the positions can you be aware of the options that are available and thus develop a firm, informed commitment to your own beliefs and values about curriculum.

VIEWS OF CURRICULUM THEORIZING

In spite of the diversity of thought and the conceptual conflicts among curricularists, there are some general points of agreement. Two of them are

1. What we do in curriculum is of fundamental importance to our students and society, the process of education, and the development of our own field.
2. Curriculum development is a heavily value-laden activity and is never value-free.

There is also general agreement that important as curriculum is, there are no individual well-developed theories, let alone a unified comprehensive theory of the entire field to help guide us in our work. Attempts have been made to formulate theories, and theorizing activities based on alternative views continue, but these are only tentative beginnings in developing comprehensive theories about curriculum. We proceed in our work without the benefits of established theories, but with the help of considerable efforts to formulate consistent sets of beliefs and practices.

Various labels have been attached to groups of curricularists who have compatible views and conceptualizations of curriculum, and these will be reflected in the discussion in this section. These labels should help clarify the field conceptually by showing similarities and differences among the works of scholars and practitioners. Labels of any kind, however, are helpful but incomplete terms to use. A label helps us group the diversity of thought and practice according to some criteria, but a single label is rarely representative of all aspects of an individual's contributions to a group and can even erroneously represent some aspects of his or her work. Thus, it is important to remember that the categories and labels should not be viewed as either/or positions. Some curricularists could be classified in more than one group, depending on which one of their works is focused on. It is also important to recognize that within any single label or category of scholars there is considerable diversity.

Traditional Approach

The most dominant, persistent, and generally accepted theoretical approach to curriculum is the one familiar to all of us—we experienced it during our own education and undoubtedly studied it somewhere in our preparation as professional educators. For most curricularists this is the position to which they were first introduced. Many study it exclusively and proceed in their work with a firm commitment to it. Those who emphasize the similar types of curricular outcomes called for by this approach have been called by a variety of terms: traditionalists (Pinar, 1978), structuralists (Huenecke, 1982), intellectuals (Schubert, 1980), and academics (Gay, 1980). Those who discuss compatible ways to develop curriculum to achieve the outcomes desired by traditionalists have been called technologists (Eisner, 1985), behaviorists (Klein, 1980), and social behaviorists (Schubert, 1980) because the processes they advocate reflect a scientific, reductionistic, linear, and rational approach to curriculum development. (Confusion about labels seems to occur in the literature between the desired outcomes dealing with subject matter and intellectual development and the processes of developing curricula using a scientific, technological paradigm. Interchangeable labels are given for both, but I consider the outcomes desired and processes of curriculum development to be conceptually distinct, although highly interrelated.) The work of this group of curricularists is easily found. Their publications are abundant, most practice is based on it, and their position is strongly supported by impressive research compatible with the approach. It is represented by the work of scholars such as Franklin Bobbitt, Ralph Tyler, Hilda Taba, George Beauchamp, John Goodlad, and Francis Hunkins.

This position emphasizes the role of organized subject matter, often in the form of the disciplines, in the outcomes and processes of curriculum development. The outcomes desired deal primarily with predetermined, logically organized skills or bodies of knowledge that all students are to learn and with the development of their intellectual capacities. The importance of the affective domain is noted in rhetoric, but is usually conspicuously absent in practice.

To develop curricula from this perspective, a behavioristic, reductionistic (reducing complex tasks to smaller component ones for teaching and learning), scientific, technological, rational process is used. The curricularists' responsibilities are to organize effectively and efficiently what is to be taught and learned. The curriculum is carefully planned and organized prior to classroom engagement: Goals and objectives are determined; content is selected and logically organized, often in the form of a textbook; teachers are trained to present it efficiently and effectively; and student learning is objectively measured as to a way to determine the effectiveness of the curriculum.

The teacher is seen as the conveyor of the curriculum, which is planned at a higher level of authority than the classroom. Teachers are expected to implement the planned curriculum faithfully, and implementation problems become important topics of study. Teaching is guided by principles gleaned from research, and learning is viewed as predictable and measurable (Klein, 1986). Teachers are prepared to be authorities in what students are expected to learn, and the teachers' task is to impart their knowledge with a high degree of professional and pedagogical skill. The role of the students is to learn, with little variation, the material presented. External motivators such as grades, tangible rewards, and threats are used to ensure that students do, indeed, learn what is expected of them.

Curriculum workers subscribe to this dominant view of curriculum for many reasons. It may be the only one they ever study and know about; it is compatible with many forces in our culture; it is advocated by prestigious lay persons, scholars, practitioners, and theorists; and it is compatible with traditional expectations of schooling. Practice based on this value position helps students achieve many of the goals of schooling advocated in the current so-called reforms. The spotlight today is clearly on this conception of curriculum.

Alternative Theoretical Positions

There are curricularists, however, who do not agree with this approach, but view curriculum in alternative ways. They are diverse in their beliefs, but united in their discomfort with the traditional approach. Their views, which in the past have not been prominent in the literature, practice, research, or calls for reform about curriculum, are featured in this book. Those who work from alternative theoretical positions start with different beliefs and values about curriculum; possess different visions about what schools ought to do; base their work on fields such as art, phenomenology, psychoanalysis, literature, critical theory, and neo-Marxism; and believe that the functions, purposes, and practices of curriculum ought to be very different from those typically found in our schools.

The mainstream organizations and journals were not initially receptive to the work of those with alternative curriculum perspectives. It was necessary, for example, for them to begin a special interest group (now known as Critical Issues in Curriculum) within the American Education Research Association and to start their own journal, *The Journal of Curriculum Theorizing,* to support discussion and dissemination of their work. Their efforts to communicate have been rewarded over the years, and they have made dramatic gains in their recognition and involvement in major publications and organizations. But their work was somewhat scattered in the curriculum literature, and until recently was not often presented in publications specializing in their views. (There are a few clear exceptions to this generalization. See, for example, Macdonald and Zaret, 1975; Pinar, 1975; Grumet and Pinar, 1976; and Pinar, 1988.)

This book reflects the importance that those with alternative perspectives have now achieved in curriculum discourse. Each of the authors views curriculum in unique ways. Some of these scholars might be loosely referred to as reconceptualists (a label that makes many scholars, both within and outside of the group, uncomfortable). Reconceptualists often emphasize two of the curriculum perspectives noted earlier: the development of self as the major function of curriculum, and the interrelationships of the norms, values, and expectations of the broader society and schooling. Other curricularists, not always identified as reconceptualists but also disagreeing with the traditional approach to curriculum, form a different group, also mentioned earlier, which emphasizes the importance of the teacher in developing knowledge about curriculum. Yet another group studies the accumulated wisdom and heritage of the field from perspectives that differ from the traditional approach. It is these shared characteristics that provided a structure for grouping the authors in this book. The remainder of this section discusses briefly each of these groups of curricularists. Each group represents a tentatively distinguishable, similar, but still evolving position about what is important in curriculum and what is needed as a basis to teach and learn about curriculum. The caution should be repeated, though, that in their other writings, some of these authors may also share characteristics that overlap with scholars and practitioners from other groups.

Scholars Emphasizing Self-Understanding. One group of contemporary curriculum theorizers base their approach to curriculum not on the behavioral or natural sciences as the traditionalists do, but on fields such as phenomenology, psychoanalysis, literature, and art. These scholars share a basic orientation that emphasizes the development of the individual and the creation of personal meaning in learning. They have been called reconceptualists (Pinar, 1978), experientialists (Gay, 1980; Schubert, 1980), humanists (Klein, 1980), generic theorizers (Huenecke, 1982), and self-actualizers (Eisner, 1985). Focus on the learning of sacrosanct subject matter—that is, subject matter so important that all students must learn it—is minimized, if not rejected outright. Organized subject matter is important only insofar as each student affirms its relevance to him or her. Those who fall within this group are not anti-intellectual nor do they minimize our accumulated wisdom and knowledge. However, they do not believe intellectual development or learning for any purpose is best achieved by having students acquire a preordained body of knowledge and skills on a schedule imposed by others outside of the classroom or through teachers' behaviors that are based on research they consider alien to both teaching and learning. Instead, they advocate the personalization of curriculum. Subject matter is important only to the degree that students have experiences through which they can attach personal meaning to what is learned. Reflection on the personal meaning of content and experience by each student is highlighted.

Learning is viewed as holistic, not as hierarchical discrete tasks within specific domains of human behavior, and learners are believed to be intrinsically motivated. The role of the teacher is usually perceived as that of a co-learner with students, pursuing topics of personal interest that students and teacher have selected together. The curriculum emerges through a process of teacher–student planning. Curriculum thus comes from inside students and cannot be successfully imposed on them by outside "authorities." Classroom practices reflecting this conception allow ample time for self-examination and personal reflection in various forms and ways. Schools must be organized to help students achieve personal growth and accept their own personal identities—not on the basis of easy administration that denies personal characteristics and interests of students. These scholars, who build upon some of the work of Dewey, include Paul Klohr, James Macdonald, Ted Aoki, Esther Zaret, Bernice Wolfson, William Pinar, Max van Manen, and Madeleine Grumet. Their most distinguishing shared contribution to our field is their commitment to helping students grow and become self-actualizing persons.

Scholars Emphasizing the Role of the Teacher. Yet another group of scholars whose work moves away from traditional curriculum scholarship emphasize the importance of the teacher's role in the curriculum. As schooling is conceived and practiced today, the teacher is a very powerful influence on what students learn. Attempts in the past have tried to by-pass the teacher by introducing programmed and "teacher-proof" materials, but with little success. The influence of the teacher on curriculum and the teacher as a source of fundamental curriculum knowledge is beginning to be recognized and seriously studied. Scholars sharing this perspective emphasize the practical knowledge and wisdom about curriculum that teachers develop as they make myriad classroom decisions daily. These scholars clearly recognize the teacher as a major curriculum decision maker and reject views of the teacher as merely a technician who is supposed to implement a curriculum planned on high. They advocate helping teachers become even more skillful curriculum developers, and expect curricula to reflect the uniqueness of every group of teachers and students. These scholars, who build upon the work of Joseph Schwab, include Michael Connelly, Jean Clandinin, Freema Elbaz, and Joel Weiss.

Scholars Emphasizing Society.   Others who are also called reconceptualists or sometimes social reconstructionists (Eisner, 1985) emphasize the importance of the interaction of societal norms, values, and expectations in curriculum and schooling. Many share a basis for their work in neo-Marxist thought and base their curriculum research and practice on critical theory. The intent of the curriculum is to help build a better society and improved human relationships—to foster social change through the strong involvement of the surrounding community.

These scholars emphasize the impact of societal forces on the structures of schooling and on both the implicit and explicit curriculum. They are critical of the traditional curriculum and the existing structures of schooling that help perpetuate the current educational system, which they see as unequal and maintaining the status quo in society. They persistently point out that the structures used in schooling (grade levels, textbooks, standardized tests, and teacher–administrator relationships, for example) are created by humans and thus are amenable to change. These structures should not be accepted as givens of American education, but challenged whenever they impede the development of the type of society we want to create in our schools, communities, states, nations, and world. Since social realities are constructed, they must be carefully studied by students so that they can be modified to help improve the world. Thus, curriculum workers within this group advocate using social issues and problems as essential content for the curriculum in order to help develop a more just and humane social order. Subject matter for them comes from issues and problems in the social and physical world around the students and what must be done to improve it. Organized content fields in the form of the disciplines are important to the extent that they can be brought to bear on issues and problems under study.

This group resists the deprofessionalization of teachers through some of the practices of the traditional approach, such as building "teacher-proof" curricula, defining teaching as a technology, developing curricula at levels beyond the school and classroom that are to be implemented regardless of local conditions and values, and imposing on all students a common core curriculum, as usually defined. Rather, they emphasize the importance of the participatory curriculum for each classroom, in which teachers and students would experience the democratic process—not where students would study democratic processes as intellectual content.

These scholars, who also build upon the work of John Dewey as well as George Counts, Harold Rugg, and Theodore Brameld, include Michael

Apple, Alex Molnar, Jean Anyon, Henry Giroux, and Nancy King.[1] They persistently and effectively document the effect of curricular and schooling practices on students and our society. These scholars raise our consciousness about the assumptions we make and the values we hold about curriculum, and the relationship of these to the broader society—as it exists now and as it might exist in a more ideal form.

Scholars Emphasizing Curriculum as a Field of Study.   There is yet another group of scholars who view curriculum in alternative ways. These scholars focus their study on the overall field of curriculum, that is, its history and accumulated knowledge. They emphasize the contributions of scholars who were forerunners of current alternative views of curriculum, and suggest different interpretations of curriculum history and the impact of historical events in curriculum on our knowledge. They document important developments in the field and highlight critical issues that must be viewed from varying perspectives, not just the traditional one. These scholars include O. L. Davis, Jr., Herbert Kliebard, Dwane Huebner, Edmund Short, William Schubert, and Barry Franklin.

These conceptualizations and alternative theoretical views of curriculum are not idle dreams or semantic arguments. They are intended to—and do—influence curriculum theory, research, and practice, and contribute significantly to the richness of the field. These creative alternatives do not reflect curricular concerns in isolation but are intended to affect the totality of schooling in America. They value different outcomes of the curriculum, advocate different classroom practices and learning materials, require new roles for students and teachers, foster fundamental reforms in teacher education, suggest different procedures for teacher supervision and evaluation, and clearly point out the need for different forms of student evaluation.

These theoretical positions are, however, in need of continued development and debate. Each is incomplete and requires further development. Each, too, must address the research and practical implications of the theoretical approach. Each must be studied in a variety of practical situations that reflect the array of educational situations found in our schools. Both the continued development of the theoretical positions and the study of practical settings are essential to a comprehensive position in curriculum. The study of curriculum practice is as important a source for curriculum knowledge as is curriculum theory, and they must be viewed as interactive, one enhancing the other. As scholars and practitioners engage in these needed activities, the curriculum field will be enriched by their efforts.

---

[1] I wish to acknowledge the use of Schubert's important work, *Curriculum Books: The First Eighty Years* (1980) in helping me trace some of the historical development of curriculum thinking.

CONCLUSION

Some students and teachers of curriculum will value the alternative approaches presented in this book. Others will deplore, condemn, or dismiss the diversity in the field of curriculum as represented here, and may perhaps attribute it to the youth of the field, the contrariness of the participants, or superficial semantic battles. The diversity may even be seen as a hopeless morass of verbiage. Such students of the field may reject any alternative thinking about curriculum and retreat to the comfort of the tried-and-true, the practices they have engaged in for many years, the dominant value system and approach that are so pervasive in the literature and in our schools. Yet other curricularists may decide that some diversity is needed in the field, but recommend greater effort and commitment by theorists, teachers, and students of curriculum to develop a single, integrated approach or comprehensive theory of curriculum that will incorporate at least some of the various positions discussed in this chapter. By contrast, others may consider that the diversity and complexity of the field are to be valued, respected, encouraged, studied, and understood (Klein, 1986; Walker, 1982). They believe the diverse positions reflected in this book significantly enrich the debate about the fundamental issues and values inherent in the curriculum field and contribute to its development in important ways.

This chapter has presented my views of the structure of the field of curriculum and the alternative perspectives represented in this book. As such, you may take exception to some of my discussion, note omissions and discrepancies, and propose other ways of viewing the important activities in which curricularists engage. My study of the field has focused on determining which of these ideas extend and strengthen my beliefs about curriculum theory, research, and practice. I have found much in the ideas discussed here that challenges my work. The one conclusion I have reached is that no single approach in curriculum will do all that we hope for and expect from our schools in helping students grow and develop today and prepare for their lives in the twenty-first century. Perhaps it may ultimately be shown that with all the goals for American schooling that have general support, several approaches are needed. We want and need too much from our schools to rely on only one approach; we must continue the search for meaningful alternative approaches and encourage diversity in the curriculum field. For me, the diversity in the field holds great promise, enriches the debates about curriculum, proposes intriguing ways to grapple with the complexity of the field, and emphasizes the fundamental importance of curriculum theory, research, and practice.

It is up to you, the serious student and teacher of curriculum, to consider the values and approaches to curriculum reflected in this book and introduced in this chapter, and then decide for yourself which approach is best for you. But your choice must be an informed, deliberate one that is based on a comprehensive knowledge base of the options available. If this book helps you to make a more informed decision about what you believe is important about curriculum, it will have achieved its purpose.

REFERENCES

Eisner, Elliot W. (1985). *The Educational Imagination: On the Design and Evaluation of School Programs.* New York: Macmillan.

Gay, Geneva. (1980). "Conceptual Models of the Curriculum Planning Process." Chapter 7 in *Considered Action for Curriculum Improvement,* 1980 Yearbook of the Association for Supervision and Curriculum Development. Alexandria, VA: Association for Supervision and Curriculum Development.

Grumet, Madeleine, and William F. Pinar. (1976). *Toward a Poor Curriculum.* Dubuque, IA: Kendall/Hurst.

Huenecke, Dorothy. (1982). "What Is Curriculum Theorizing? What Are Its Implications for Practice?" *Educational Leadership, 39* (4), 290–294.

Klein, M. Frances. (1980). "A Curriculum Perspective and the Beginning Teacher Evaluation Study." Chapter VI in *Time to Learn.* Washington, DC: National Institute of Education.

Klein, M. Frances. (1982). "Independent Study." *Encyclopedia of Educational Research,* 5th Ed. New York: Free Press.

Klein, M. Frances. (1985). "Curriculum Design." *International Encyclopedia of Education: Curriculum Studies,* T. Husen and N. Postlethwaite, Eds. Oxford, England: Pergamon Press.

Klein, M. Frances (1986). "Alternative Curriculum Conceptions and Designs." *Theory Into Practice, 25* (1), 31–35.

Kliebard, Herbert M. (1975). "Reappraisal: The Tyler Rationale." Chapter 5 in *Curriculum Theorizing: The Reconceptualists,* William F. Pinar, Ed. Berkeley, CA: McCutchan.

Macdonald, James B., and Esther Zaret (Eds.). (1975). *Schools in Search of Meaning.* Washington, DC: Association for Supervision and Curriculum Development.

Pinar, William F. (1975). *Curriculum Theorizing: The Reconceptualists.* Berkeley, CA: McCutchan.

Pinar, William F. (1978, September). "Notes on the Curriculum Field 1978." *Educational Researcher, 7,* 5–12.

Pinar, William F. (Ed.). (1988). *Contemporary Curriculum Discourses.* Scottsdale, AZ: Gorsuch Scarisbrick.

Schubert, William H. (1980). *Curriculum Books: The First Eighty Years.* Lanham, MD: University Press of America.

Schwab, Joseph J. (1970). *The Practical: A Language for Curriculum.* Washington, DC: National Education Association.

Walker, Decker F. (1982). "Curriculum Theory Is Many Things to Many People." *Theory Into Practice, 21* (1), 62–65.

2

An Evolutionary
and Metaphorical Journey
into Teaching and Thinking
About Curriculum

J. DAN MARSHALL
National College of Education

JAMES T. SEARS
University of South Carolina

Being aware of oneself as the instrument of one's teaching and aware of the story that makes one's life sensible allows for greater change and growth as well as greater intentionality in teaching choices.

(Ayers, 1988, p. 20)

THE EVOLUTIONARY JOURNEY

About Teaching

As Frances Klein has shown, curriculum practitioners, teachers, and scholars alike have continuously wrestled with questions of appropriate knowledge, context, and approaches to teaching curriculum. Klein's own curriculum thought and work, as well as her work with her mentor John Goodlad, is testimony to the persistent importance of these questions. Attention to such concerns is also evident in the edited collection by Edmund Short (1970), *A Search for Valid Content for Curriculum Courses;* the synoptic text, *Curriculum: Perspective, Paradigm, and Possibility,* by William Schubert (1986); and the journal, *Teaching Education,* edited by Craig Kridel.

The evolution of curriculum pedagogy parallels the development of curriculum as a field of study. *Teaching and Thinking About Curriculum* is a set of interrelated essays written by curriculum scholars who teach curriculum. Though they share this academic endeavor with hundreds of others in colleges and universities across the United States, Canada, Australia, and Great Britain, their concepts of curriculum set them apart from most of their colleagues. They, like growing numbers of others, engage in contemporary or reconceptualized curriculum discourse (Pinar, 1988).

This book reflects what William Pinar (1988) has labeled the "second wave" of curriculum reconceptualization, "which started as an opposition to the mainstream and tradition of the field [and] has become the field" (p. 7). The environment that provides the most obvious and straightforward path for the exchange of these ideas between curriculum teachers and their elementary and secondary colleagues is the higher education classroom—the backdrop for these essays on contemporary curriculum pedagogy. Indeed, its focus on teaching is what sets this book apart from others that address contemporary curriculum thought (see, for example, Macdonald & Zaret, 1975; Molnar, 1987; Pinar, 1975). The need for such a focus is critical, given that "the major ideas which constitute the contemporary field of [curriculum] study have yet to make their way to colleagues in elementary and secondary schools" (Pinar, 1988, p. 13).

The 13 core essays in this book are stories of classroom teaching in which contemporary curriculum ideas are foremost, and contemporary curriculum discourse prevails. Within these classrooms curriculum-as-subject-matter is no less complex (or captivating) than the lived curriculum created and recreated through the teaching-learning dialectic. Bringing together 24 curriculum teachers to discuss their pedagogy recognizes the value of their classroom work and reflects "a social process whereby individuals come to greater understanding of themselves, others, and the world through mutual reconceptualization" (Schubert, 1986, p. 33). *Teaching and Thinking About Curriculum* mirrors the synergistic relationship between curriculum thinking and curriculum teaching, between the curriculum teacher and the curriculum student, and among the generations of curriculum teachers.

About Empowerment

Each of these curriculum teachers aims to empower students through curriculum studies. "Empowerment," however, has become an educational buzzword in the 1980s. So that our message will not be misunderstood, we will explain our use of the term "empowerment."

The Oxford English Dictionary informs us that "empower" originally surfaced in 1654 and meant to authorize or license. According to this definition, some person or formal body with power sanctions or approves the transmission of that power to another person or formal body. In 1681, a second use of "empower" emerged: to enable or permit. Here, a person or body with power affords an opportunity for another person or body to develop power. The notion of direct transmission is diminished, and responsibility for empowerment is shared by the enabler and the enabled.

Though subtle, the differences in these definitions of empowerment clearly distinguish contemporary from conventional curriculum teachers, when viewed within the teaching-learning context. From the conventional perspective, one empowers students by imparting *a priori* knowledge and specific skills that allow them to work within the existing social system. This model, *empowerment-as-authorization,* is wielded by a single person or small group of like-minded persons; curriculum students are empowered to work within the limited framework provided by this individual or group.

This neo-conservative conception of empowerment pervades education. Masked in the rhetoric of reform, teacher education policies and programs have resulted in increased centralization of power, greater standardization of the curriculum, less teacher autonomy, and a more technocratic orientation to schooling. On their own, as well as through major educational organizations like the Association for Supervision and Curriculum Development (ASCD), entrepreneurs do a thriving business promoting workshops, distributing "how to" manuals, and marketing videocassette recordings with prepackaged and distilled versions of empowerment. Within these contexts, empowerment means providing teachers and students with the knowledge and skills needed to do what others prescribe. Madeline Hunter and her now-infamous formula for successful teaching is a classic example of the appropriation of this empowerment model toward nonliberating ends. Her disciples welcome her vision of the teaching-learning process as an applied technological science in which direct teaching results in expected learning outcomes (see Costa, 1984; Gibboney, 1987). Like some huge and tragic pedagogical pyramid scam, those furthest from the apex receive the least amount of her power and are simultaneously thwarted from realizing their own (see Garman & Hazi, 1988).

The alternative conception of empowerment, *empowerment-as-enablement,* differs in form, process, and intent. To begin, the form is idiosyncratic. Teachers become empowered or enabled in different circumstances, for different reasons, and in different ways. Their power is created and realized by them—not received from or bestowed by others. Each of the essays that follow suggests that empowerment is a deeply personal process of meaning making within particular historical, cultural, and economic contexts.

This model of empowerment further recognizes that one's realization of power is a process begun but never completed. When teaching is viewed as a fundamentally dynamic and political act, the folly of static "empowerment packages" becomes evident and the concept of "lifelong learning" becomes a reality.

Finally, the intent of empowering students through curriculum studies is to enable them to recognize, create, and channel their own power. This is achieved in large part because the learning environment expects students to be active, responsible participants. One cannot enable students who act (or are expected to act) as passive receptors of another's power. When students share the burden of the classroom dialectic, classrooms become incubators in which ideas are germinated, shared, nurtured, argued, acted upon, and often transformed by teacher and students alike.

Transmitting a generic recipe for empowering educators or for preparing prepackaged sets of curriculum materials to empower students is antithetical to the conception of empowerment-as-enablement and at odds with the premise of this book.

About This Book's Development

During the past 20 years, curriculum teachers and scholars have at least recognized, if not engaged in, some fascinating curriculum peregrinations. The story of these explorations has been detailed elsewhere (see, for example, Benham, 1981; Klohr, 1980; Miller, 1978: van Manen, 1978). The result is that "conventional curriculum wisdom" is no longer taken for granted by all those associated with the field. Instead, a group of recent curriculum dissidents, known for better or worse as reconceptualists, have brought unique existential and structural perspectives to the study of curriculum. Broad in scope and pluralistic in focus, this ongoing reconceptualization of curriculum thought reflects empowerment-as-enablement.

For those who think about curriculum in the less conventional ways noted earlier by Klein, the teaching of curriculum is problematic. As a teacher, one is forced to recognize one's own values and beliefs when determining the content and activities to be shared and experienced by students. Furthermore, one's instructional practices cannot be transmission-oriented; students must be expected at least to transact with, and ideally to help transform, contemporary curriculum ideas (Miller & Seller, 1985). This book explores such challenges in pedagogy and describes unique approaches adopted by its contributors.

The genesis of this book was a session conducted in 1986 at ASCD called "Teaching Curriculum." A surprisingly large number of curriculum teachers attended and expressed an interest in developing and sharing new ideas for their work. We were encouraged to learn of others' attraction to curriculum pedagogy and began to work on ways to establish some form of communication among curriculum teachers. A network? A newsletter? A book?

A similar, more elaborate session took place the following year at ASCD's conference under the sponsorship of the ASCD-affiliated Curriculum Teachers Network. During that conference, we discussed the feasibility of a book about curriculum teaching with Teachers College Press (TCP). With their encouragement, we contacted some 300 curriculum professors, inviting them—or their colleagues—to submit abstracts for a book about contemporary curriculum teaching.

Forty-five curriculum teachers responded. Ten persons were selected to blind review complete sets of these submissions. Eight of these readers were curriculum professors and two were graduate students in curriculum and instruction. After lengthy discussions with us, each reviewer judged the submissions according to thematic appropriateness, strength of rationale, organization, interest, and the writer's apparent degree of commitment to curriculum teaching. These reviews were completed in August 1987.

Twenty writers whose abstracts received strong ratings from the reviewers were asked to submit an elaborate outline of their proposed chapter. From those, we made final selections in late October and submitted a prospectus to TCP in December. When the project was finalized early in 1988, the writers set to work. We arranged gatherings to coincide with two major professional conferences that spring so that all the participants met and talked with us, the TCP editor, and each other about this collective, collaborative endeavor. We also encouraged writers of closely related chapters to exchange drafts and share reviews of their work throughout the writing process.

About This Book's Organization

Core Chapters.   The stories of 14 curriculum teachers make up the core of this text. They are organized into four areas, corresponding to the four parts of the book—self, teacher, community, and field—which serve as contextual perspectives for curriculum thought and action. These resemble similar categories within the curriculum literature, such as Schwab's (1970, 1971, 1973) "commonplaces" (learner, teacher, subject matter, and milieu) and the contextual domains (personal, instructional, institutional, and societal) created by Sirotnik and Oakes (1981) for identifying and organizing contextual variables for curriculum evaluation. Furthermore, as Beyer notes later, our categories reflect the kinds of major curriculum questions addressed by the field: personal, practical, political, and theoretical.

The origin of these contextual perspectives is significant. We did not consciously bring these perspectives into play; they emerged as we studied the elaborate outlines submitted by prospective authors. Writers spoke from different platforms or contexts, some more clearly bounded by one perspective, others a bit more expansive. We have maintained and employed these perspectives primarily as an organizational scheme for the book. For us, they depict starting points for these authors and simultaneously represent perspectives from which curriculum may be viewed.

Purposefully autobiographical in nature, stories within each part illuminate these teachers' "personal practical knowledge" (Connelly & Clandinin, 1988) and constitute a form of teacher lore—"a valuable and neglected area of study for the understanding of praxis in education" (Schubert, 1988, p. 22). Each story is preceded by the author's own biographical statement. This emphasis illuminates the reflective nature of contemporary curriculum thought and pedagogy.

Part Discourse.   Following the chapters in each part is a brief commentary, written by another teacher whose work has been influential in reconceptualizing curriculum thought. Once labeled as "discontents" (Jackson, 1981), these *contestaires* have long challenged conventional thinking about curriculum. Despite the emergence of a generation of teachers and scholars who have built upon their collective insights, they continue to question the field.

Completing the part focusing on "self" is Maxine Greene, whose more than two decades of educational labors provide her with a perspective on reality (and teaching) similar to those of Bowman/Haggerson, Doll, and Kantor. Her eloquent and evocative writing reflects her struggle to understand curriculum through introspection. Greene (1988) describes this vantage point as follows:

> Troubled by impersonality, by abstract vantage points, I wanted people to name themselves and tell their stories when they made their statements. I came to believe (or I was taught) that "reality" referred, after all, to interpreted experience. Resisting the notion of a finished, predetermined, objective reality, I became fascinated not merely with multiple modes of interpretation, but with all that fed into interpretation from lived lives and sedimented meanings. (p. xii)

Ted Aoki, whose curriculum work is probably (and unfortunately) best known to Canadian teachers and scholars, follows the "teacher" part. Central, here, is a realization and respect for the role of teacher as curriculum creator. Those adopting this as their primary vantage point focus on the classroom environment as curriculum laboratory and the interactions therein between teachers and their students. The relationships between learners and teachers, central to the chapters by Miller and Wood, have been themes important to Aoki for years in his efforts to broaden and humanize curriculum inquiry. As Aoki (1979) writes: "I find it important to centre curriculum thought on a broader frame, that of man/world relationships, for it permits probing of the deeper meaning of what it is for persons (teachers and students) to be human, to become more human, to act more humanly in educational situations" (p. 4).

The "community" part represents a starting point for curriculum thought and teaching that assert the importance of structural forces on education. Michael Apple, whose incisive and prolific writing has focused attention on these structural forces, concludes this part. The chapters by Pink, Beyer, Donmoyer, and Erdman all suggest an expansion of vision similar to that of Apple himself: a query into "how power operates in our society . . . Who benefits? In what ways? How are relations of domination and subordination reproduced and challenged in existing cultural, political, and economic forms of interaction?" (Apple, 1986, p. 14).

William Pinar, who is seen by many as the major spokesperson for and defender of curriculum reconceptualization, completes the "field" part. The chapter authors—Short, Schubert, Shaker, and Kridel—ground their pedagogical actions and thoughts in the field of curriculum as they simultaneously work to understand and expand it. An eclectic scholar and vigorous advocate for this "changing landscape of curriculum study," Pinar (1978) notes that "as curricularists we must address ourselves to the historically-established concerns of the curriculum field" (p. 9). He continues: "The production of curriculum knowledge is important to the advancement of the field. However, if this production does not originate in an emancipatory intention . . . then no fundamental movement in the historical situation can occur" (p. 11).

In recent years, each of these contributors—Greene, Aoki, Apple, and Pinar—has played a very important role within the curriculum field: As a *contestaire,* each has challenged the established order and continues to contribute to the expansion of thinking about curriculum. The ideas they present here serve to promote as well as model curriculum discourse of the sort they encourage in their own curriculum teaching. They do not critique the chapters, but use them as a platform to reflect on the teaching of curriculum.

Concluding Essays. The volume's concluding essays by Louise Berman and Wells Foshay represent yet another layer of discourse. Both of these distinguished curriculum teachers and scholars are genealogical descendants of Hollis Caswell, author of the curriculum field's first synoptic textbook.

Caswell's own students, particularly Alice Miel—Berman's mentor—and Foshay, have all kept alive the spirit of cooperative, democratic inquiry (Schubert et al., 1988). The twin essays penned by these two prominent veteran curriculum teachers and respected writers place the teaching and thinking of curriculum in a context spanning several generations of thought.

Evident, by now, is our intent for this volume to be a genealogy of thought and practice in the teaching of curriculum. The voices of these 20 contributors reflect the rich tapestry of a regenerated curriculum discourse. Such conversations have been the lifeblood of teaching and thinking about curriculum throughout this century. These and other discussions will be catalysts for future rebirths of our field.

Ongoing Conversation. In the truest spirit of such dialogue, our book contains one final layer of discourse: a conversation among three curriculum teachers who have been enormously influential in our lives and the lives of many of the writers in this book. These *conversations parmi animateurs* are thoughtful commentaries of three persons whose ability to present complex ideas in an easily understandable form has inspired generations of curriculum teachers. Their conversations are woven throughout the book.

Paul Klohr was introduced to the curriculum field as a graduate student participant-observer in the experimental University School at Ohio State University. Later, he became director of this school, the most radical of the thirty schools in the Eight Year Study. Described in the classic *Were We Guinea Pigs* (1938), the school was directly influenced by the curriculum thinking of Boyd Bode, Laura Zirbes, and Harold Alberty. As one of Alberty's students, Klohr has "kept alive a commitment to a deep level of reflection on values and liberal democratic discourse" (Schubert et al., 1988, p. 143). Klohr has had a significant impact on the reconceptualization of curriculum discourse over the years and was the major professor of four of the writers in this book.

Another of Klohr's students engaging in the book's continuing dialogue is Norm Overly. Overly has devoted his curriculum energies to the unstudied curriculum, lifelong learning, and, more recently, global and cross-cultural curriculum work. His involvement in the World Council of Curriculum & Instruction, his theologically grounded insights, and his long tenure as professor of curriculum at Indiana University continue to influence curriculum workers, teachers, and scholars.

The third participant in the book's ongoing conversation is O. L. Davis, Jr. A past president of the Association for Supervision and Curriculum Development, Davis's curriculum genealogy can be traced back through his mentor, Harold Drummond, to Harold Rugg. Like most of the curriculum teachers in this book, Davis is a generalist at heart. His scholarly efforts have focused on the teaching and content of social studies, textbook development, curriculum history, and liberating education.

Few of us develop thoughts and practices in isolation. We read and reflect upon the work of our predecessors and, in the best of circumstances, grow into our professional selves under the guidance and encouragement of one or more mentors. This book is our conscious attempt—through its introductory chapters, its multilayered core, and its concluding essays—to illuminate these roots. We do not suggest that the work of these "junior" curriculum teachers is in some linear way an effect of their more senior colleagues and mentors. Our message is quite the contrary: A dynamic reciprocity of thought is at work among and between those who appear in this book, just as it is among all curriculum teachers (who seek to empower) and their students. Lasting relationships emerge between those who find excitement and importance in curriculum work and their students. This realization, we believe, lies at the heart of *Teaching and Thinking About Curriculum.*

THE METAPHORICAL JOURNEY

Most teachers know the power of metaphors. We use them in our classrooms to prompt thinking, invite the making of relationships, and encourage the asking of questions. Metaphors are vehicles that illuminate the structures of our thinking and disclose new avenues for our understanding. Metaphors are reciprocal bridges between the group and each of its members, through which conjured images can lead one or many from the group to discover latent meaningfulness or reeling epiphany. Most important, metaphors are elixirs.

The book's four contextual perspectives (self, teacher, community, and field) are conceptual frameworks for teaching and thinking about curriculum. To explore the potential value of such frameworks, we have developed six metaphors: the garbage can, the photographer's lens, the earth, ripples on water's surface, the Magic Cubes, and the Venn diagram. Each metaphor reflects a distinctive conceptualization of *Teaching and Thinking About Curriculum.*

There are several advantages of exploring these metaphors. First, they encourage reflection about the grounded perspective (or the lack of one) that each of us brings into our classroom. Second, they suggest the problems and possibilities of other grounded perspectives. Third, they provide a conceptual template for examining the 13 chapters that form the core of this book. These perspectives, we believe, form a useful construct for making

Table 1 Six Teaching Metaphors—Comparisons and Contrasts

Metaphor	Relationship Among Four Perspectives	Primacy of Perspectives	Variety of Perspectives	Primacy of Teacher
Garbage Can	None	None	None	None
Lens	Discrete Unconnected	Singular No Primacy	Finite Partly Open System	High
Earth	Interrelated Fixed and Hierarchical	Multiple Primacy	Finite Closed System	None
Ripples	Interconnected Iridescent	Multiple No Primacy	Infinite Open System	Moderate
Magic Cubes	Discrete Interconnected	Multiple No Primacy	Finite Closed System	High
Venn Diagram	Discrete Connected or Unconnected	Multiple No Primacy	Infinite Open System	High

sense of how the curriculum scholars represented in this book approach their teaching. Table 1 compares and contrasts the teaching of curriculum when explored through the six metaphors.

The Metaphor of the Garbage Can

Engaged in the humdrum life of a curriculum teacher, there are those who profess no contextual perspective to their teaching. These curriculum teachers spend little or no time considering what they're doing or why. Easy availability, expediency, and convention underlie their unreflective selection of a particular text, weekly assignments, and resource materials. Educational resources or curriculum approaches that are no longer in vogue, such as writings from the radical romantic educators of the 1960s or Taba's inductive curriculum development model, are tossed into the garbage can of obsolescent materials. A similar fate can be expected for Hunter's model of effective teaching or Adler's model for curriculum design.

Persons whose curriculum teaching was represented by this metaphor probably would not bother to look at this book. If they did, they might argue that one should not adopt any of the four platforms or perspectives, but should attempt instead to remain objective in one's approach to teaching. If they read the book, they might argue that the different pedagogical perspectives it presents don't even exist within the "established curriculum field." Worse yet, they might—without developing strong feelings about it one way or another—order it for their curriculum classes because they wanted to have "the very latest" thinking available for their students.

In short, the garbage can metaphor suggests that unreflective curriculum teaching adds nothing to our field. This metaphor further implies that the unreflective use of good resources is poor pedagogy; expedient use of poor material is pedagogical malpractice.

The Metaphor of the Lens

Photography is an art and a science. The photographic *context* that composes a snapshot, such as conditions of light, background setting, and subject, is a critical consideration for the photographer. The *technology* of photography, such as the type of camera lenses and developing equipment and materials, determines the range of possible photographs. Finally, the *photographer* brings his or her own experience, purpose, interest, and feeling to the picture-taking process.

In the teaching of curriculum, there are some teachers, like amateur photographers, whose most immediate concern is the classroom experience at the moment (the picture). These teachers use the conceptual lens of curriculum provided to them by their professional mentors. A person who has studied under professors emphasizing policy analysis or neo-Marxism may find the "community" lens, reflected in the essays of Beyer, Donmoyer, Pink, and Erdman, most salient. Another person, steeped in phenomenological tradition, may engage in introspection while reading the Doll, Bowman/Haggerson, and Kantor essays, which focus on "self." These readers, however, may be unfamiliar or uncomfortable with other lenses and may ignore or skim quickly through essays from other parts. Pleased with their pictures, they may have no desire to expend time and resources in acquiring other lenses.

Other teachers of curriculum, like journeymen photographers, seek to acquire as many lenses as possible. Boasting only a superficial knowledge about the uses and limitations of each, they will read this book's 13 core chapters, borrowing assorted terms (such as Doll's "post-modernism") and incorporating interesting techniques (Kridel's use of biography, for example) into their teaching. Their students may be impressed (or appalled) at their apparent academic knowledge and pedagogic skill. In the classroom, however, there is an absence of a well-thought-out perspective about the teaching of curriculum.

More knowledgeable and experienced curriculum teachers have a greater number of tools at their disposal. For them, the decision to use a particular lens is dictated by the classroom context and educational purpose. While the photographer may choose to use a wide-angle lens within a panoramic setting to capture as much scenery as possible, the master curriculum teacher may elect to start from the perspectives of first-year teachers in an introductory graduate level course to build upon their professional concerns and interests. In this case, the lens of "teacher" and the essays of Miller and Wood would be most relevant.

Adopting the metaphor of the lens, the apprentice, journeyman, and master curriculum teacher share several assumptions about the teaching of curriculum. First, the four perspectives (self, teacher, community, field) are discrete and unconnected. In a given situation, the curriculum teacher focuses through the lens of *one* perspective. Though this single perspective need be only the starting point, in less sophisticated hands it becomes the ending point as well. Second, each perspective has a particular power and serves a specific function. Like the metaphor of the lens, the questions that are asked and the resources that are tapped vary with the perspective that is used. Third, the variety of perspectives, like camera lenses, is finite and limited by the extant knowledge and methods. Thus, there are only three ways to enhance one's teaching and thinking about curriculum: improve existing lenses, invent new ways to employ existing lenses, or create new lenses.

The Metaphor of the Earth

As any elementary school child might know, the earth is composed of four major parts. At the center of the earth and extending outward some 800 miles is the inner, liquid core. Surrounding this is an outer core composed of liquid nickel-iron, which is approximately 1400 miles thick. The Gutenberg Discontinuity separates the earth's core from the mantle, which is composed of silicates that appear as olive-green rock. The crust of the earth, composed of basalt and granite, ranges from three miles thick at the ocean depths to forty miles beneath mountain ranges.

Unlike the metaphor of the lens, the metaphor of the earth acknowledges the presence and interconnectedness of all four contextual perspectives. These four components exist in a fixed relationship to one another. In reading the essays in one part of this book, there may be a preference to view one of these perspectives as the "core" of teaching curriculum. For example, Andrea Bowman and Nelson Haggerson, writing from the perspective of "self," articulate the importance of the enfoldment process in the teaching of curriculum. From the inner core, "self," the reader may choose to expand to the outer core, which might be "community" values, policy, and ideology. In this instance, the reader might enfold Robert Donmoyer's multiple conceptions of politics into his or her *personal* meaning of curriculum teaching.

The curriculum teacher who adopts the metaphor of the earth also makes several assumptions. First, the four earthen components are discrete but interrelated in a hierarchical manner. With self as the inner core and field as the outer core, for example, the teaching of curriculum through a historical and biographical perspective will be mediated through the self. Self is the core around which the other three perspectives enclose. Second, each perspective, composed of unique elements, was formed differently. The perspective of the "field" of study, for example, was formed earlier in this century through curriculum workers and scholars such as Charters, Dewey, Rugg, and Zirbes. The perspective of the "community" in curriculum thinking was formed through the interdisciplinary application of political science, sociology, and cultural anthropology. Third, there are *only* four earthen layers. These exist independently of the knower. The substance of teaching and thinking about curriculum, like the layers of the earth, exist independently of human thought. Through human thought they await discovery. Thus, this metaphor suggests that readers who wish to expand their knowledge and skill in teaching and thinking about curriculum ought to concentrate on these four contextual perspectives and pursue further reading and resources suggested by the chapter authors.

The Metaphor of Ripples

Tossing a stone into water creates ripples on its surface. Like the earth's layers, these ripples are isomorphic. But, at the same time, they are amorphous; there is a center, but it is fleeting. Unlike the always extant earth's layers, these ripples result from the act of tossing the stone. Unlike the metaphor of the camera lens and photographer, the nature of the thrower is less important than the size of the stone that is thrown and the nature of the water into which it is cast.

The metaphor of the ripples suggests that the contextual perspectives discussed in this book are not only interconnected but iridescent. Thus, Janet Miller's concern for teachers' contexts is inextricably tied to her own experiences and reflexivity as she tries to see the world in new ways. George Wood's interest in working with and learning from teachers in the Appalachian area is conceptually related to his changing understanding of the meaning of a democratic community and the power of ideology reflected in concepts such as resistance and empowerment.

Adopting this metaphor, the reader of this book may identify the ripple's center as the "field." Short's concern for the absence of meaningful curriculum inquiry, for example, requires that curriculum teachers impart knowledge and skills in order for their students to challenge the trend of curriculum trivialization. From the "field" as the center for teaching and thinking about curriculum emanate the perspectives of self, teacher, and community. This center, though, is neither static nor permanent. Like its effluent ripples, it is an artifact of the teaching moment. Thus, starting curriculum teaching from the perspective of the "field" is a purposeful decision that one acknowledges as transitory. The duration of this teaching moment (a class period, several weeks, a semester) is less dependent on the teacher (the stone thrower) than on the content in hand (the type of stone thrown) and the breadth of the students' prior knowledge and experience (the expansiveness of the body of water). Thus, in a curriculum course for college seniors, raising the question of worth by examining three central tendencies in the curriculum field, as William Schubert advocates in this book, may be limited to one class period. At the doctoral level of study, however, an entire course may have this as the organizing center for discourse and action.

Implicit in the metaphor of the ripples is that these four perspectives are products of our own intellectual construction. The lens and the earth exist independently of us. The ripples cannot exist without the stone thrower. However, the presence of the stone thrower guarantees neither the appearance of ripples nor their quality: The nature of the ripples is defined by the combination of the thrower, stone, and water.

The Metaphor of the Magic Cubes

Several years ago many people were fascinated by a set of four, four-colored cubes. Over the past decade, thousands have toyed with though relatively few have mastered its challenges. The commonly sought goal for players of the Magic Cubes is for each of the four cubes to display one solid color as they are set adjacent to one another.

Unlike the metaphor of the ripples, the person manipulating the cubes is of central importance. His or her conceptual ability (or perhaps sheer perseverance) is crucial in successfully rotating the Magic Cubes to depict one particular pattern. Like the metaphor of the earth, this is a closed system. There is a finite number of cubes and colors. Unlike the lens metaphor, all possible elements are visible and must be used. Unlike the earth metaphor, no particular component is more central than another. The player's task is to work with the elements at hand and abide by the established rules.

The metaphor of the Magic Cubes suggests that the effectiveness of curriculum teaching is determined primarily by the knowledge and skill of the teacher. Further, all four contextual perspectives for the teaching of curriculum must be acknowledged and integrated into the teaching act. No particular perspective is favored over another. Thus, one may begin with "community," but in the process of manipulating this section, other perspectives are also handled. Each perspective, then, is integrally related to the others. For example, Beyer's position (in Chapter 8) that curriculum deliberation is a normative enterprise includes not only an awareness of how education is linked to social contexts and a vision of alternative worlds and forms of language, but also the necessity to develop practices and strategies that enable those alternative visions to take hold in classrooms. To do so, Beyer moves from the community context of language and politics to the context of the teacher and the classroom context wherein alternative visions are tested and contested.

Within this metaphor, each perspective is discrete. Unlike the metaphor of the ripples, the metaphor of the Magic Cube suggests that though the "community" and "teacher" perspectives are interconnected, they are neither interchangeable nor amphibolous. Each perspective is idiosyncratic, reflecting a distinctive set of assumptions.

The Metaphor of the Venn Diagram

Venn diagrams show areas of commonalities and differences among sets within a known universe. In the universe of natural numbers, for example, the sets of integers, whole numbers, and irrational numbers would display areas of intersection as well as areas of disjunction. In the universe of animals, the sets of mammals, pets, dogs, and cocker spaniels would show four circles of various intersections.

The four curriculum perspectives displayed through a Venn diagram suggest aspects within each that overlap one or more perspectives, as well as other areas where no intersections occur. If one of the three primary colors or the absence of color represents each of the four perspectives, then areas of overlap not only denote commonalities but produce new colors. For example, red overlapping blue creates green; yellow, blue, and red produce black.

Adopting this metaphor to the book would suggest that the reader, depending on level of curriculum knowledge and intellectual skill, may reconstruct and combine in novel ways the ideas of these authors as well as his or her own ideas generated from reading their essays. So, for example, the reader may intellectually intersect William Pink's observation that "curriculum inquiry should be the primary focus of the building level faculty" (see Chapter 9) with Paul Shaker's contention that "phenomenological and depth psychological curriculum can motivate students to learn about the process of education while gaining insight about their own development" (see Chapter 14). The result might be a vision of a middle school in which students join in partnership with teachers in evaluating the effectiveness of their school's curriculum.

This metaphor thus allows one to view the more straightforward aspects of what will be represented in the following chapters. "Knowledge construction" is a theme found throughout these four perspectives; journal writing is discussed by many of the authors. How are these concepts and practices helpful to the reader? How might they assume different meanings at their intersection points? By definition, the Venn diagram metaphor requires each perspective to maintain some part of its uniqueness while simultaneously intersecting with each of the other three perspectives in proportionally different respects. Together, the perspectives form the diagram's quadripartite center.

CONCLUSION

The goal of *Teaching and Thinking About Curriculum* is to encourage reflective and critical thought about the teaching of curriculum. By design, the book explicitly rejects a narrow, static conception of curriculum and pedagogy. Instead, it aims to illuminate efforts toward broadening and enriching a changing curriculum field.

The essays that follow are rooted in the intellectual traditions of critical theory and phenomenology. The essayists' insights are grounded in their weekly classroom struggles to translate reconceptualized curriculum ideas into everyday practice for themselves and their partners in learning. Their work exemplifies some of the best efforts to extend curriculum reconceptualization beyond scholarly theorizing to the pedagogy of college and university teachers and, ultimately, into the schools and classrooms of their students.

We believe that the reader will recognize the empowering spirit that underscores the work of these curriculum teachers. Whether they work with preservice teachers, master's students, or doctoral candidates, their shared intent is to create an environment in which their students create meaning. Common to such a pedagogical environment are themes like student action, knowledge production, and the normative dimension of curriculum work. You will recognize these and other themes recurring throughout the book amid a rather broad spectrum of curriculum ideas.

Teaching and Thinking About Curriculum celebrates the breadth and depth of the curriculum field in general and curriculum pedagogy in particular. Everyone represented in this text reflects a deep commitment to curriculum work—a commitment often promoted and nurtured by mentors, other predecessors, and contemporaries. Such is the legacy of contemporary curriculum scholarship and the never-ending hope of curriculum teachers working with the very people who will reconceptualize the way curriculum is practiced in elementary and secondary schools in the future.

REFERENCES

Aoki, T. T. (1979). *Toward curriculum inquiry in a new key.* Paper presented at the Conference on Phenomenological Description: Potential for Research in Art Education, Montreal, Quebec, April 6–8. (ERIC Document Reproduction Service No. ED 182 808)

Apple, M. W. (1986). *Teachers and texts: A political economy of class and gender relations in education.* New York: Routledge & Kegan Paul.

Ayers, W. (1988, May). *Giving headaches: On teaching and the reform of teacher education.* Paper presented at the Midwest Region Holmes Group Conference, Chicago.

Benham, B. J. (1981). Curriculum theory in the 1970s: The reconceptualist movement. *Journal of Curriculum Theorizing, 3,* 162–170.

Connelly, F. M., & Clandinin, D. J. (1988). *Teachers as curriculum planners.* New York: Teachers College Press.

Costa, A. L. (1984). A reaction to Hunter's "Knowing, Teaching, and Supervising." In P. L. Hosford (Ed.), *Using what we know about teaching* (pp. 196–203). Alexandria, VA: Association for Supervision and Curriculum Development.

Garman, N. B., & Hazi, H. M. (1988). Teachers ask: Is there life after Madeline Hunter? *Educational Leadership, 69,* 669–672.

Gibboney, R. A. (1987). A critique of Madeline Hunter's teaching model from Dewey's perspective. *Educational Leadership, 44* (5), 46–50.

Greene, M. (1988). *The dialectic of freedom.* New York: Teachers College Press.

Jackson, P. W. (1981). Curriculum and its discontents. In H. A. Giroux, A. N. Penna, & W. F. Pinar (Eds.), *Curriculum and instruction* (pp. 367–381). Berkeley, CA: McCutchan.

Klohr, P. R. (1980). The curriculum field: Gritty and ragged? *Curriculum Perspectives, 1* (1), 1–7.

Macdonald, J. B., & Zaret, E. (Eds.). (1975). *Schools in search of meaning.* Washington, DC: Association for Supervision and Curriculum Development.

van Manen, M. Reconceptualist curriculum thought: A review of recent literature. *Curriculum Inquiry, 8* (4), 365–375.

Miller, J. L. (1978). Curriculum theory: A recent history. *Journal of Curriculum Theorizing, 1* (1), 28–43.

Miller, J. P., & Seller, J. (1985). *Curriculum.* New York: Longman.

Molnar, A. (Ed.). (1987). *Social issues in education: Challenge and responsibility.* Alexandria, VA: Association for Supervision and Curriculum Development.

Pinar, W. F. (Ed.). (1975). *Curriculum theorizing: The reconceptualists.* Berkeley, CA: McCutchan.

Pinar, W. F. (1978). Notes on the curriculum field, 1978. *Educational Researcher,* 7 (Sept.), 5–12.

Pinar, W. (1988). *Contemporary curriculum discourses.* Scottsdale, AZ: Gorsuch Scarisbrick.

Schubert, W. H. (1986). *Curriculum: Perspective, paradigm, and possibility.* New York: Macmillan.

Schubert, W. H. (1988). *Teacher lore: A basis for understanding praxis.* Paper presented at the Annual Meeting of the American Educational Research Association, New Orleans, April 5–9.

Schubert, W. H., Schubert, A. L., Herzog, L., Posner, G., & Kridel, C. (1988). A genealogy of curriculum researchers. *Journal of Curriculum Theorizing, 8*(1), 137–183.

Schwab, J. J. (1970). The practical: A language for curriculum. Washington, DC: National Education Association.

Schwab, J. J. (1971). The practical: Arts of eclectic? *School Review, 79,* 493–542.

Schwab, J. J. (1973). The practical 3: Translation into curriculum. *School Review, 81,* 501–522.

Short, E. C. (Ed.). (1970). *A search for valid content for curriculum courses.* Toledo, OH: The University of Toledo.

Sirotnik, K. A., & Oakes, J. (1981). A contextual appraisal system for schools: Medicine or madness? *Educational Leadership, 39,* 164–173.

Conversation parmi animateurs

O. L. DAVIS, JR.
University of Texas at Austin

PAUL KLOHR
Ohio State University

NORM OVERLY
Indiana University

KLOHR: *Teaching and Thinking About Curriculum* seems to be expressing the kind of diversity required in creating "empowerment." It is distinctive evidence of a paradigm shift in the field of contemporary curriculum discourse that was hardly in the picture a decade ago, and certainly not 20 years ago. I think this book signifies a fresh impetus in the field that is far more diverse than what we saw before. And, by its very diversity, it is most significant. To use Maxine Greene's expression, this book is evidence of the "opening of spaces" that is required in the current scene when there is clearly a limited view of the nature of curriculum.

OVERLY: Of course, Paul, not everybody during the 1950s and 1960s was a conformist. I think back to my work with you. You were as much an encourager as a nurturer. I remember a close friend of mine who took courses with me who really disliked the things you did. My reaction was totally opposite to his. He found little substance in your courses because you didn't tell us how to develop curriculum. You were suggesting a different paradigm, although I don't know that we were using that word then. You did such things as suggest that we take models from anywhere—music, physics, or chemistry—and play with them in terms of what they might suggest to us about curriculum. That kind of reassociation and creative experimentation seemed inappropriate to him. It dented his understanding of a university education and his scientific model of what curriculum ought to be about.

33

DAVIS: The scientific model of curriculum: Our generation didn't do too well in this regard. By and large, people decided either to do research or not to do research. And, socially acceptable research—30 years ago—was seen as empirical. During those years people like Jim Macdonald, Jack Frymier, Dave Turney, and I met. Every time we got together and talked about our curriculum efforts, we realized we were just adding futility onto futility. But, our first work was all empirical. And, having done it may be seen, in some respects, as a way of giving ourselves legitimacy as university professors. Later when we did other things, we could say, "Well, at least there was a time when we 'counted.'"

KLOHR: My career was different from yours, O. L. I didn't have that scientific set of guidelines thrown onto my work. I came through Ohio State when Bode's philosophical tradition was still very strong. Harold Alberty, my mentor, had just finished his work with Bode. Their orientation was normative—the kind of thinking that attends to basic kinds of value questions that undergird curriculum. So, I guess I'm saying that so much of contemporary curriculum emphasis does not attend to such questions. Of course, the value of this collection of essays is that it deals very basically with what I would call foundational or value-oriented sorts of questions, which have pretty well been abandoned in the last several decades. This kind of thinking provides a vitality in the field that it hasn't had since back when Harold Alberty and Laura Zirbes were active. And, of course, they depended on major philosophers like Dewey and Bode—such thinkers have passed out of the picture. There are very few philosophers any more addressing those questions.

OVERLY: You know, speaking of Dewey reminds me of others who influenced my thinking about curriculum and teaching. I remember Marion VanCampen and Verna Walters, with whom I did my undergraduate and master's work. These were people in their late 60s who were products of Teachers College and the progressive education era. Actually, I never read John Dewey until I became a doctoral student. Until then it was Dewey filtered through my teachers. And they tended to talk more about William Kilpatrick, whom they saw as more of a practitioner.

DAVIS: Your mention of practitioner drew me back to the title of this book, Norm: *Teaching and Thinking About Curriculum*. I had a tough time starting out as a curriculum teacher. Getting away from graduate school brought me face-to-face with the fact that I was operating by myself. What I drew on for my teaching of my curriculum course was my own recollections of Bill Van Til and Harold Drummond at Peabody, and later, a short association with William Alexander. That was it! I didn't have any sense of their work with other people or examples of their struggles with coming to grips with teaching. In the development of their ideas I did, but not in teaching courses.

OVERLY: That certainly is one contribution of this volume. But, I felt constrained by its organizational framework. People aren't people alone: We are people in relationships, in communities, in roles. For analytical purposes, I suppose we can break these interrelationships out into the four perspectives [self, teacher, community, and field] that this book does, as long as we recognize that it all fits together; that we're only trying to understand the whole. In that sense, these perspectives are a useful heuristic device. In other words, they don't reflect the world as it is but rather the world as one sees it.

KLOHR: Well, for me, Norm, these four categories hold up very well. As I reflect about my own thoughts of the curriculum field and my own teaching within the field, my recollections fit without my forcing them into categories. The distinctions hold up well as themes of continuity that ran through my own career and my own rather autobiographical thinking of the field. For me, that gives the categories a kind of double support: They are based on these authors' chapters as well as on my own experiences. The other comment I would make about the categories is that, while they are discrete enough to give insight into my own work, they are also clearly interrelated.

OVERLY: Here we do agree. Each of these perspectives must be tied together. While it is possible to present them individually, I would be concerned if we prepared people to think or teach about curriculum from only one of these perspectives. The dialogues going on in these essays and our discussions about curriculum—in fact the way this book is organized—provide an opportunity to engage individuals in a truly holistic and complex study of curriculum.

DAVIS: That's interesting, Norm. Have you read Bill Pinar's book, *Contemporary Curriculum Discourses?* What struck me as I looked through it was the anomaly in his title. Discourse has to do with both individuals' statements as well as others' responses to them. While I recognize the importance of Bill's latest effort, I think this collection of essays may very well represent the first conspicuous public effort to involve a larger community in genuine discourse—not in just "talking at." Engaging people such as Wells Foshay, Maxine Greene, Ted Aoki, Bill Pinar, Frances Klein, Louise Berman, and Michael Apple—as well as, to some extent, the three of us—is testimony to this.

PART I

TEACHING
FROM THE PERSPECTIVE
OF SELF

Is the teaching of curriculum a reflection of ourselves? Does our classroom teaching manifest our internal struggles as we work through curriculum ideas and reflect on prior experiences? To what extent is our conception of teaching curriculum predicated on our understanding of the teacher-student role and the relationship between teaching and learning? Such questions arise when we teach and think about curriculum from the perspective of self. Speaking from their experiences as public school teachers and professors in higher education, the authors of these three chapters share the impact that their personal experiences and journeys toward self-understanding have had on their conceptions of teaching and thinking about curriculum.

Arguing against the traditional conception of curriculum and instruction rooted in failed notions of behaviorism and mental development, William Doll in Chapter 3 posits a post-modern view of teaching and thinking about curriculum. Doll advocates teaching curriculum through a process of "re-visioning." Beginning with the self, Doll (and his students) move beyond self through the critical examination of personal and private thoughts exposed to public scrutiny. Within the classroom, the teacher's challenge is to maintain an "essential tension" between the comfort of familiar concepts and methods (both his or her own and the students') and alternative approaches and ideas. As disequilibrium is experienced, opportunities for genuine learning occur; teacher and students engage in reflective, personal relationships based on trust and mutual understanding.

This model of teaching curriculum through reflection and interaction is also represented well in the dialogue between professor and doctoral student that takes place in Chapter 4. Using the metaphor of the fan, Andrea Bowman and Nelson Haggerson assert that students must develop a personal curriculum if they are to understand the nature of curriculum and be effective curriculum developers and teachers. These authors echo the importance of self-struggle and personal risk as students enfold themselves into the curriculum and unfold themselves to others in the class. Through the use of journals, aesthetic assignments, peer supervision, action research, and role playing, students create new views of themselves while constructing and expanding their views of curriculum.

In Chapter 5 Ken Kantor unfolds his story of three years of teaching high school English during the 1960s and how those years helped to shape his present curriculum teaching. Kantor's current conception of curriculum is mediated through his life experiences and their re-interpretation. He argues that the course of study cannot be delivered in a historical or cultural vacuum; it is the situation-specific context that provides the meaning for knowledge and understanding. The contexts from which he draws his understanding of teaching and thinking about curriculum include working with Eddie James, an eleventh grade student; advising student writers of the school's literary magazine; and teaching *The Scarlet Letter.* Based on these and other experiences, Kantor proposes five underlying principles for the teaching of curriculum.

3

Teaching
A Post–Modern Curriculum

WILLIAM E. DOLL, JR.
Louisiana State University

I came to professional education through the back door—teaching while taking my master's in philosophy. After a decade of teaching and administrating, I enrolled in Johns Hopkins for doctoral work—Steve Mann was my mentor—partly because Hopkins was light on formalism and heavy on substance: only five required courses, no minimum hours for a Ph. D., and strong contact with the professors. For one year I read in the philosophy of science. I also read virtually all Dewey wrote and did my dissertation on his theory of change—experience from a pragmatic perspective. Richard Rorty is now reviving this perspective.

After Hopkins I went to SUNY–Oswego, where I read Piaget and Bruner, developed a "structuralist" teacher preparation program, and did administration again. After 14 years "Upstate," Mary, Will, and I went to Redlands, California, where I directed the university's teacher preparation program. In California I was introduced to process thought, post-modern thought, and Ilya Prigogine's thought.

Currently I use the rubric of post-modernism to expound the theory of change, growth, and development I have derived from Dewey, Piaget, Bruner, Prigogine, and now Whitehead. I am working on a book, A Post-Modern View of Curriculum, *and am enjoying my new-found academic life at Louisiana State University.*

The pupil's progress is often conceived as a uniform steady advance undifferentiated by change of type or alteration in pace.... I hold that this conception of education is based upon a false psychology of the process of mental development which has greatly hindered the effectiveness of our methods. (Alfred North Whitehead, 1929/1967, p. 17)

I began my teaching career in a small, country-day school in the Boston suburbs, teaching Latin and algebra to eighth graders. My methods were simple: I followed the book; my students followed me. For Latin declensions and conjugations I used a stopwatch—shades of Frederick Taylor. Not only did my students memorize, they memorized under time constraints. Often this sort of pressure, 20 seconds on the stopwatch, brought tears to the eyes of both my male and female students. However, such "toughness" was approved of by both parents and administration.

My first movement away from such a "modernist" methodology— simple, linear, closed—occurred in the winter of my second year. On Fridays, after lunch, I would let the students play games—chess, checkers, puzzles, and so forth. One young boy, Beezy, not adept at recitation within the 20-second rule, liked to explore math puzzles. One particular Friday Beezy chose the "monkey in the well" problem: A monkey 30 feet down a well climbs up 3 feet each day but slides back 2 feet each night. How many days will it take for the monkey to climb out? The catch, of course, is to find the day on which the 3-foot climb is not followed by a 2-foot descent, since the climb puts the monkey out of the well. Then, as now, I did this type of problem using a diagram and marking off the daily progress. Beezy, however, developed a formula: $30 = n(3-2) + X$. With the X as a 2, the numerical difference between the day counted and the height climbed, on the twenty-eighth day the monkey climbed his final 3 feet: 28, 29, 30. Beezy not only solved the problem better and faster than I did, but he had a methodology categorically superior to mine. In Jerome Bruner's terms, he was able to work in the symbolic mode while I was limited to the iconic. It seemed to me that my insistence on memorization and timed-response was a bit beside the point. My student was thinking in ways categorically different from and superior to mine. What was I doing to empower his natural ability, his level of competence? Sadly, I had no answer to this question.

INFLUENCES ON TEACHING DEVELOPMENT

The foregoing, over 30 years ago, started me on my quest for a better way, a way that Dewey (1934/1964) says is "radically different" from both "external imposition" and internal "unfolding" (p. 8). The radical difference, of course, is that instead of separating the external from the internal, in typical Cartesian fashion, this new way integrates these two so that in union each is transformed. This way accepts neither the rigidity of behaviorism nor the unboundedness of romanticism. Change is seen as necessary, natural, and potentially productive, but is kept within boundaries and integrated with more conventional approaches. In this quest for the better alternative, I continued teaching, went to graduate school in both philosophy and education, and read heavily in the writings of John Dewey, Jean Piaget, and Jerome Bruner. Collectively these three helped me see that Whitehead was right: Our conception of education is and has been based on a false psychology—behaviorism—and on a false view of mental development—simple and repeated associationism.

Individually each has helped me move toward my present, post-modern view of teaching. Dewey has helped me see the importance of reflection, with an emphasis on the prefix "re." He argues, in the early pages of *Experience and Nature* (1929/1958), for conceiving of experience at two levels: (1) a concrete, practical, active level; (2) an abstract, reflective, refined level. "The distinction is one between what is experienced as the result of [physical activity or doing] and what is experienced in consequence of . . . reflective inquiry" on those doings (pp. 4–5). Level 2, of course, emerges from level 1 and is really a transformation of the original experience. Whereas level 1 is hands-on experience, level 2 is an intellectual revisiting of that experience. It is a looking back to what has already occurred to connect that doing with other doings, and to envision other possibilities and alternatives. At its best, our curriculum methods have paid attention to level 1. But virtually no attention has been paid to level 2. What this second level means to me as a teacher is that books should be re-read, papers should be re-written, and tests should be re-taken—all with the expressed purpose of re-visioning both the work in question and one's initial reactions to that work. It is this dual thrust of the external integrated with the internal that provides the basis for transformatory experience.

I have worked mostly with re-writing at the graduate and adult levels of education; that is, with those who already possess a high degree of maturity and hence benefit quickly from a re-visioning process. In these classes, in both education and the humanities, I often assign two or three relatively short papers (six to eight pages). No other writings are required. But for each paper handed in to be graded, I require a full-length, complete, typed, first draft. I comment extensively, without grades, on these first drafts. I also comment on the "final" draft and offer the opportunity, which most take, of doing a "post-final" re-write. Thus, every paper is written twice, and usually three times. This procedure is not different from my own writing habits and produces solid work in a short time. It does, however, inflate grades; but my goal is to produce competent writers and thinkers, not to maintain a uniform distribution of grades. The tail must not wag the dog.

To help further my students' development and to make certain their re-visioning is empowering and not narrowing or overfocused, I have them read and critique both their colleagues' and my writings. Every semester I submit some of my own work to the same first, final, and post-final scrutiny they undergo. Writing, and with it analytical thinking, becomes a community process. The students sharpen their analytical and creative skills by scrutinizing not only their own work but also that of their colleagues and their teacher. This process obviously takes a great deal of curriculum time and involves personal pain. Time and pain seem to me necessary ingredients for transformation.

Such a two-tiered, re-visioned view of experience as I am elaborating forms the heart of what Dewey means by reflective inquiry as well as his famous transformation of personal "ises" into public "oughts." This process encourages us to begin with ourselves but then to move beyond ourselves— "for development involves a point *toward* which as well as one *from* which" (1934/1964, p. 8). The key is to so integrate the *toward* with the *from* that neither dominates or is subservient to the other; development is a continual process of reconstruction, of submitting one's personal and private thoughts to public scrutiny.

While Dewey cannot be considered post-modern—the movement began in German architecture and literary criticism a few years after his death—any curriculum that emphasizes reflection, re-visioning, and re-doing is not the usual modernist curriculum we know. In fact, the notion of "re" is very much part of feedback loops in systems biology, of computer graphics in chaos theory, and of deconstruction interpretations in post-structural literary theory—themselves all parts of the post-modern movement. Thus, while Dewey is not post-modern, I believe his educational ideas can be best understood from this framework.

Jean Piaget has also helped me see the need for disequilibrium or pain (noise to the behaviorists) in the curriculum. The modernist paradigm, which I argue underlies Western thought from Copernicus through Einstein (Doll, 1983) and which still dominates the social sciences, including education and curriculum, has no place for disequilibrium as a positive, creative force. Newton's world was one of simple order: predictable in its movements, uniform in its applications, steady in its mechanism. Such a clock-like world of mechanical objects has allowed education to assume the validity and reality of I.Q., predictability, grades, averages, linear sequencing, and ends separated from means. In short, the Newtonian, modernist world view undergirds the very essence of our contemporary curriculum—a flat, set course with hurdles students are to run. However, if we, along with Prigogine and Stengers (1984), see the universe filled not with orderly orbs spinning perpetually in divine harmony, but with strange objects—quasars, pulsars, exploding galaxies, stars collapsing into black holes that devour all they can ensnare (pp. 214–215)—then our concept of curriculum will be more turbulent, less set.

While Piaget, like Dewey, cannot legitimately be called a post-modernist—the sequential ordering and uniformity of his stages mitigates this—he does draw on interactive biological systems, not on linear mechanics, for his basic model. Piaget saw that progress is constructed and evolutionary, not copied or imposed. As he was fond of saying, "Knowledge is constructed, not copied" (1971, p. 28). Within this constructive process disequilibrium plays a key role. No matter how it occurs, nonbalance or disequilibrium "produces the driving force of development . . . [without it] there would not be increasing re-equilibration" (1977, p. 3). In his process triad—equilibrium, disequilibrium, re-equilibration—Piaget has given us a model we can use in curriculum as a real alternative to the behaviorist, modernist one we have adopted. In his model there needs to be a tension between the comfort of equilibrium and the discomfort of disequilibrium. The challenge to the teacher or curriculum maker is to keep this tension in the right proportion, in what Thomas Kuhn (1977) refers to as an "essential tension"—so that reflective re-equilibrium can occur.

In the dozen or so years I have been working on this Piagetian model as a curriculum alternative to the Tyler rationale, I have been far more successful with the equilibrium and disequilibrium phases than with the re-equilibrative transformations. It is quite likely I never saw the time between conception and birth as needing a nurturing process, a point Bruner (1973) considers crucial for intellectual growth. I mistakenly assumed that once equilibrium and disequilibrium came in contact with one another, like sperm and egg, re-equilibrated transformations would automatically, soon, and miraculously occur. While I have not given up on the elements of self-generation, spontaneity, and miraculousness—in fact, along with Paul Davies (1988) I see them as essential ingredients of a new "cosmic blueprint"—recently I have been far more aware of my role as intellectual midwife in bringing ideas into the light and action of life. Like knowledge, curricular processes, too, must be constructed. To lay curricula out in too much preset detail is to produce a trivialized curriculum.

Awareness of my new role began to take shape when one of the teachers I had in a graduate curriculum course said the only thing she learned from my course was "how not to teach." I had refused to lay out in clear, unambiguous, and non-negotiable terms the goals, methods, and evaluative procedures the students were to follow. I still refuse to do this, believing it must be done conjointly; this is the very stuff of curriculum process. However, I now frame my disequilibrative remarks—"One of your tasks as teachers is to create chaos in the classroom"—in a much broader human and intellectual context. I ask my students to "suspend disbelief in my competence," to remain open to evidence of my competence as the course emerges, and to demand of me a showing of that competence. Again, the notion of an essential tension, as well as a faith in community processes, becomes crucial here.

A PROCESS APPROACH

What I have been advocating so far and what has worked well for me as a teacher and curriculum designer—at elementary school, undergraduate, graduate, and adult learner levels—is an emphasis on process. While Dewey, Piaget, and Bruner have all advocated process, the concept became empowering for me only in recent years, when the "California experience" brought me in contact with post-modern and process thought. While there is certainly nothing uniquely "California" to either of these movements, it is there I came in contact with both. Process thought, particularly in its theological aspects, is founded on the work of Alfred North Whitehead (1925, 1929), as interpreted by his pupil Charles Hartshorne (1948). In simple terms, it argues that the reality of thought lies *in* experience not *outside* experience. We construct thought, we do not discover it. The mind is an organizing concept, not a blank tablet to be imprinted. Curriculum designers must realize that we are inside, not outside, experience. As Maurice Merleau-Ponty (1960) has expressed it:

> So long as I keep before me the ideal of an absolute observer [a tacit assumption the modernist curriculum continually makes], of knowledge without a point of view, I can see my situation as being founded on error. But once I have acknowledged that through this situation I am connected to all actions and to all knowledge that is meaningful to me ... then my contact with the social in the finitude of my situation is revealed to me as the starting point of all truth ... [and] since we are inside truth and cannot get outside, all I can do is to define truth within the situation. (pp. 136–137; personal translation)

This shift from an absolute observer outside experience—Newton's *deus ex machina*—to a participator inside is the transition I have made as a curricularist and as a teacher, from my early modernist days to my present postmodernist ones.

While Dewey, Piaget, Bruner, and Whitehead have all aided me in making this transition, one statement from Donald Schön (1983) has been my beacon. As modified by me, from *practitioner* and *client* to *teacher* and *student*, it reads as follows:

> In a reflective contract between teacher and student, the student does not agree to accept the teacher's authority, but to suspend disbelief in that authority—to remain open to evidence of the teacher's competence as it emerges. (p. 296)

Here, the student and the teacher are asked to form a personal relationship in which the teacher has the opportunity to practice the craft of teaching and the student evaluates the teacher on actual performance, not on external, professional, or institutional criteria. In such a reflective relationship, the student "agrees to join the teacher in inquiry in trying to understand what the student is experiencing and to make that understanding accessible" (p. 296).

The student, operating from a position of trust, must be willing to share embryonic and emerging thoughts and to reflect on them both logically and psychologically. The teacher must not abuse this trust, but must "agree to help the student understand the meaning of the advice given and the rationale for it." In this latter role the teacher needs to be "readily confrontable by the student; and to reflect with the student, on the tacit understanding each has" (p. 296).

Obviously, the relationship here is not between equals; each individual has a different role to play. But it is a relationship wherein these roles intersect in an open, honest, potentially transformative manner. The curriculum is not preset, but, in Dewey's terms, is oriented in a definite direction. In short, it is a process where ends take particular formation through the mutual interaction of teacher and student, where each participates from a perspective that is shared with the other and each is open to the transformation of individual experience.

Using this concept, I have been able to reduce the anxiety associated with disequilibrium and to work with my students from first grade on in helping them develop their own tacit understandings. With graduate and adult students, I can state these goals and methods directly, as well as request that they keep me honest in my dealings with them. With younger students, I can use examples only. In the area of mathematics, which I teach once a week in a public school classroom, I never use a teacher's guide or an answer book. I do the problems they do, and we explore what we see in these problems together. We share our insights. Sometimes they make up the problems for the day's activity, sometimes I do, sometimes their classroom teacher does. But always we reflect together on the nature of the problems, on what they mean, how they can be interpreted, and on variations that can be produced. Together we learn a great deal, not only about mathematics and its structure but also about our own perceptions and ways of organization. Again, transformations take place.

POST-MODERNISM

I'd like to close this chapter with a few words on post-modernism. At one level it is both an architectural and a pop-culture movement that puts together an eclectic combination of various styles, foods, and designs. Architecturally, the A.T.&T. building on Madison Avenue in New York City is post-modern: It combines Roman arches at the base, with functionalist Bauhaus block design in the midsection, topped off with Chippendale spires. At a trendy restaurant in Los Angeles, one can order a "post-modern" lunch of overdone hamburger, Wonder bread, and Grolsch beer. On another level, post-modernism is a serious attempt to move beyond the rigid formalism and dichotomous categories modernism has set up—in literature, the sciences, epistemology, theology, and mathematics. As one post-modern commentator phrases it:

> [The concept] represents a critical reappraisal of modern modes of thought, religious belief and moral conviction. It invites a deepening suspicion of the rigid dichotomies modernity has created between objective reality and subjective experience, fact and imagination, secular and sacred, public and private. (Waters, 1986, p. 113)

Post-modernism is a movement that accepts the universe as complex, self-generating, and evolving. It is a universe that is always in the process of Becoming, not one that has been rigidly set in Being. It is a universe in which development will depend, in part, on us and our actions. It has, I believe, a tremendous heuristic power for curriculum development. Now when my students tell me they have learned how not to teach, their frame of reference is very different from that of a decade ago.

REFERENCES

Bruner, Jerome. (1973). On the perception of incongruity: A paradigm. In J. Anglin (Ed.), *Beyond the information given.* New York: Norton. (Original essay publication, 1949.)

Davies, Paul. (1988). *The cosmic blueprint.* New York: Simon & Schuster.

Dewey, John. (1958). *Experience and nature.* New York: Dover. (Original publication, 1929.)

Dewey, John. (1964). The need for a philosophy of education. In R. D. Archambault (Ed.), *John Dewey on education.* New York: Modern Library. (Original essay publication, 1934.)

Doll, Wm. E., Jr. (1983). Curriculum and change: Piaget's organismic origins. *Journal of Curriculum Theorizing, 5*(2), 4–61.

Hartshorne, Charles. (1948). *The divine relativity.* New Haven: Yale University Press.

Kuhn, Thomas. (1977). *The essential tension.* Chicago: Chicago University Press.

Merleau-Ponty, Maurice. (1960). Le philosophie et la sociologie. In *Collection Idées.* Paris: Gallimard.

Newton, Isaac. (1972). *Mathematical principles of natural philosophy (Principia*—3rd ed., rev.). Cambridge: Harvard University Press (Original publication, 1729.)

Piaget, Jean. (1971). *Science of education and the psychology of the child.* New York: Viking.

Piaget, Jean. (1977). *The development of thought: Equilibration and cognitive structures.* New York: Viking.

Prigogine, Ilya, and Stengers, Isabelle. (1984). *Order out of chaos: Man's new dialogue with nature.* New York: Bantam.

Schön, Donald. (1983). *The reflective practitioner: How professionals think in action.* New York: Basic Books.

Waters, Brent. (1986). Ministry and the university in a postmodern world. *Religion and Intellectual Life,* 4(1), 113–122.

Whitehead, Alfred North. (1925). *Science and the modern world.* New York: Macmillan.

Whitehead, Alfred North. (1929). *Process and reality.* New York: Macmillan.

Whitehead, Alfred North. (1967) *Aims of education.* New York: The Free Press. (Original publication, 1929.)

4

Empowering Educators Through the Processes of Enfolding and Unfolding Curriculum

ANDREA C. BOWMAN
University of Northern Iowa

NELSON L. HAGGERSON
Arizona State University

I, Andrea C. Bowman, am an assistant professor and Coordinator of Student Teaching at the University of Northern Iowa. I completed an Ed.D. in Curriculum and Instruction at Arizona State University (1987), where my major professor and mentor was Nelson L. Haggerson.

My current teaching beliefs began unfolding in my first year of teaching (1969) when I attempted to apply the educational theories taught to me in my teacher preparation program at San Jose State College (now SJSU). I found myself questioning the way reading was "supposed" to be taught in my elementary school. Students appeared more absorbed in the reading process when they had a voice in selecting their reading material than when they followed the preset curriculum (basal readers).

As I continued teaching, I gained the confidence I needed to explore alternative curricular possibilities. Then, as I was working on my doctorate and teaching classes in teacher education, I discovered that the ideas I had tried out in the elementary school setting were based on research and were even practiced in some places! With the assurance that "my" ideas were shared by others, I proceeded to give my university students more ownership for their learning. I also listened carefully to the students as they unfolded their curricula, and their voices became enfolded in my subsequent courses.

I, Nelson L. Haggerson, am a professor of education at Arizona State University. I completed a Ph.D. at Claremont Graduate School (1960), where my advisor (mentor) was Clyde Curran. His advisor was L. G. Thomas.

I see the roots of my mytho-poetic teaching soul in my first position as a teacher of high school mathematics and Latin. I found the most effective entree into teaching/learning plane geometry was through both the environment and the imagination. Students began geometry with photos and movies of designs in the environment, before we ever touched proofs, logic, and measurement. In Latin class we all gained a healthy respect for mythology as we read and enacted those myths in both English and Latin.

A major influence in my university teaching, in which enfolding and unfolding of curricula is now the thrust, was the "human potential" movement of the 1960s and 1970s. Bill Coulson, Director of the Center for the Study of the Person, and several of my colleagues, among them Susan Cummings, Warren Kingsbury and Naomi Wamacks, as well as students Mary Catherine Dunn and Lynette Knight, all formerly of Arizona State University, gave me courage, example, and faith in the mytho-poetic, collegial, and empowering posture of teaching.

We would like to invite you to enfold yourself in our dialogue as you read this chapter. While not a transcription of a specific conversation, we believe the dialogue format best captures the essence of an ongoing exchange. Our discussion started in a curriculum class where we met as doctoral student and professor. Now, after several years, it is difficult for us to decide whose thoughts sparked which ideas. Ours has been a spirited dialogue, and we would like you to engage in it with us, and to reflect with us on some of our discoveries about curriculum as an agent for empowerment.

ANDREA: Nelson, have you made any recent discoveries about the enfolding and unfolding of curriculum in what Doll (Chapter 3) sees as our post-modern world?

NELSON: I recently visited the Boston Museum of Fine Arts and accidentally came upon an exhibit that I entitled "The Enfolding and Unfolding of Fans." As you know, we had already submitted the title of this chapter as "Empowering Educators Through the Processes of Enfolding and Unfolding Curriculum." All of a sudden I found a metaphor that helped me further conceptualize the processes. As I carefully examined each of the fans in the exhibit, I began to make notes on the uses and aesthetics of fans. Fans have been used as masks, therapy, language, memory aids, almanacs, maps, stories, political messages, worry beads, as well as aids for comfort. Fans are beautiful, mysterious, magical, surprising, coquettish, satisfying, stimulating, and enrapturing. Fans are often so dynamic they appear to have a life of their own.

ANDREA: The fan is the process and the product in which the creator enfolds the story to be unfolded; it is the curriculum! The creator lends life to the fan, which then takes on a life of its own and, in turn, affects the lives of those both actively and passively experiencing it.

NELSON: I think this poem, using another metaphor, portrays your thought.

> THE SCULPTURE [THE FAN]
>
> The artist walking by
> picked up a lump of clay
> and moistened it.
> With fingers warm he smoothed,
> plucked, shaped and urged
> his life into the form.
> Spirit from his spirit
> danced in clay.
> It caught the music
> of his heart, and breathed.
>   (Haggerson, 1971)

ANDREA: These metaphors help when considering enfolding and un-folding the curriculum.

THE CURRICULUM AS SELF

NELSON: Yes, they do in a number of ways. When teaching my doctoral curriculum class I want students to understand and experience, to the great-est extent possible, various curriculum views and metaphors. One of these is the curriculum as self. At the very beginning of the class I ask students to make a list of 10 activities they really like to do. We talk about those for a while, and then I ask them to list 10 experiences they want to have, and finally 10 things they need to do this semester. We talk about the patterns appearing in their reporting; the differences between likes, wants, and needs; and priorities for attaining their likes, wants, and needs. I then ask each to translate a need into a goal that the student would like to fulfill during the semester. We discuss the translation process and analyze priorities for attaining the goal. Finally we do an action plan that includes ways of attaining the goal, a time line, and ways to assess progress. That action plan becomes the student's personal curriculum for the semester. As teacher, I also select a goal and develop and carry out a personal curriculum. At various times during the semester we report to the class on our progress. Students often report progress, problems, and changes in their personal curricula through journal entries.

ANDREA: What stands out about the personal curriculum in this class?

NELSON: Typically students find that they are the curriculum. They discover that to carry out a personal curriculum, they have to change, they have to struggle; a few are not able or willing to attain their goal. However, those who are willing to take the risks discover that they are enfolding themselves into the curriculum and that as they share with members of the class publicly, or me through their journals, they are unfolding their curricula. In a way, the students find themselves more confident, more open, more willing to take risks: They experience being empowered.

ANDREA: In retrospect, discovering the curriculum as self was an energizing experience, which I can now see as the foundation for reaching the goals I had set for myself. There was that unforgettable curriculum class, you know the one I mean, where we were all struggling with self. The course title was Curriculum and Instruction, but we were all struggling to find meaning in a doctoral program. Much like Kantor (Chapter 5), the curriculum was enfolded in our autobiographies. As we kept journals, created aesthetic pieces (prose, poetry, drawings, fans), role-played, danced, and inquired, we unfolded our changing selves and allowed others in the class to contribute to that process.

NELSON: As I listen to you recollect, it occurs to me that the process of enfolding and unfolding is recursive. Do you see it that way?

ANDREA: Yes. As I discovered more of myself—my strengths, my weaknesses—I was able to share those with other members of the class. They, in turn, went through a similar process, and in the course of our interactions we created new views of ourselves as curricula. And so the process goes; it is recursive (see Chapter 5). It is also empowering.

NELSON: How do you mean?

ANDREA: We took some risks. We gave ourselves permission to look back on our lives, to explore new domains; we allowed others to look at our lives and our creations. I wrote my first poetry, and in doing so, discovered a new way of expressing joy and grief. The satisfactions gained from these experiences encouraged us to want more, to explore additional facets of curriculum; we unfolded the fan a little further. We gained confidence in our reflective skills and in our interactions with others. As we related our own curricula with curriculum literature, we realized the need for expanding our perspectives on curriculum.

NELSON: That reminds me of a way I am currently thinking about inquiring into curriculum as self: the process of heuristic inquiry. Let me tell you a little about that process. I took the idea from Douglass and Moustakas (1985). The first phase of heuristic inquiry is immersion. One has a need, a fear, a problem, an idea. The immersion phase of the inquiry is explicating the personal situation as fully as possible. The second phase is acquisition. Once the personal situation has been examined, other perspectives are brought into the picture. We look at the literature on the subject, we ask others about similar experiences, and we observe others in similar situations. Finally we come to a realization, which is the last phase of heuristic inquiry.

ANDREA: Have you been able to try out this process?

NELSON: Yes, I recently chaired a doctoral dissertation in which the candidate used heuristic inquiry. Scott (1987) studied the nature of radical adult life transitions and the healing processes in their aftermath. She had recently made a radical transition in her own life. She was hurting, fearful, joyful, resentful. She shared her experience as a beginning point (immersion). She then found others who had gone through radical life changes, and she read literature about the phenomenon (acquisition). She came to realize that the transition was a "confrontation of limited self-conception and vision with a greater reality," (p. iv) which enhanced her own empowerment.
This sounds like the naturalistic curriculum research you did on the transitions made by students becoming teachers.

VOICES OF THE CURRICULUM

ANDREA: Yes, that was a very satisfying study to do. As a teacher, I reexperienced some of my own early struggles and excitement while I was becoming a teacher. As a teacher becoming a teacher of teachers, I identified with the experience of transition. How good it felt when a student called me "professor" for the first time. And how awkward it felt, at times, to have the responsibility for helping students become teachers, without the authority of being a "real" professor. As a student of research becoming a researcher, I experienced the surprise of seeing a study unfold the way I had read about studies unfolding. As a person becoming myself, I sensed an increased trust and faith in myself as a teacher, a teacher of teachers, a researcher, and a person. I was empowered.

NELSON: Why did you decide to do that study?

ANDREA: My career goal was to become a teacher educator. To accomplish that goal I needed to better understand the socialization process of students becoming teachers. I decided to take a closer look at students in the process of becoming teachers, to gain a better understanding of them and to translate those findings into a curriculum that would facilitate the socialization of teachers. At the time, I was working with students who were studying to become teachers in a public school setting that was supportive of their growth. It seemed desirable to look at these students in that setting, hoping to gain an understanding about their experiences as they made the transition from student to teacher.

NELSON: Tell me more about your study.

ANDREA: I conducted a naturalistic study (Bowman, 1987). I gathered data by means of observation and interviews and through journals kept by preservice teachers and me. From the data, I constructed seven biographies of preservice teachers. Through analysis and interpretation of the biographies, I developed a number of themes, which served as bases for propositions I formulated and were eventually used in forming a curriculum construal (a conceptual framework that serves as a heuristic for curriculum development). I took these propositions, combined them with facets of empowerment (enablement, permission, desire, consequence, and information), and explicated a curriculum component (statement) to form the construal.

NELSON: So, whose voices are enfolded into the curriculum construal?

ANDREA: Well, in essence I developed a preservice teacher curriculum based on preservice teacher needs and construed it in such a way that, by fulfilling their needs, it would also empower them, give them confidence in themselves, and give them permission to use their talents and skills. In a word, a curriculum to emancipate them from the methods-techniques-skills syndrome. So, voices of the preservice teachers and my voice were enfolded into the construal. The notion of voices inspired a poem, which I used to dedicate the study.

MAY I INTRUDE UPON YOUR LIFE?

May I intrude
Upon your life?
May I stop
And look awhile?
Combine your voice
With my experiences?
May I write a story
Which will let others
Know you?
Learn from you?
Be touched by your life?
(Bowman, 1987)

I have just talked about the voices of students and teachers (that is, myself) that are enfolded into the curriculum. Have you experienced other voices in the curriculum?

NELSON: As a matter of fact, I discovered the place of other voices a couple of years ago. Dr. Vasant Merchant, editor of the *Arizona Humanities Association Journal,* asked me to prepare an article for an issue on "Humanities and Education for World Peace." That issue was to serve as a curriculum for peace studies. When it became clear that I was going to Japan in the summer of 1986 for a world peace conference, and would be there on August 6, the date the dropping of the Atomic Bomb is remembered, I asked if I could write the article upon my return.

While in Hiroshima I attended the Hiroshima Peace Memorial Ceremony and several sessions of the Peace Summit. I visited the Peace Museum and the bookstore in Peace Park. The museum had many photographs, some paintings, and a number of artifacts. At the bookstore I found a book by Eleanor Coerr (1977) entitled *Sadako and the Thousand Paper Cranes.* It is the story of a Japanese girl, Sadako, who died at the age of 11 from leukemia, and for whom the "Child's Statue in Memory of the Atomic Bomb" was erected. Earlier in the day we placed thousands of paper cranes at the foot of her statue. As I read Coerr's book, I realized that Sadako's voice was heard through her story, and that the story was itself witness to the feelings, hopes, fears, and mysteries of a people. Hence, the story as witness became a part of the peace curriculum (Haggerson, 1987).

I want to add to that discovery by telling you about my finding that the photographs, especially the black-and-white photographs, were also witness. The photographs in the museum depicted the tragedy in a way no other media could have. The black-and-white photographs portrayed the essence of the situation. I saw there a part of the peace curriculum that I had never imagined. It was a voice of a tragedy to which photographs were witness. Through the photographs as witness, we heard the voices of photographers as they enfolded into the curriculum of peace.

ANDREA: As our curriculum is unfolding, it reminds me of the fan with its many dimensions. It, too, is a witness bearing the voices of artists depicting the culture of a given time and place.

NELSON: Yes, I agree. I also think of the scientist as witness, and while we are talking about a peace curriculum, I can relate to Nicolescu (1986) who writes about the "scientist as bearing witness." She conjectures that our conception of reality as only objective or subjective results in one of the major schisms of our times. There is the world out there, and there is the world created by humankind. However, there is a third possibility, which seems to conform to modern scientific knowledge: "The real" is the result of interaction between the world and the human being, the two facets of one and the same reality. It is to this interaction, well described by Doll (in Chapter 3), that the modern scientist could truly "bear witness" (p. 29). As we develop the peace curriculum, we surely should listen to the voices of Pauling and Tutu (speakers at the peace conference who bore witness to the interaction of the physical reality and the human reality in violent and nonviolent interaction).

ANDREA: Indeed, if the curriculum is to be viable, we must listen to creditable voices in the many forms in which they bear witness. And we need to search for and be open to other voices that may tell us of new perspectives.

UNFOLDING CURRICULAR ACTIVITIES

NELSON: In the last conversation, we emphasized the enfolding of voices into the curriculum. Now let's talk about the empowerment that accompanies the unfolding of curriculum. How are you enhancing empowerment in your student teaching curriculum?

ANDREA: There is a powerful network among student teachers. They consult with each other about assignments, positive and not-so-positive classroom experiences, and problems of adjusting to a new community and a new classroom. They also enjoy each other's company outside the school environment.

As I reflected on this network, I realized it could be expanded to better help them with their curricular decisions and instructional practices. I had one group of student teachers discuss a lesson in pairs after each taught a lesson that the others had not seen. As a facilitator, I suggested questions and supervision strategies that they could use to enhance their dialogue. Having had little previous experience with peer supervision, the student teachers reported that they liked this process. They did not feel, however, that they had enough strategies to adequately help one another. So, incorporating their suggestions, I used a peer supervision activity with the next group of student teachers during their orientation day activities. I divided them into small groups and asked each group to brainstorm a list of possible questions and supervision strategies that would be helpful to themselves and their peers. Each group then shared its list with the entire class for clarification and further suggestions. I didn't contribute any suggestions. Their ideas were sufficient to begin a simplified form of peer supervision. I collected the lists of questions and suggestions and compiled a set for each member of the group. When they met the following week, I gave them the list, asked them to divide into pairs and, using the questions and suggestions, try out a peer supervision conference about a lesson they had taught during the week. At the end of that activity, I asked them to share reactions to the peer supervision. They contributed further questions and strategies that they had found useful. They practiced this activity each week at their seminar, thereby expanding their repertoire of questions and strategies for peer supervision.

Student teachers began using these techniques on occasions other than the seminar. They not only felt empowered to employ these strategies but were able to assist each other in becoming better teachers. They reported that not only the peer supervision activities but also other cooperative activities strengthened their support for each other, which, in turn, strengthened their existing network.

NELSON: It sounds to me like you were giving permission to the student teachers to unfold their ideas, thus empowering them to strengthen their own teaching and peer support.

ANDREA: Yes, and it keeps growing. As the student teachers are unfolding their curricula, I am learning from them how to better facilitate their

professional growth. This is an example of empowerment through the unfolding of curriculum.

How are you thinking about and teaching the unfolding curriculum process with graduate students?

NELSON: Last spring I volunteered to teach a new course, Introduction
to Graduate Studies, along with my regular graduate curriculum course and
naturalistic research course. You remember I mentioned earlier that I ask
each of my doctoral students in the curriculum class to do a personal curriculum, and that I take on the development of a personal curriculum myself?
Well, last spring I took as my personal curriculum goal the conceptualization
and implementation of the Introduction to Graduate Studies course. I had
been given a syllabus from the previous instructor, but I didn't think it met
the needs of our students at that time. I concurred with the course goal
stated by my predecessor: "To empower graduate students so they could go
about their graduate studies more effectively and independently." My teaching style and knowledge background, however, didn't match her course format. I decided to approach the course as an introduction to what I called
"disciplined inquiry," a term and set of phenomena that I thought were descriptive of the nature of the knowledge explosion. The study, I thought,
would contribute to the empowerment of education students. Actually, I
used what we are calling action research in the process: I conceptualized
the entire course and then attempted to develop a sequence of activities and
materials that I tried out each week in class. I changed as the needs demanded and I documented the changes, the reasons for the changes, and the
outcomes. The course, then, was based on my ideas, feedback from students,
and constantly checking with other colleagues to see what they perceived
to be the needs of their graduate students. I also reported periodically to the
graduate curriculum class, as did other members of the class. As the course
unfolded, I began to get a sense that students were making connections with
their other courses and with their teaching.

ANDREA: How would you summarize the substantiative aspects of your
personal curriculum, which turned out to be the content of Introduction to
Graduate Studies?

NELSON: As I view it, my personal curriculum was a manifestation of
the unfolding curriculum. Reports from students, colleagues, and my own
observations indicated to me that my unfolding curriculum was also empowering to both of them. I called my personal curriculum report a "Modest
Proposal." Let me summarize it. One aspect is that education is disciplined
inquiry having as its domain ways of thinking about the educative processes,

practices, skills, and all of their attendant relationships. Also, education is disciplined inquiry guided by rules. Education is disciplined inquiry that has a historical frame of reference. And, education is disciplined inquiry that includes a community of scholars (Haggerson, 1988).

This modest proposal is an example of the ever-unfolding curriculum called Introduction to Graduate Studies.

Andrea, where are we now in our dialogue about empowering educators?

A LANGUAGE OF CURRICULUM

ANDREA: We set the stage for discussing the processes of enfolding and unfolding curriculum through metaphor: the fan. We explained the empowerment processes through the identification of curriculum with self, through the voices that contribute to the curriculum, and through the activities used in unfolding the curriculum. We now need to look at the language through which we communicate our views about curriculum. How would you describe that language?

NELSON: I like to describe the language as "mytho-poetic" (Macdonald, 1981; Pinar, 1988). In thinking about and teaching curriculum, we find the language of the "mytho-poetic" empowering to ourselves and others. It is an appropriate language for the post-modern age in which we live.

ANDREA: It seems to me that when we use the term "language" here we are talking about not only the formal language of words and symbols and the nonverbal language of behavior, but also the inner (tacit) language of being that facilitates our curricular actions (Cassirer, 1946).

NELSON: Yes, and, as I see it, the language of the mytho-poetic is figurative (Haggerson, 1985). It is the language of stories, myths, metaphors, pictures, witnesses, poems, possibilities. Not only have we used figurative language in addressing the notion of "empowering educators through the processes of enfolding and unfolding curriculum," but we advocate figurative language as a prominent part of the school curriculum. Inherent in figurative language are expressive objectives, multiple opportunities, varied interpretations, and multiple metaphors. Perhaps our curriculum, in an even more inclusive metaphor than the fan, is expressed by the following poem:

ONENESS

The oneness of it all is
A house of many mansions,

Multiple levels of consciousness,
Numerous degrees of caring, and
Infinite individual personalities . . .
Juxtaposed in dynamic
    relationships
   called a
    Universe! [Curriculum]
      (Haggerson, 1971)

UNFOLDING THE RISKS

ANDREA: As much as I think we should end this piece with your poem, I think we would be neglecting an important aspect of our enfolding and unfolding curriculum, which we have both experienced. For as much satisfaction as we have gained with this curriculum process, we have also experienced frustration and at times a sense of uncertainty. There are some risks involved for both students and teachers.

NELSON: Yes. I have sensed that some students do not fully participate in the process for some reason or another. An unfolding, enfolding curriculum requires the students to become active agents in their own learning. A few seem uncomfortable with that notion. Some hide behind the expression, "Just tell me what I have to learn for the test." Others say, "I know what I believe about the teaching/learning process. Don't expect me to change my views." It appears, though, that these students are afraid to take the risk of reflecting on self as it relates to the curriculum.

ANDREA: As a teacher I have sometimes felt vulnerable and uncertain with the unfolding, enfolding process. I let the students know that I can learn from them (Kantor also did this when he asked his students to give him suggestions for writing his chapter). And, as does Doll, when he allows his course design to be constructed "conjointly" by professor and students, I give up some of the control to the students. That can be frightening. Sometimes the students are also frightened, at first. Once in a while I want to toss out the whole idea, write a series of lectures, and just tell the students what I want them to know. I think that might be easier. However, when I begin to feel this way, I look back on students' comments about the courses: "We had to think, not memorize." "I didn't feel intimidated by you . . . I was relaxed, so I learned more." "It was a refreshing way to learn . . . we learned from each other." Such comments help me to reconsider. Even though there are risks, the process is satisfying to both the students and the teacher.

And so our dialogue continues with each other, with our students, with our colleagues, and with you. We have discovered that the enfolding and unfolding of curriculum is a powerful (empowering) way to teach and learn. We have further discovered that our unfolding dialogue, including the use of metaphor (the fan), is a necessary part of that empowering process.

REFERENCES

Bowman, Andrea C. (1987). *Perspectives of becoming a secondary teacher: A pre-student teaching experience.* Dissertation. Tempe, AZ: Arizona State University.

Cassirer, E. (1946). *Language and Myth.* New York: Dover.

Coerr, Eleanor. (1977). *Sadako and the thousand paper cranes.* New York: Putnam's.

Douglass, B. G., & Moustakas, C. (1985). Heuristic inquiry: The internal search to know. *The Journal of Humanistic Psychology, 25* (3), 39–55.

Haggerson, Nelson L. (1971). *To dance with joy.* New York: Exposition Press.

Haggerson, Nelson L. (1985). Curriculum as figurative language: Exalting teaching and learning through poetry. *Illinois School Research and Development, 22* (1), 10–17.

Haggerson, Nelson L. (1987). Ironies of the Pacific: Educational imperatives. *Arizona Humanities Association Journal, 6* (5), 53–56. Also appears in *WCCI Forum, 1* (1), 63–66.

Haggerson, Nelson L. (1988). Reconceptualizing inquiry in curriculum: Using multiple research paradigms to enhance the study of curriculum. *Journal of Curriculum Theorizing, 8* (1), 81–102.

Macdonald, James B. (1981). Theory-practice and the hermeneutic circle. *Journal of Curriculum Theorizing, 3* (2), 130–138.

Nicolescu, Basarab. (1986). Science and tradition. *Parabola, 11* (1), 28–35.

Niebuhr, R. R. (1986). Looking through the wall: A meditation on vision. *Parabola, 11* (1), 6–18.

Pinar, William. (1988). Introduction. In W. Pinar (Ed.), *Contemporary Curriculum Discourses.* Scottsdale, AZ: Gorsuch Scarisbrick.

Scott, Andrea C. (1987). Understanding the experience of leaving a way of life. Dissertation. Tempe, AZ: Arizona State University.

5

Both Sides Now

Teaching English,
Teaching Curriculum

KEN KANTOR
National College of Education

My interest and work in curriculum reflect a relationship (often a tension) between a generalist view and a content-specific (English language arts) perspective. That relationship began to come into focus for me in my doctoral study at Stanford University in the early 1970s. I am indebted to my major advisor, Alfred Grommon, for urging me to examine the history of English education, to Elliot Eisner and Decker Walker for making me aware of curriculum theory, to David Tyack for his emphasis on looking at primary sources, to Lawrence Thomas for his insights into Progressive education (and particularly the work of Dewey), to Fannie Shaftel for her experiential method and example as a scholar-practitioner, and to fellow doctoral students Dan Donlan and Dwaine Greer for helping me maintain the connection between the personal and the professional. Many others since then have also influenced me strongly, notably colleagues and students at Bowling Green State University and the University of Georgia through their commitment to a humanistic model of English teaching and curriculum, and present associates at National College of Education in their continual relating of theory to practice, and practice to theory. In a sense, I have now come full circle, teaching courses in curriculum, instructional leadership, qualitative research, and linguistics and writing, and thus bringing into greater balance the universal and the content-specific. I return to a starting point, however, only to begin the discovery process anew.

> The events in our lives happen in a sequence in time, but in their significance to ourselves they find their own order, a timetable not necessarily—perhaps not possibly—chronological. The time as we know it subjectively is often the chronology that stories and novels follow: it is the continuous thread of revelation. (Eudora Welty, 1983)

At the heart of this chapter is an autobiographical narrative of my three years of teaching high school English in southern California, and an interpretive discussion of ways in which that experience relates to my later teaching of courses in English curriculum history and theory. The account is recursive as well as linear, revealing both how impressions of my professional and personal life have been clarified in light of experiences since then, and how my present teaching of curriculum is given meaning through an understanding of the past. In the words of Andrea Bowman and Nelson Haggerson (Chapter 4), the curriculum is the "story to be unfolded."

Specifically, the story explores my English teaching in light of weaknesses stemming from inexperience and naivete, and successes based on instincts and actions that proved sound with respect to contemporary curriculum theory. Thematically, the story draws inspiration from music of the late 1960s. During that time Joni Mitchell wrote the song "Both Sides Now," which serves as the title of this chapter and strikes the necessary note of uncertainty: After more than 20 years of life as a teacher of English and curriculum, I sometimes feel that "I really don't know life at all." But as William Doll argues, in Chapter 3, uncertainty and discovery are essential to the post-modern curriculum in which we are engaged.

RETURNING TO THE SCENE

But I was so much older then.
—Bob Dylan, "My Back Pages"

The place was the San Joaquin Valley of southern California, the time August 1967. I had just gotten married and had left a large state university in the Midwest, after earning a master's degree in English and spending two more years in a doctoral program, also in English. I had taken a job teaching secondary English, for four main reasons: (1) I wanted to teach at the high school level; (2) I wished to avoid the draft (the superintendent of this district had written a letter to my draft board citing the need for English teachers); (3) I wanted to escape the midwestern winters (in January 1967 we had suffered through a 26-inch snowfall); and (4) I had an older brother, other relatives, and friends living in the Bay Area (any place in California seemed as good as any other). So Nancy and I set off on our honeymoon trip across the United States to begin our life together and meet whatever adventures were ahead of us.

My assignment was eleventh grade English, three advanced and two general level classes, with a focus on American literature. The students were from largely middle and lower-middle income families, white, black, Hispanic, and a few Asian-American. A number of the white students were descendants of the "Okies"; their ancestors, as described in Steinbeck's novel *The Grapes of Wrath,* had populated the migrant work camps nearby. (Steinbeck's depiction of the Okies was a sensitive issue; it was only shortly before we arrived that the book was allowed to be displayed on the school library shelves.) Many of the Hispanic students were children of migrant farm workers; some were in school only part of the year, having to "follow the crops" to other places. They and the black students lived in largely segregated neighborhoods on the east side of town, literally across the tracks.

My memories of this period lie firmly within the context of the times, particularly the events of 1968. Several of those events were to touch us directly. The assassination of Martin Luther King, Jr. in April 1968 led to racial unrest and conflict at our school. The assassination of Bobby Kennedy occurred in Los Angeles, just a hundred miles south of us. In the Democratic primaries, George Wallace received his greatest California support in our county. Nancy and I spent the summer of 1968 in Chicago and left just before the Democratic Convention in that city; on TV screens in motel rooms across the country, we watched protesters and police in their violent clashes. In Delano, just north of us, Cesar Chavez was leading the migrant farm workers in a nationwide grape boycott. A number of male students in my classes were talking about or preparing to join the military service and very possibly would be sent to Vietnam. And the recently elected governor of California was an ex-actor named Ronald Reagan. This was the larger context, then, in which my teaching of high school English in these years took place.

The idea of context assumes a major role in my teaching of curriculum courses at the college level. I emphasize that the teaching of English (or any other subject) does not occur in a vacuum and must be related to larger social, cultural, political, and historical issues. Certainly such matters as censorship, dialect differences, and "back-to-basics" are intimately tied to attitudes within the larger community and society, as well as the particular backgrounds of individuals. As Doll illustrates in his reference to the thoughts of Merleau-Ponty (Chapter 3), it is the specifics of situations that give phenomena their curricular meaning.

HESTER PRYNNE AND HUCK FINN LIVE!

It was September 1969 and the first day of my elective course in nineteenth-century American novels. We had just initiated our new English elective program for eleventh and twelfth graders, and I was eager to teach the nine-week course centering on *The Scarlet Letter, Huckleberry Finn,* and *The Red Badge of Courage.* To begin the discussion of *The Scarlet Letter,* I had students read the first chapter, in which Hester Prynne is seen on the scaffold in the town marketplace, jeered at by the crowd for her sin of adultery. I then asked the students how they felt a modern-day "Hester" might be treated by the larger society. The discussion was lively and engaged, with most students agreeing that while a pregnant teenage girl might not be subject to the same public ridicule as Hester, she might be criticized or rejected in more subtle ways.

At the end of class, one girl who had been quiet during the discussion came up to the front, slammed her book on my desk, and angrily declared that she was not taking this course. Later that day her father called and explained to me that she had gotten pregnant the previous year and had a child out of wedlock. He said she felt that many of the comments in the class discussion were directed against her, and though he had tried to persuade her to talk with me, she had adamantly refused and insisted on being transferred to another class. The next day she was no longer in my class.

This incident remains with me as a dramatic example of how powerfully literature can relate to our lives and how students in responding to literature bring their experiences and values to bear on their interpretations. Several years later in my doctoral study in English education, I read Louise Rosenblatt's classic work *Literature as Exploration* (1938), and I understood clearly what she meant by her discussion of the dynamic transaction between reader and text. I emphasize this idea strongly in my teaching of curriculum courses.

I can remember other instances of such transactions from that earlier time. *Huckleberry Finn,* despite the controversial nature of the references to Nigger Jim throughout, spoke strongly to many students about issues of race and morality. A few identified with Huck striking out on a raft down the Mississippi, as they shared his anti-establishment views and desire to escape from a corrupt society. (I recall reading about a halfway house at the time called "Huckleberry's for Runaways.")

I had less success with teaching *The Red Badge of Courage.* I'd thought that with the immediacy of Vietnam, students would identify with Henry Fleming's uncertainties and loss of innocence. (When I saw the film "Platoon" recently, I related the anguish of the main character to Henry's realizations about the harsh realities of war.) But perhaps because of that frightening immediacy, my students showed less interest in the themes of *Red Badge.* At the end of the course, I asked them to rank order the three novels in terms of their preferences. The overwhelming favorite was *The Scarlet Letter.* This surprised me initially, because I didn't think students would find Hawthorne's Puritan ethic very appealing. On reflection, though, it struck me that the issue of sexual morality in the novel connected strongly with the feelings of the adolescents in my class. It seemed that they were searching for a set of values, a clear sense of right and wrong in a world that seemed increasingly less morally secure. The sexual revolution was occurring around them, bringing with it both expectations of freedom and confusions about responsibility. This highlighted for me a central dilemma of literature teaching: how to help students develop an appreciation for connotation and ambiguity while their stages of development and the circumstances of their society seemed to demand a singular and literal set of truths. Again, as I stress with my college students, literature cannot be separated from the context of the values, conflicts, and contradictions that it represents.

TOMMIE SMITH, JOHN CARLOS, AND DERON JONES

All because of the color of his skin.
—Bob Dylan, "Oxford Town"

Deron Jones was a black student in my eleventh grade general level class. He sat in the back of the room and was very quiet; sometimes I'd find him with his head down on his desk. His written work was good, though, and showed genuine thinking ability; this countered any suggestions that he was "nonverbal." Later that year I saw evidence that he was anything but nonverbal. He was talking to a friend after lunch about the 1968 Summer Olympics, specifically the raised-fist black power salute of athletes Tommie Smith and John Carlos as they stood on the winners' stand. In talking about this incident, Deron was animated and fully engaged, fluent and articulate.

Later I was able to relate this observation to my reading of sociolinguistic studies, particularly the work of William Labov (1970) on black dialect. The clear finding here was that the language of black students was in certain ways different from, but not inferior to, the language of white students. It was primarily when required to meet the demands of "standard English" in school settings that black students seemed uncommunicative and nonverbal. The "deficit hypothesis" of various psychologists and linguists was being challenged and largely discredited. Deron's language ability with peers outside the classroom made it evident that his writing proficiency was no accident, as it related to his abilities in oral expression.

In linguistics courses I have taught more recently, dialectal differences represent a major topic. It is difficult for many students to overcome their biases; many still see the language of black or Hispanic people as inferior to that of middle class whites. To address these prejudices, I have students talk and write about personal experiences in which they were discriminated against because of the way they spoke. I also have them interview others regarding attitudes toward dialect speakers. One interesting action research project involves documenting and analyzing individuals' responses to tape-recorded passages reflecting various dialects. The issue here is not simply one of linguistic understanding, but of a social and cultural understanding that results in greater respect for the language, perspectives, and values of people of different backgrounds.

As I mentioned earlier, racial tensions surfaced dramatically at the time of the King assassination. Black parents and students had already begun to protest the use of Confederate symbols at the school; athletic teams were called the Rebels, the Confederate flag was paraded at football games, and the marching band played "Dixie." The King assassination aggravated these tensions, and students, at times, erupted in violent confrontations. Wishing to address racial questions more directly, I had decided to teach the play *A Raisin in the Sun* (Hansberry, 1959), about a black family in Chicago attempting to move into an all white neighborhood. What I found among the students was prejudice and lack of awareness certainly, but also a greater willingness to establish understanding than seemed to be the desire of their parents. Discussion of the play allowed us to explore especially the dilemma of tradition versus change. Some argued, for example, that the Confederate symbols represented an important tradition of the school and community; others countered that racism was also a tradition, but one not deserving of being maintained. And reading *A Raisin in the Sun* helped them to consider racial issues in personal terms, because they could see Walter Younger and his family as human beings with strengths and weaknesses, but more important, with dreams and aspirations for a better life.

SIROCCO: SEEKING A VOICE

Sirocco was the name of the school literary magazine, referring to a hot southerly wind, and thus avoiding the negative associations of Confederate symbols. In my first year, I offered to be faculty advisor to the magazine. The previous advisor willingly turned over the job, counseling me that I could get away with publishing pieces that expressed political views, but not any

dealing with sex. Sirocco also became an after-school club, meeting errati-
cally during the year and more frequently near publication time in May
when matters of editing, layout, and printing had to be attended to.

The magazine contained poems, stories, personal essays, illustrations,
and photographs dealing with a variety of personal and social themes. In the
1970 issue, many of the pieces originated in my elective courses in creative
writing. One of the benefits of the elective program was that students from
both general and advanced levels were combined in the classes. In preparing
the creative writing courses, I had expressed the view that high academic
achievers had no monopoly on creativity; I was later pleased to discover that
prominent English educators (Dixon, 1967; Moffett, 1968) held the same
view. That position is still central to my teaching of curriculum and methods
courses in writing. As inspiration for writing, I used photographs, short
films, and song lyrics, especially those written and sung by the poets of the
day: Bob Dylan, Joni Mitchell, Simon and Garfunkel, Aretha Franklin, Judy
Collins, The Beatles, Jimi Hendrix, and Janis Joplin. I gained some reputation
for this; one student told me she'd take my Creative Writing course if I prom-
ised not to play Simon and Garfunkel's "Sounds of Silence." Recognizing that
the song had already become clichéd, I agreed to her request.

Many of the writings were quite personal, dealing with feelings about
loneliness, hope, anger, happiness, death, beauty, reality, and fantasy. Following is one student's expression of passionately felt emotions and of the dilemmas those emotions posed for her:

> I want to screech, to scream
> To wax, to wane.
> To be violent, troubled
> To be ripped asunder with grief and despair
> To explode in inexpressible joy.
> To be raw, to be stark
> At the soul of my being.
> My passions intense
> Gross sensitivity.
> But I'm moderate.
> And I won't attain release from soft comfort
>   by drifting.
> I must violently emerge.
> A second birth, so to speak.

Often students' feelings in these writings would be tied to themes of
nature. Some writings were pastoral in subject matter and tone; others connected ideas about nature to ecological problems. A number of students also
confronted family and generational questions (at a time when, we recall,
they were advised not to trust anyone over 30). Still others wrote humorous

pieces. The lighter pieces represented a minority, however; most students seemed to be thinking and writing about serious matters. The war in Vietnam weighed heavily on students' minds; their writings about it often reflected anger and despair. The assassination of Martin Luther King, Jr. inspired several powerful poems, by both black and white students. Others wrote more generally about racial issues; one poem written by a young black woman is especially striking.

SNICKERS BAR

Midway
through a melted snickers bar,
I realize that
the only man on the bus, drunk and talking
out
of
his
head, is a black man.
When is Eldridge coming back?
I need things to think about.
Contents: Cocoa, powdered milk, egg whites,
        soybean oil,
salt (emulsifier added), caramel. . . .
Looking out of the window into the ghetto,
you long for nicer thoughts,
Burn Babylon Burn.
4:15, Where's my brother?
Who is my brother? The Biafran?
        The Nigerian?
Maybe in my mind,
I am fooled . . . Mr. A saxon?
Peanuts always get stuck between my teeth anyway.

What impresses me as I look back at many of these writings are the ways in which the students personalized larger social and political issues. Again, it was a time when national and world events were pressing and real, and young people expressed ideas and feelings about those events in terms that showed their caring and concern. Like the fan to which Bowman and Haggerson refer in Chapter 4, *Sirocco* was "a witness, bearing the voices of artists depicting the culture of a given time and place."

Some students attested specifically to the power of writing for asserting convictions and making sense of things; one young man ended his poem about writing in this way.

What to write about
ain't hard to find

> and I
> for one
> like to write
> because I think
> the things I wonder
> about, are important and real,
> not pure, not pretty, not new
> man, they're here and I
> am part of them.

Writings like these testify to the importance of a constructivist view of curriculum as articulated by Doll (Chapter 3) and Bowman and Haggerson (Chapter 4). Courses in writing that I teach at the college level have at their center a view of writing as a process of discovery, as a means for thinking and learning and, above all, meaning-making. Students do a great deal of expressive writing in journals and experiment with various purposes, audiences, and forms. In doing so, they create their own curriculum of meaning.

"WITH A LITTLE HELP FROM MY FRIENDS"

For all the excitement of learning I was beginning to see in my classes, teaching was often difficult. Some students remained unmotivated, racial tensions continued to ferment just below the surface, the larger community held political views contrary to my own, and the demands of teaching five classes a day and handling other responsibilities began to take their toll. Given these pressures, I was fortunate to have the support and friendship of a number of colleagues.

I remember Bob, an energetic and committed English teacher, a voracious reader of literature, sociology, and political science, and a haunter of bookstores. His shelves at home were lined with books and journals two and three deep. More important, his personal reading was the primary source for his teaching. He stocked his classroom with paperbacks and magazines, and would often bring in articles and editorials reflecting a range of opinion on issues like Vietnam, civil rights, legalization of marijuana, abortion, and so on. Bob was not afraid to have his students deal with controversy; he taught me a great deal about courage in teaching.

And there was Reg, a photography teacher and our next-door neighbor. I especially recall evenings with Reg, watching the Steve Allen show, playing darts, dancing to Motown songs at Saturday night parties, and taking off on spontaneous weekend camping trips to Pismo Beach in Reg's jeep. I also remember watching the draft lottery on television with Reg, all of us breathing a sigh of relief when his number came up far down the list.

There were others too: Paul, the assistant principal who defended my teaching of *A Raisin in the Sun* to skeptical parents; Dave, the principal who maintained a reasoned position and a cool head during the racial conflicts of 1968; Larry and Rachel who organized our skits for the Faculty Follies and Democratic Party fundraisers; Barry, the art teacher who coordinated our informal faculty play-readings of "Macbird" and "School for Scandal"; and Mark, a conservative and intelligent science teacher who argued with me about education and human nature and helped me strengthen my convictions. And one who provided a negative memory, a football coach who worked in his spare time as a grower, one day bringing a large bunch of beautiful green grapes into the teachers' lounge, placing them on the coffee table, and sitting back smugly to see who supported the boycott and who didn't.

Finally, there were the students—young women and men, black, white, Chicano, coming of age in a very uncertain time. One group, composed of various mavericks, attached themselves to Bob, Reg, Nancy, and me, showing up at our apartment at various hours of the evening and weekends to visit. We'd usually listen to music, have soft drinks and cookies, and talk, sometimes about serious topics, sometimes not. Mostly, I think they simply wanted to express their ideas and feelings to adults who were willing to listen.

And one student especially: Bonnie, in the eighth-period advanced English class my first year. It was a small group of about 15 students, and Bonnie took a seat in the back corner near the door, apart from the others. She was tall and thin, wore horn-rimmed glasses and long dresses, and sat at her desk in an angular fashion, observing the world in her own unique way. She wasn't a loner, though; she entered willingly into discussions and spoke passionately about her support of liberal causes. I looked forward to this last class of the day and the bright, interested students in it, particularly Bonnie.

One morning two years later, Bob gave me a ride to school and told me that Bonnie had been killed in a car crash the night before. Her sister Sharon, who was then in my creative writing class, came to me later that morning, her face pale and her eyes dark with tears, and told me she'd be attending the funeral in the afternoon. Not knowing what else to say, I told Sharon I was very sorry to hear about Bonnie. I wasn't able to concentrate well on my teaching for several weeks. Later in the year, Sharon wrote two moving poems about Bonnie's death and asked that they be published in *Sirocco*.

Reminiscing about these people in my life, I am struck by the importance of a sense of community. This is something I strive to bring about in my writing courses in particular, as we write together and share our creations with each other. In Bonnie's spirit, this is both an independent and interdependent activity. In a graduate course entitled The Teacher as Writer, which I taught this past semester, I joined with students in developing and carrying out what Bowman and Haggerson (Chapter 4) might call an "action plan" for a "personal curriculum." My own plan involved the writing of this chapter. I shared with the students my prewriting sketches and successive drafts, and they responded with praise for what they saw as strengths and suggestions for what might be improved. I'm pleased to say that this final version reflects many of their recommendations. More important, the approach allowed me to relinquish much of my role as dispenser of knowledge and to enter with my students into a community of teachers and writers.

"THE CIRCLE GAME"

We're captive on the carousel of time.
—Joni Mitchell, "The Circle Game"

Reviewing these experiences leads me to assert five theoretical positions, which serve as underlying principles for my teaching of curriculum. First, curriculum needs to be defined in terms of personal, lived experiences, rather than through some set of objectives, strategies, notions of scope and sequence, and artificial scenarios. As Doll (Chapter 3) would suggest, this personal view of curriculum reflects the post-modern alternative to the ordered Newtonian perspective. An appropriate mode for curriculum inquiry, then, is narrative (Connelly & Clandinin, 1985), as the stories of teachers' and students' experiences and interactions become texts for discovery and interpretation. I am submitting here my own narrative for that kind of analysis, and welcome any perspectives on it that go beyond my interpretations of these events.

Second, it is important for curriculum studies to be content-specific, and not simply generic. Some recent ASCD publications have indicated a renewed interest in curriculum and teaching within specific content areas (Brandt, 1988; Jones, Palinscar, Ogle, & Carr, 1987). In the present case, I've attempted to draw relationships between the events I've described and current theory in the areas of response to literature, psycholinguistics and sociolinguistics, composing processes, and cultural literacy. This last issue is especially crucial, as we attempt to gain a fuller sense of what literacy is about. This effort should certainly go beyond the narrow elitist views put forth by conservative proponents like Allan Bloom (1987) and E. D. Hirsch (1987). As a beginning point, it needs to recognize the "outside curriculum" (Schubert & Melnick, 1987), which is so important to students' lives. For students in my classes in the late 1960s, cultural literacy meant an exploration of their personal identities in relation to a society that many of them saw as promoting prejudice and discrimination, militarism, conformity, self-interest and materialism, and political and religious hypocrisy. To the extent that students shape their growing identities through transactions with literature and through speaking and writing in their own voices, they are building their cultural literacy.

Third, curriculum teaching and inquiry should respect the interplay between practical and theoretical knowledge, and the validity of teachers' experience and expertise (Bolster, 1983; Clandinin, 1986; Elbaz, 1983; Lampert, 1985; McDonald, 1986; Zeichner & Liston, 1987). Though my own practical knowledge as a beginning teacher was limited and led me to make many misjudgments and mistakes, it also allowed me to take some risks and at times make decisions that were beneficial for the growth of students and myself. And as I have gained experience in teaching, so have I developed a greater sense of the dialectic of theory and practice and an appreciation for "practice-as-inquiry" (North, 1987). This awareness can also bring about a greater sense of community, as the teacher is perceived, in Doll's terms, as a co-learner engaged in the same processes of transformation as his or her students (see Chapter 3).

Fourth, our sense of curriculum must be contextualized not simply in terms of classrooms, schools, and communities, but also with respect to social, political, cultural, and historical issues. The students I taught in the late 1960s were certainly shaped by their backgrounds and environments, as was I. But they were also shaping themselves, questioning the assumptions of their backgrounds and society. And as their teacher, I had to recognize that my teaching of English was a political act, especially in teaching novels like *The Scarlet Letter, Huckleberry Finn, The Ox-Bow Incident, The Great Gatsby,* and *Fahrenheit 451;* plays like *A Raisin in the Sun, Death of a Salesman,* and *Our Town;* poems by Langston Hughes, Emily Dickinson, Walt Whitman, and contemporary songwriters; and essays by Henry David Thoreau and Martin Luther King, Jr. To have attempted to be politically and value-neutral, of course, would have been to convey political and value judgments.

Additionally, I had to learn to understand better the relationships between cultural stability and cultural change. Coming as I did from a liberal Jewish background, my views were very different from many I encountered, especially among those who supported the war in Vietnam and criticized the civil rights movement and other progressive causes. Particularly in southern California, parents were concerned about the increased availability of marijuana, LSD, and other drugs; the sounds and lyrics of hard rock and psychedelic music; the political views of figures like Timothy Leary and Eldridge Cleaver; and the hippie/activist culture in Berkeley, San Francisco, and some parts of Los Angeles. They did not want to "lose" their children to those influences. I can see more clearly now how my teaching and curriculum views were threatening to those parents, who feared that critical thinking about social issues would lead their children to reject the values they had worked so hard to instill.

Finally, the recursive nature of the account presented here represents an important model, I think, for curriculum theory and history. As Eudora Welty says (in the excerpt with which this chapter begins), past, present, and future are not simply linear and chronological, but instead are intertwined in dynamic and continually revealing ways. Writing this essay has represented for me both a retrospective and projective process (Perl, 1980). We look at what we have said or done to gain a sense both of its own meaning and of how to move forward. My years of teaching (and of living) seem like a kaleidoscope of shifting intentions, perceptions, and relationships. We are indeed, as Joni Mitchell sang, "captive on the carousel of time," but if we strive to construct meaning from our experience, we return to the beginning point with a clearer and renewed awareness of who we are and where we fit in the larger scheme of things. In Bowman's words (Chapter 4), we create "new views of ourselves." Autobiography, then, becomes a key to understanding of the self, of the times and places in which we have lived, and thereby of the nature of curriculum.

REFERENCES

Bloom, A. D. (1987). The closing of the American mind. New York: Simon & Schuster.

Bolster, A. S., Jr. (1983). Toward a more effective model of research on teaching. *Harvard Educational Review, 53* (3), 294–308.

Brandt, R. (Ed). (1988). *Content of the curriculum.* 1988 ASCD Yearbook. Alexandria, VA: Association for Supervision and Curriculum Development.

Clandinin, D. J. (1986). *Classroom practice: Teacher images in action.* Philadelphia: Falmer Press.

Connelly, F. M., & Clandinin, D. J. (1985). Personal practical knowledge and the modes of knowing. In E. W. Eisner (Ed.), *Learning and teaching the ways of knowing* (pp. 174–198). Eighty-fourth Yearbook of the Society for the Study of Education, Part II. Chicago, IL: University of Chicago Press.

Dixon, J. (1967). *Growth through English.* Oxford: Oxford University Press.

Elbaz, F. (1983). *Teacher thinking: A study of practical knowledge.* London: Croom Helm.

Hansberry, L. (1959). *A raisin in the sun.* New York: Random House.

Hirsch, E. D. (1987). *Cultural literacy: What every American needs to know.* Boston: Houghton-Mifflin.

Jones, B. F., Palinscar, A. S., Ogle, D. S., & Carr, E. G. (1987). *Strategic teaching and learning: Cognitive instruction in the content areas.* Alexandria, VA: Association for Supervision and Curriculum Development/North Central Regional Educational Laboratory.

Labov, W. (1970). *The study of nonstandard English.* Urbana, IL: National Council of Teachers of English.

Lampert, M. (1985). How do teachers manage to teach? Perspectives on problems in practice. *Harvard Educational Review, 55* (2), 178–194.

McDonald, J. P. (1986). Raising the teacher's voice and the ironic role of theory. *Harvard Educational Review, 56* (4), 355–378.

Moffett, J. (1968). *Teaching the universe of discourse.* Boston: Houghton-Mifflin.

North, S. M. (1987). *The making of knowledge in composition.* Upper Montclair, NJ: Boynton/Cook.

Perl, S. (1980). Understanding composing. *College Composition and Communication, 31* (4) 363–369.

Rosenblatt, L. (1938). *Literature as exploration.* Chicago: D. Appleton-Century.

Schubert, W. H., & Melnick, C. R. (1987). Study of "outside curriculum" of student lives. *Journal of Curriculum and Supervision, 2* (2), 200–202.

Welty, E. (1983). *One writer's beginnings.* New York: Warner.

Zeichner, K. M., & Liston, D. P. (1987). Teaching student teachers to reflect. *Harvard Educational Review, 57* (1), 23–48.

Contestaire

MAXINE GREENE
Teachers College, Columbia University

Interpretation and Re-Vision:
Toward Another Story

I am reminded, once again, of how the notion of "self" for me refers to what is in the making, what is not yet. John Dewey (1916) said it in one way when he wrote that the self is not ready-made, "but something in continuous formation through choice of action" (p. 408). At the same time, he identified self with interest: "The kind and amount of interest actively taken in a thing reveals and measures the quality of selfhood which exists" (p. 408). This connects for me with Jean-Paul Sartre's view of project, which has to do with the relation between the human being and an object that human being is trying to bring into being. In fact, each person is characterized by his or her going beyond a situation and by what he or she succeeds in making of what he or she has been made. Certainly, this is one way of looking at curriculum. Sartre (1963) spoke of "a flight and a leap ahead, at once a refusal and a realization," and of knowing as a "moment of *praxis*, even its most fundamental one" (p. 92).

The three papers provoking me to a renewed pursuit of myself as teacher educator and curriculum theorist are all concerned with the curriculum as project, one that involves the becoming of the teacher even as it confronts the uses of curriculum in unfolding, enfolding, and empowering. The ideas of recursiveness and re-visioning are related provocatively to an emerging dialogue, to life stories, and to ongoing processes of writing and articulating that give form and sense to the flow of experiences. Clearly, this would mean little if it did not in some fashion open the way to community or prepare the ground for a public space.

Granting our familiarity with ideas of disequilibrium and dissonance, and our recent interest in what James Gleick calls the "new science" of chaos (1987), we all on some level seek a framework, a consensus, something on which we can depend. Like many other philosophers, I was deeply struck by Richard Rorty's (1979) new interest in "edifying philosophy," the point of which is "to keep the conversation going rather than to find objective truth" (p. 377). Rejecting dependable rational frameworks and "universal commensuration," Rorty chooses to turn away from systems in the way the "great edifying, peripheral thinkers" (namely Dewey, Wittgenstein, and Heidegger) did (p. 368) and try the modes of hermeneutics or interpretation. This introduces, of course, ideas of vantage point, perspective, and multiple discourses into considerations of curriculum. In doing so, it not only brings us into confrontation with relativism; it demands that we take positions, as never before, on one-dimensional, conservative views of what E. D. Hirsch (1987) chooses to call "cultural literacy." I am reminded of the voice sounding in Ken Kantor's work, the protests and demands and celebrations not yet resolved.

Looking about at the newcomers surging on to our shores and taking heed of the objections being raised to the expansion and differentiation of curricula (like the new curriculum at Stanford University), I realize we are in tension. The tension has to do with the relationship between curricula we devise today and what we think of (and cherish) as the democratic tradition, or our heritage, or our core values, or our norms.

Yet, as William Doll reminds us, we are living in what is called a time of "post-modernism." Jean-Francois Lyotard (1987) chooses to describe the "postmodern condition" as one in which people can no longer appeal to "some grand narrative" like "the Enlightenment narrative, in which the hero of knowledge works toward a good ethico-political end" (p. 73). Not only does post-modernism, in this sense, exclude proofs of the validity of narrative statements as it does the rational agreements we associate with consensus; it has to allow for a variety of language games. These not only include the symbolisms of chemistry and calculus, but "machine languages, the matrices of game theory, new systems of musical notation, systems of notation for nondenotative forms of logic . . . the language of the genetic code" (p. 86). I am reminded of Michel Foucault (1973) telling about his laughter at the recognition that the cultural codes we live by and the orders of discourse we follow are arbitrary, subject continually to revision (p.

xvii); and I continue to wonder how we can integrate this with our thinking about curriculum.

To think of modernism, in contrast to this, is to think of more or less self-sufficient, autonomous forms of art and representation, in no way connected to historical and social contexts. Although Picasso, Braque, Joyce, Eliot, and Brecht still hold far more than purely aestheticized, frozen possibilities—at least for those willing to disclose the transgressive in them and the persisting outrage—they have been thrust into an airless imaginary space of ideal reflection, separated from what is humdrum and everyday and "real." The import of this, at least for me, is to find ways of reconstituting such texts through our teaching, restoring their emancipatory value, making conceivable what Walter Benjamin (1978) described as "the disintegration of the aura in the experience of shock" (p. 194). It is a matter of releasing readers to achieve a range of texts as meaningful against the landscapes of their own lived lives. I would place considerable emphasis, however, on the care and attentiveness required for the achievement of texts, the "reading" of visual forms, the opening of works in the social sciences or the natural sciences. I recall Dewey (1934), with painting in mind, talking about work that had to be done by the percipient as well as by the artist. "The one who is too lazy, idle, or indurated in convention to perform this work will not see or hear. His 'appreciation' will be a mixture of scraps of learning with conformity to norms of conventional admiration and with a confused, even if genuine, emotional excitation" (p. 54). Sartre (1949), writing about engagements with literature, said the reader must be "conscious of disclosing in creating, of creating by disclosing. . . . If he is inattentive, tired, stupid, or thoughtless, most of the relations will escape him. He will never manage to 'catch on' to the object" (p. 43). Both are talking about the kind of self-chosen discipline and sense of craft that make possible a moving beyond—a creation of a synthetic form that surpasses what is written; the making of the kinds of connections in the reader's or percipient's experience that permit him or her to know moments of freedom, to look at things as if they could be otherwise. This can be nurtured, indeed it must be nurtured, with a clear consciousness of the affiliations that form the context of the text or painting: the sociopolitical moment; the biography of the artist; the history of texts, images, or forms.

This raises the question once again of the point of choosing curriculum as project, curriculum as possibility. It is a matter of enabling students to find their voices, to think about their own thinking, to open themselves to others, to perceive continuities in their experience, to deal with disequilibrium and dissonance and chaos. There remains, as ever, the matter of participant membership; there remains the significance of what Hannah Arendt (1961) called the "common world." I have often turned to her paragraph on education, where she made the point that education "is where we decide whether we love our children enough not to expel them from our world and leave them to their own devices, nor to strike from their hands their chance of undertaking something new, something unforeseen by us, but to prepare them in advance for the task of renewing a common world" (p. 196). She was interested in change and continuity; she was concerned about the individual perspective and an emerging shared interest, or "in-between." Focally, she was concerned about renewal, about moving beyond through the creation of a space of dialogue and human action. It was for her (as it had been for Dewey) a public space, marked by an articulate public—no longer silenced, no longer mystified. It was the kind of space in which persons could pursue themselves as distinctive beings *because* they were participants in ongoing conversation, because they were aware of social insufficiencies, because they were committed to transform. To me, that is the consummation of a view of curriculum rooted in a concept of "self." Text, content, discipline, multiplicity, laughter—and, in time, the constitution of a truly human world.

REFERENCES

Arendt, H. (1961). *Between Past and Future*. New York: Viking.

Benjamin, W. (1978). *Illuminations*. New York: Schocken.

Dewey, J. (1916). *Democracy and Education*. New York: Macmillan.

Dewey, J. (1934). *Art as Experience*. New York: Minton, Balch and Co.

Foucault, M. (1973). *The Order of Things*. New York: Vintage Books.

Gleick, J. (1987). *Chaos*. New York: Viking.

Hirsch, E. D. (1987). *Cultural Literacy: What every American needs to know*. Boston: Houghton-Mifflin.

Lyotard, J-F. (1987). "The Postmodern Condition." In K. Baynes, J. Bohman, & T. McCarthy (Eds.), *After Philosophy: End or Transformation?* (pp. 73–94). Cambridge: MIT Press.

Rorty, R. (1979). *Philosophy and the Mirror of Nature*. Princeton: Princeton University Press.

Sartre, J-P. (1949). *Literature and Existentialism*. New York: Citadel Press.

Sartre, J-P. (1963). *Search for a Method*. New York: Alfred A. Knopf.

Conversation parmi animateurs

O. L. DAVIS, JR.
University of Texas at Austin

PAUL KLOHR
Ohio State University

NORM OVERLY
Indiana University

KLOHR: Well, I suppose if I were identifying some point at which my interest in self emerged, it would be my early work with Ross Mooney at Ohio State. He was working with ideas reflected in a collection of essays published in 1956 called *The Self*. Clark Moustakas was the editor. As I recall, Abraham Maslow, Carl Rogers, Erich Fromm, and Carl Jung contributed to it. Mooney conducted psychological studies highlighting self-perceptions of reality. This research, conducted at the Visual Demonstration Center, located at Ohio State, provided evidence of the striking realization that when you check on reality, a good portion of it is in *you*—it's not "out there." So, Mooney developed the infinity sign as representing reality and suggested that you have to deal with the part that's inside the loops as well as the area outside the symbol.

DAVIS: I think Bill Doll does a nice job elaborating on this "inside–outside" relationship in his discussion of post-modernism. From a literary perspective, Ken Kantor's stories about his journey to selfhood are equally powerful. I find these stories tremendously beneficial in that they offer, as good literature does, an opportunity to think, "By golly, that's similar to what I did. I remember how this situation came up." Or, "Gee, I wish I had done that kind of thing." Writings like these foster the development of subconscious memory and encourage personal reflection about our teaching. As curriculum teachers get together in the future, my guess is that we will talk about such things as how I did this in my classroom and how I came to be aware of these kinds of insights into myself as person and as teacher. In that respect, these writings are tremendously important.

KLOHR: I agree, O. L. The use of literature is a powerful tool for introspection. So, too are the performing arts. About the time I was introduced to Dewey's *Art as Experience*, both Mooney and Zirbes were becoming interested in creativity. So, running through my early years at Ohio State was this growing concern about how we could think about a curriculum that involved the self. During that time, I became director of the University School. The core of our curriculum was the performing arts. What this resulted in, in the way that one reported to students and to parents about what was happening, was a very moving demonstration of Maslow's self-actualization. Between kindergarten and twelfth grade one could sense this development of self as it was manifested in the curriculum.

OVERLY: I'm trying to highlight the importance of self by using the novel *The Name of the Rose* in my curriculum course. It's a murder mystery set in the fourteenth century. The reason I picked it, in the first place, was because of the historical context. Students look at the curriculum implications of the novel: life in the monastery, the library, the control and censorship of knowledge, and the controlled society. From there, I suggest that a book is useful as a metaphor for curriculum because of the way in which you go about constructing a novel of a particular type: What goes into the selection of content, the perspective of the person, and the evaluation that takes place are not unlike curriculum concerns. And, like the curriculum, the novel takes on a life of its own so that meanings come out of it that the author did not even intend. It's not the author's purpose to tell the people what it means; the readers have to find the meaning for themselves. This, of course, is a radical concept to many of my students.

KLOHR: Well, this more phenomenological orientation stressing the importance of self, the making of meaning, and the intuitive side of human beings was certainly foreign to curriculum leaders a generation or two earlier. As I mentioned, my earliest work was with Mooney—and with Alberty, who was redoing the secondary curriculum. Alberty's work was inspirational and logical, but he had very little support in his professional career. He had the philosophical support of Bode, but that was about it—a kind of extension of Dewey. But now we have this much broader base in psychology, sociology, and critical theory.

Much of my curriculum work seemed, initially, more intuitive. Its good to find, 48 years later, a group of people who are thinking this way.

DAVIS: It seems to me, Paul, that each of us, as curriculum teachers and scholars, has been affected by the perspective that we bring to our work. As we talk about this notion of the self, it's not just knowing ourselves better but knowing ourselves better as teachers. Who are we as teachers? In a sense, our teaching efforts to engage an individual to go on a journey—maybe with us and maybe not, maybe a short one, but for some a longer one—is a journey into ourselves.

OVERLY: I'm reminded of how I came into the curriculum field most directly from being a missionary teacher. This is a very important part of who I am. Now, when I say "missionary" I don't mean "missionary as converter," but "missionary as witness." Whether we intend to or not, we witness our beliefs by what we do and who we are. My challenge is to help others know who they are and what they believe and why they believe it—whether it's religion or education. For me, personal reflection is the critical component. I can't teach anything unless I am helping people to reflect on how they interact with what they're learning. In my own practice, the autobiographical has grown out of an effort to encourage students to think for themselves, an effort to get them to break away from the banking concept of education and assume responsibility for their own learning. It's an emphasis on a holistic perspective that I think is grounded in Dewey's view of learning as the making of meaning from the gradual incorporation of new ideas in terms of current personal understandings.

KLOHR: This notion of engaging people in personal reflection, I think, is a critical role of the curriculum teacher and the curriculum developer.

OVERLY: There are other ways, of course, to make meaning. But I believe that no matter what kind of meaning we make, behind it all are ourselves. To have the fullest understanding possible, we need to recognize that. Otherwise we will be fooling ourselves about the nature of the interpretation we are making. We will believe we are being objective; that we are using only the best research findings; that we have separated ourselves successfully from the teaching-learning act.

PART II

TEACHING FROM THE PERSPECTIVE OF THE TEACHER

Despite the history of failed curriculum efforts that have ignored the pivotal role of the teacher in curriculum development and implementation, few of us place the teacher at the starting point when developing syllabi or preparing to teach courses in curriculum. For some curriculum teachers, the classroom teacher and the institutional context within which he or she works are viewed as impediments to learning about curriculum or as obstacles to our curriculum agendas. For others, the teacher and the context of the school room are viewed in unproblematic terms: We simply fulfill their and/or their districts' expressed needs.

The authors in this part assert that the perspective of the teacher ought to ground our teaching and thinking about curriculum. Rejecting romantic and technocratic views of classroom teachers and their roles in curriculum development, these authors invite their students to challenge taken-for-granted conceptions of the curriculum, while acknowledging and honoring the contexts within which they work.

Drawing on the imagery of a prism, Janet Miller in Chapter 6 describes how she encourages her students, as teacher-researchers, to examine curriculum from different angles and to assume more active roles in the process of curriculum creation. Employing "dialogue journal-writing," verbal dialogues, and annotated bibliographies, Miller challenges her students to question and transcend their positivistic and patriarchal conceptions of teaching and curriculum. Miller also explores with students ways in which they, as classroom teachers, can create alternative educational settings for themselves and their students. With each activity, she and her students experience another turn of the prism.

In Chapter 7 George Wood takes us into three classrooms

where teachers, as curriculum workers, are developing curricula for an emerging democracy. Arguing that recent curriculum proposals and reform efforts further disempower teachers, he explores the negative consequences for the civic mission of the curriculum and discusses the formation of a grass roots organization, the Institute for Democracy in Education. Throughout this rendering, teachers take and hold center stage. Wood concludes by outlining a curriculum for democratic empowerment by the work of teachers at the Institute.

6

Teachers as
Curriculum Creators

JANET L. MILLER
Hofstra University

I began my doctoral studies at The Ohio State University in 1974 through the encouragement of William Pinar, mentor for my master's degree at the University of Rochester. My master's work followed seven years of teaching high school English in upstate New York. I completed my Ph.D. in curriculum theory, mentored by Paul Klohr, and in humanities/English education, mentored by Donald R. Bateman, in 1977. These individuals, and the graduate students with whom I studied, including Bob Bullough, Craig Kridel, Paul Shaker, George Dixon, and Libby Carr Brown, continue to influence my thinking about curriculum and teaching. As mentors, scholars, and friends, they serve as models that I attempt, in modest ways, to emulate.

The value I place on community among my colleagues started to develop when I began to teach high school English in 1966, and was nourished by dear friends and wildly creative teaching colleagues, Kay McIntosh and Arlene Kakareka. Perhaps teaching in an area of New York State that demanded resourcefulness and provided ample opportunity, on cold winter nights, for reflective consideration of our work enabled me to view teaching from perspectives that other contexts might not have encouraged. I since have felt an urgency in my teaching to look for connections and, in my own search, to encourage my students to do their own looking and connecting. That urgency persists, even though I am no longer compelled by the frozen winter landscapes of Massena, New York to find places where warmth and community abide.

A triangular prism hangs from a thin filigree thread in my study window. I look through it into the yard outside whenever I notice the refracted colors slowly moving around the room as the day progresses. Peering through the prism, I watch just-budding forsythia blur into golden clumps of color, separated now from the distinct arching of branches and framed in a new version of spring. Later, as the sun sets, the forsythia reappear as golden, violet, blue, and orange dots across the table where I sit writing. Both points of seeing present shifting versions of the environment surrounding me; these versions depend not only on the slight motion of the hanging crystal itself but also on the angles from which I look through and around the prism.

I use the image of the prism when I teach and think about curriculum; it is a way of encouraging students to look at curriculum from various angles as well as to consider their active roles in the creation of these points of view. At the same time, the prism's refracted colors provide an image of curriculum as reflection of a particular context, itself in constant flux and yet captured for the moment as a representation of reality. The intersection of these contradictory and simultaneous points of viewing provides entry into a way of teaching and thinking about curriculum that acknowledges both the constructed nature of curriculum and the varying perspectives that teachers and students contribute to that construction. Concurrently, the moving dots of color remind us that no one construction necessarily signals completion or a comprehensive view.

My teaching of curriculum is about vision, in a sense, then, and about the difficulties I experience when I try to see the world in new ways. Teaching, for me, also is about the tensions I feel in encouraging and inviting students to consider curriculum as a prismatic study, without imposing the boundaries of my vision on their own points of view. Yet, as Pagano (1988) notes, ways of looking can be as conventional and constitutive as ways of talking. To examine my own sources of authority, in self-reflexive and autobiographical voice (Martin & Mohanty, 1986; Pinar & Grumet, 1976), is to concurrently invite students to become readers, writers, and revisers of their own stories, their own versions of educational experience. These perspectives ground my teaching and thinking about curriculum and challenge versions of institutional contexts that perpetuate teachers' visions of their roles as consumers and dispensers of others' constructions of knowledge (Apple, 1986; Mooney, 1975).

As a curriculum teacher, I believe that teaching itself is a constantly evolving form of curriculum, a particular way of interacting, interpreting, questioning, and re-visioning that involves students in these processes in a reciprocal and self-reflexive manner. As I explore the ways in which these processes might contribute to teachers' conceptions of themselves as curriculum creators—in search of their freedoms in order that they might provoke young persons to go in search of their own (Greene, 1988)—I will note the difficulties inherent in these approaches to curriculum teaching.

These include discrepancies in context and position of students and teachers, the institutional constraints of such contexts, and the continuing dominance of the positivist paradigm in conceptions of pedagogy, research, and curriculum. I will also describe ways in which I use dialogue journal-writing, autobiographically situated reading and theorizing assignments, and critically oriented teacher-as-researcher projects that especially draw on feminists' explorations of reciprocal and interactive research processes. These serve as concrete examples of students and teachers collaboratively attempting to see and create curriculum as a form of human *praxis,* that process of reflecting and acting, interpreting and changing (Bernstein, 1971) that helps to shape our worlds (Huebner, 1975).

TEACHERS' CONTEXTS

Before I share my image of the prism as metaphor for curriculum studies, I invite my graduate students, the majority of whom are themselves teachers, to share their definitions of curriculum. Students record their versions of curriculum through short entries in their curriculum journals. These entries often take the form of personal vignettes of particular teaching episodes or remembrances of curriculum experienced as students. This writing provides an introduction to journal-writing that constitutes one of the self-reflexive processes of our curriculum class. It also begins to highlight the varieties of curriculum conceptions with which we will grapple.

I invite the class to share their versions of curriculum with one another, and this most often provides an opening into the contexts within which these teachers work. Although I never require the sharing aspect of our journal-writing, I find that most teachers are eager to voice not only their conceptions of curriculum but also the frustrations and anxieties that they experience in attempting to implement curriculum that often has been created, chosen, and standardized by others in the form of textbooks or state mandates.

Most teachers initially speak of curriculum as "content that we must cover or squeeze into" predetermined structures of time, measurement, assessment, or knowledge. One teacher spoke of her feeling that she and her students were "galloping across the curriculum" to reach the objectives that the "learning specialists" had specified. Other images that emerge in teachers' definitions of curriculum include those of entrapment or enclosure: They speak of feeling "boxed-in" or "confined" by the curriculum; some describe their work as looking for ways "out of" or "around" or "beyond" the mandated texts and performance objectives.

One second-year high school English teacher, Ben, expressed his concerns about his apparent lack of control over the externals that characteristically disrupt all teachers' professional lives. His initial definition of curriculum included his perceived demands of the "mandated" curriculum and its exclusionary effects.

> I find myself constantly questioning the content and methodology. I feel odd because I'm not clear on ways out of the curriculum. I don't want to speak out because of my inexperience. Mostly, I feel that content needs to be completely revamped to open up and direct the kids in more expansive ways. I just wonder how I can make it work for me, and how I can fit in.

Contextual Discrepancies

The linear and bounded ways in which teachers often initially define curriculum reflect the still-dominant model in educational discourse and practice. That model of technical rationality posits that professional activity consists of instrumental problem solving made rigorous by the application of scientific theory and technique (Schön, 1983). As a curriculum researcher, I am aware of the many critiques within the educational community of the positivist paradigm in which this model of technical rationality is situated (Bredo & Feinberg, 1982; Mischler, 1979). I also support and participate in forms of curriculum inquiry that propose alternative conceptions of curriculum discourse and research (Pinar, 1988). As a curriculum teacher, one of my central challenges is to acknowledge the contexts in which my students work (Cornbleth, 1988) and simultaneously to acknowledge the perspectives from which I seek to question the structures of those very contexts.

The trick is to do this not only without imposing my own versions of curriculum on students, thus forming yet another boundary on their notions of curriculum, but also without denying the positions from which each of us speaks. No matter how often I refer to my seven years of public school teaching experience or how often I enter schools to work with teachers in classrooms and inservice contexts, I now teach and think about curriculum from the position of a university professor. Given the hierarchical structure of schooling, this position as traditionally conceived gives my voice authority and "expert" status. Thus, to acknowledge in traditional and hierarchical ways the contexts of elementary and secondary teachers is not necessarily to enter, or to speak from, those contexts, but rather to view them from afar, from only one flat plane of the prism.

As a woman working in academe, however, I am aware of the marginalization of my perspectives within conceptions of teaching and research activities that remain male-identified (Miller, 1988). Thus, I can remember and focus on the marginalization that all teachers experience within the existing structures of elementary and secondary schools. Moving teachers to the center of the dialogue is one of my major goals in teaching curriculum.

I do not teach, however, in a perfectly analogous situation to those of my students. Although I wish to teach curriculum from nonimpositional but contextualized perspectives, I do not want to preempt my students' descriptions of their situations by naming or categorizing their contexts for them. I see this as a major balancing point for those who wish to teach curriculum in ways that encourage us all to uncover the particularity and contingency of our knowledge and practice and to see meanings as situational (Lather, 1988).

How might I respond without rejection or preemptive labeling, then, to teachers' definitions of curriculum that reflect positivistic and patriarchal conceptions of teaching and curriculum? How do I honor teachers' situations and, at the same time, honor my own (Berlak, 1988)? How do I support and yet not impose alternative visions of curriculum that I believe might extend the boundaries, and thus the possibilities, of teachers as curriculum creators? In posing these questions as the backdrop against which I teach curriculum, I invite students to enter into these dilemmas with me. Our dialogue and debates that ensue from these questions, as well as those that emerge throughout our work together, become curriculum. One student described this process in her journal: "I am beginning to see that we are *doing* what we have been talking and reading about."

Contextual Voices

As we begin to read from a variety of curriculum texts, I ask students to record in their journals their reactions, questions, and musings about curriculum. I begin a process of reading and responding to the journal entries, thus creating a layer of dialogue with individual students that enlarges our class-based discussions. As a teacher, dialogue journal-writing allows me to hear subtle variations in students' tones and points of view, reinforcing the need to attend not only to the variations among contexts but also to the shifting perspectives within individual and collective texts. As a co-learner, my participation in dialogue journal-writing enables my students to hear similar variations and contradictions within my various contextualized voices. I am both teacher and learner, and, like my students who teach, I struggle with the institutional constraints and expectations of these often dichotomized roles.

We read and respond to one another in writing and in dialogue, not as interpreters of one another's texts, but as creators and questioners and revisers of our own. As we engage with one another through the telling and reading of our stories, we sense the incompleteness of the stories themselves (Brodkey, 1987). As Grumet (1988) reminds us, although our stories come from us, we cannot be reduced to them. However, Grumet notes that, in the telling, we may diminish the distance between the private and public poles of our experience.

> As we study the forms of our own experience we are not searching only for evidence of the external forces that have diminished us; instead, we are recovering our own possibilities, ways of knowing and being in the world that we remember and imagine and must draw into language that can span the chasm that presently separates what we know as our public and private worlds. (p. 532)

The written and verbal dialogues between and among students and myself take the form of vignettes—small personal stories of our everyday understandings of teaching and curriculum. Feminists argue that, for women, these stories may reveal different knowledges that may conflict with, and are never reflected in, the dominant stories a culture tells about social life (Harding, 1987). Similarly, I believe that there are possibilities that we may recover in the telling of these small stories of the women and men who teach and who have been marginalized by the model of technical rationality. One possibility is the hope that, by knowing the ways of others' histories, we may be encouraged to see beyond and through our own (de-Lauretis, 1986). Thus, with the written and verbal dialogues, we begin turning the prism, not to forget the "forces that have diminished us" but rather to begin to look in new and undiminished ways at ourselves within our teaching contexts.

Written dialogue between the English teacher, Ben, and myself begins to address these small shifts from perceived external constraints on the teaching role to consideration of relationships and actions among teachers and students.

BEN: In a sense, this is self-imposed, but I still feel as though I'm working with someone else's context. But I feel that I'm learning so much everyday, and it's not the kind of thing that deals with methodology. I'm learning about people, kids of every sort, adults. . . . I see that I must acknowledge people—their insides, their wants, desires, inner and outer lives.

JM: In a way, we always are working with someone else's context, if we consider the curriculum to be the creation of someone else's understandings of literature or history or science. Why do you say that this is self-imposed and not institutionally imposed? It seems

BEN: to me that you are shifting the context to yourself as teacher here and to your relationships with students and colleagues. Is this part of curriculum for you, inner and outer lives?

BEN: I say self-imposed because I can't always get away from what I think I'm supposed to do. I'm trying. For me, it's been a process of becoming more involved with the roots of my work. I teach writing, have always had a connection to it on a lot of different levels, even way before I thought about the possibility of teaching it. But suddenly, it's crept up on me. I am a writer. And that's what I must do, for me and for my students. I knew it all along, but I guess this confirms it in a big way. In order to make it as a teacher, especially of something as artful and personal as writing, teachers have to work on their creative selves. In a way, we are modeling ideal behavior for our students, but I think it's more than that. We're doing it.

JM: This is a part of your insides, your wants and desires, yes? And you are not afraid to reveal that to your students. In so doing, I think that you also are creating curriculum. You are showing, not telling, to use the writing process language, and you are inviting your students to participate in that creating process by showing them your wants and desires. What will you do with theirs?

BEN: Yes, I feel the shift. I do believe that if we allow ourselves the context for the dialectic, then we can really strengthen ourselves and our students. I'd like to pose the possibility that we as teachers could potentially be empowered by this shift in thinking and doing. But you're wrong—I'm scared. I know I won't always know what to do. And what if their wants and desires aren't mine?

Ben and I are struggling together here to feel the strength of our "inner worlds" as appropriate contexts for teaching and creating curriculum. His last question echoes my own concerns about impositional teaching. I think that his reaction to my question about students' "wants and desires" reflects my own fears about the difficulties in "spanning the chasm," through our teaching, that separates our private and public, our "inner and outer" worlds.

The dialogue journal-writing opens possibilities. For example, Ben and I could explore the possibilities of examining the gender-based differences in our perceptions and enactments of our similar concerns. We could examine the language with which we speak and write as telling about ourselves. We could establish a reflexive focus on how we construct the very examination of our teaching and curriculum processes (Lather, 1988).

At the very least, the written and verbal dialogues create a place in which the students and I can forge connections and ask questions. One student confessed that "this was the first time that I was totally honest in my

writing and in my responses because I couldn't figure out what you wanted."
As Greene (1988) observes, "Teachers, like their students, have to learn to
love the questions, as they come to realize that there can be no final agreements or answers, no final commensurability" (p. 134).

TURNINGS

As I teach curriculum, then, the students and I share the subtle shifts in
focus and in viewing perspectives. We work together to create the curriculum of our course as well as to understand the possibilities of such creation
in other schooling contexts. We do not necessarily share identical views.
Rather, we share processes of seeing, of framing, of noting the importance of
what we eliminate from our viewing as much as we notice the focus of our
interests (Marcus & Fischer, 1986).

Re-viewing Institutional Contexts

In addition to verbal and written dialogue about our collective readings
and deliberations, I ask students to prepare an annotated bibliography of
outside readings, which complement the course readings and discussions.
Here, I encourage students to select readings that represent their chosen
areas of interest in curriculum inquiry as well as reflect their areas of pedagogical expertise or concerns. Further, I encourage them to effect connections among the themes and issues that have emerged for them within our
course context and to critique the readings from any of the perspectives we
have examined.

Many students choose to read within their discipline-defined areas.
They often prefer to look for evidence of the surfacing of alternative perspectives that we have examined within the contexts of prevalent paradigms
of teaching and curriculum. In this way, I invite them to re-view their institutional contexts from various and alternative perspectives as well as to reconsider the problems and possibilities of conceiving of themselves and
other teachers as curriculum creators. I am encouraging yet another turning
of the prism, another attempt to simultaneously view our work as both creation and reflection, to acknowledge the possibilities as well as the limits of
our vision and actions.

Teachers-as-Researchers

I encourage students to continue, beyond the confines of our course
work, the self-reflexive processes that we have shared in our studies of cur-

riculum. Thus, I posit the concept of teacher-as-researcher as another opening into conceptions of teacher-as-curriculum creator.

At this point, my students are not surprised that I reject versions of teacher-as-researcher that simply replicate the procedures and intents of the prevailing positivist norm in educational research. These versions include notions of teacher–researcher collaboration that reinforce the "expert" status of those who enter classrooms to determine as well as to guide teachers' research activities. Instead, I point to the inquiry in which we have engaged together in our classroom as a form of research, and I ask students to consider ways in which their own teaching could be viewed from this perspective.

As students turn the prism on their own teaching practices and begin to look at themselves as researchers, I share examples of ongoing collaborative work among myself and five graduate students/teachers (Miller, in press) who are exploring possibilities of enacting classroom research as a form of *praxis* (Lather, 1986). This approach to research, informed particularly by feminist perspectives, is a democratized process of inquiry characterized by negotiation and reciprocity among the researchers and the researched. This research orientation necessarily includes a willingness of all involved to risk, to be actively involved in the creation of change, and to conceive of personal preunderstandings as well as classroom processes and interactions as appropriate research foci.

Within our collaborative group, we have taken aspects of this research orientation and stretched its boundaries to develop conceptions of ourselves as researchers of our own practice and of the structures that often form that practice. Thus, we are exploring conceptions of ourselves as *praxis*-oriented researchers in our classrooms and other educational settings. We are examining ways in which these conceptions might contribute to our understandings of ourselves as "knowers." With such understandings, we hope to place ourselves and our students at the center of our own teaching and research priorities. We hope, through our centering efforts, to create educational settings for ourselves and our students in which oppressive situations are exposed and rejected by all. As we explore these conceptions, however, we also are challenged constantly. We are amazed and often dismayed to discover the degree to which our notions of ourselves as curriculum conveyers, rather than creators, are entrenched, both in our understandings and in the minds of those with whom we work. We know that our explorations and attempts to become creators within our teacher-as-researcher construct are long-term efforts. Thus, we value the support and encouragement that our collaboration provides.

By participating in this collaborative investigation that aims to place teachers at the center of research and teaching processes, I have come to believe that we eventually can refocus the ways in which we conceptualize and speak about "teachers' knowledge." If we can begin to conceive of teaching as a "quiet form of research" (Britton, 1987), we again turn the prism, opening new perspectives on teachers' active agency in the creation of interactive processes in teaching, curriculum, and research.

Teachers, conducting research within their classroom contexts, then might speak of their own conceptions of their knowledge and practice. Further, I suggest that we view teacher-as-researcher possibilities especially within modes of feminist critical ethnography (Maher & Tetreault, 1988; Roman & Christian-Smith, 1988). These approaches call attention to the chasm that separates what researchers produce as reconstructions of teachers' knowledge, even when this research is conducted from a "teacher's perspective" (Clandinin, 1986; Elbaz, 1983; Perl & Wilson, 1986), and what teachers consider to be their knowledges (Elbaz, 1987).

By sharing these examples of our attempts to turn the prism yet again, I thus focus on the limitations as well as possibilities of collaborative investigations into new versions of teacher-as-researcher. Through these examples, I invite curriculum students to participate in their own inquiries beyond the confines of the graduate classroom. Such inquiries take various forms, often resulting in autobiographical accounts, framed in contexts of a "final paper" for class requirements, of students' initial attempts at viewing themselves from again another new angle. As they recount their frustrations and ambivalences in attempting to view their own teaching as a form of research, new questions are posed and new problems emerge.

In a sense, with these writings, we come full circle, closing the class with questions similar to the ones with which we began. The posing of alternative conceptions of teacher-as-researcher again confronts the pervasive influence of positivist approaches to teaching, curriculum, and research. Curriculum students speak of the frustrations of seeing their worlds and their actions in new ways and yet being unable to find openings within their schooling contexts that could give them room to act upon their revisionings.

These frustrations, expressed both in classroom dialogue and in journal-writing, provide new directions for me as a curriculum teacher. With each class, I am challenged to continue turning the prism of my own teaching. I must look for new angles from which to approach the intertwined elements of social, political, personal, and historical contexts that influence, distort, constitute, and reflect teachers' understandings and enactments of curriculum. In teaching curriculum, I continue to search for ways in which students might envision themselves as curriculum creators, not only within the context of our course but also within their own classrooms. I hope that students might begin to create openings, their own points of viewing that challenge the taken-for-granted structures and functions of schooling, which dim visions of possibilities for students and teachers alike.

The prism hangs in my study window, swaying slightly with the spring breeze. It turns, and I watch new patterns emerge in the crystal planes as blooming forsythia meld into green branches. I see that I cannot turn the prism for others in a complete or constant manner, just as I cannot possibly view all the patterned colors detailed by its movement. I struggle with the story of my own teaching, knowing that this is only half the telling and that even this half is refracting only scenes, slight segments of the processes of teaching and thinking about curriculum. Still, some students, as they leave our class, speak of never being able to think about curriculum in quite the same ways again. I view this as at least a gentle turning.

REFERENCES

Apple, M. W. (1986). *Teachers and texts: A political economy of class and gender relations in education.* New York: Routledge & Kegan Paul.

Berlak, A. (1988, April). *Teaching for outrage and empathy in the liberal arts.* Paper presented at the Annual Meeting of the American Educational Research Association, New Orleans.

Bernstein, R. J. (1971). *Praxis and action.* Philadelphia: University of Pennsylvania Press.

Bredo, E., & Feinberg, W. (Eds.). (1982). *Knowledge and values in social and educational research.* Philadelphia: Temple University Press.

Britton, J. (1987). A quiet form of research. In D. Goswami & P. Stillman (Eds.), *Reclaiming the classroom: Teacher research as an agency for change* (pp. 13–19). Portsmouth, NH: Heinemann-Boynton/Cook.

Brodkey, L. (1987). Writing critical ethnographic narratives. *Anthropology and Education Quarterly, 18,* 67–76.

Clandinin, D. J. (1986). *Classroom practice: Teacher images in action.* Philadelphia: Falmer Press.

Cornbleth, C. (1988). Curriculum in and out of context. *Journal of Curriculum and Supervision, 3,* 85–96.

deLauretis, T. (Ed.). (1986). *Feminist studies, critical studies.* Bloomington: Indiana University Press.

Elbaz, F. (1983). *Teacher thinking: A study of practical knowledge.* London: Croom Helm.

Elbaz, F. (1987). Teachers' knowledge of teaching: Strategies for reflection. In J. Smyth (Ed.), *Educating teachers: Changing the nature of pedagogical knowledge* (pp. 45–53). London: Falmer Press.

Greene, M. (1988). *The dialectic of freedom.* New York: Teachers College Press.

Grumet, M. R. (1988). Women and teaching: Homeless at home. In W. F. Pinar (Ed.),

Contemporary curriculum discourses (pp. 531–539). Scottsdale, AZ: Gorsuch Scarisbrick.

Harding, S. (Ed.). (1987). *Feminism and methodology.* Bloomington: Indiana University Press.

Huebner, D. (1975). The tasks of the curricular theorist. In W. F. Pinar (Ed.), *Curriculum theorizing: The reconceptualists* (pp. 250–270). Berkeley: McCutchan.

Lather, P. (1986). Research as praxis. *Harvard Educational Review, 56,* 257–277.

Lather, P. (1988, April). *Educational research and practice in a postmodern era.* Paper presented at the Annual Meeting of the American Educational Research Association, New Orleans.

Maher, F., & Tetreault, M. K. (1988, April). *Breaking through illusion II: The intersection of feminist pedagogy and feminist ethnography.* Paper presented at the Annual Meeting of the American Educational Research Association, New Orleans.

Marcus, G. E., & Fischer, M. (1986). *Anthropology as cultural critique: An experimental moment in the human sciences.* Chicago: University of Chicago Press.

Martin, B., & Mohanty, C. (1986). Feminist politics: What's home got to do with it? In T. deLauretis (Ed.), *Feminist studies, critical studies* (pp. 191–212). Bloomington: Indiana University Press.

Miller, J. L. (1988). The resistance of women academics: An autobiographical account. In W. F. Pinar (Ed.), *Contemporary curriculum discourses* (pp. 486–494). Scottsdale, AZ: Gorsuch Scarisbrick.

Miller, J. L. (in press). *Creating spaces and finding voices: Teachers in collaboration for empowerment.* Albany: State University of New York Press.

Mischler, E. G. (1979). Meaning in context: Is there any other kind? *Harvard Educational Review, 49,* 1–18.

Mooney, R. (1975). The researcher himself. In W. F. Pinar (Ed.), *Curriculum theorizing: The reconceptualists* (pp. 175–207). Berkeley: McCutchan.

Pagano, J. (1988). The claim of philia. In W. F. Pinar (Ed.), *Contemporary curriculum discourses* (pp. 514–530). Scottsdale, AZ: Gorsuch Scarisbrick.

Perl, S., & Wilson, N. (1986). *Through teachers' eyes: Portraits of writing teachers at work.* Portsmouth, NH: Heinemann Educational Books.

Pinar, W. F. (Ed.). (1988). *Contemporary curriculum discourses.* Scottsdale, AZ: Gorsuch Scarisbrick.

Pinar, W. F., & Grumet, M. R. (1976). *Toward a poor curriculum.* Dubuque, IA: Kendall/Hunt.

Roman, L. G., & Christian-Smith, L. K. (Eds.). (1988). *Becoming feminine: The politics of popular culture.* London: Falmer Press.

Schön, D. A. (1983). *The reflective practitioner: How professionals think in action.* New York: Basic Books.

7

Teachers as Curriculum Workers

GEORGE H. WOOD
Ohio University

Most of my learning about teaching and learning was influenced by classroom teachers. In my first job as a social studies teacher in Michigan, I had the fortune of working for Pearl Johnson. Pearl believed in me when others didn't, allowed me to make my own mistakes, and was always gentle in her criticism.

I left Michigan for doctoral work with Larry Metcalf* at the University of Illinois. Larry opened me up to thinking carefully about thinking, demonstrated to me the worthiness of a lifetime of commitment, and introduced me to John Dewey. He had help in all this from Joe Burnett, Ralph Page, and Ben Cox.

At Illinois I had the great luck to teach social studies with Mike Woods. Mike showed me in practice what Larry was giving me in theory. He is still, in my mind, one of the most outstanding teachers in America today. And he has never left the high school classroom he loves so dearly.

Now, at Ohio University, I work with the teachers of the Institute for Democracy in Education. The daily heroics of these teachers, but a sample of which is found in this chapter, inspires me to believe that there is hope for progressive, democratic schooling. Without the work of these teachers, the chapter that follows would not have been written. Among their number is my wife, Marcia Burchby. She does daily with six-year-olds what I can only write about.

In a sixth grade classroom in rural southeastern Ohio, Bill Elasky begins the year by posing a question: "What do you think are some of

---

* As this manuscript was in the final stage of being edited, I received word that Larry Metcalf died on January 31, 1989. I deeply regret that he never saw this chapter in print.

the biggest problems in our area, and what could we do about them?" What follows is an intense reflection on the lives these twelve- and thirteen-year-olds lead in Appalachian Ohio. As we might expect, unemployment heads the list of problems as over 25 percent of these children's parents are without jobs.

Questions abound: What work is here? Why are there no industries? How can we get higher unemployment benefits? And, most important, what can we do about this? No one is sure how to answer this last question—time to ponder the issue a bit longer. Upon reflection, the answer is simple—there is little if anything these students can do about the long-term, structural unemployment that plagues the area.

In the meantime, an oil truck discharges a hazardous chemical in a nearby stream, and an Environmental Protection Agency cleanup crew takes over in grand style. The students, unable to get answers from the officials on site, decide to take matters into their own hands. In a matter of days, they and Bill have come up with a plan for testing and monitoring water quality in the area's streams and rivers. Their work culminates in written reports on water quality and what can be done to improve it—reports never before available in the area.

Nancy Corbett's high school English class is at first surprised by the prospect that the focus of their compositions could be something they are concerned about. In a spirit of genuine interest, and perhaps with the desire to test their teacher's sincerity, they choose teenage pregnancy. The topic makes sense, given this urban area's rate of teen pregnancy—one in six.

The project begins in some safe ways—visits to hospitals, talks by "experts." But before long the really tough issues come up—sex, birth control, morality. Bringing it all home is a visit by a teen mother, complete with her baby, as she could neither find nor afford child care that day.

What is to be done after this experience? How to pull together the grim realities for so many teens with the genuine compassion and empathy these kids have developed? Clearly, a major factor in all of this is a lack of information about birth options and consequences. So there are now in circulation thousands of flyers "by teens, for teens" on teen pregnancy. Their intent is not to preach, but to teach. The class and Nancy now move on to teenage alcoholism and drug addiction.

A team of second grade teachers decides that the district's reading program is just not working. Their students, already hampered in
their efforts to learn to read by a lack of books at home and the high
illiteracy rates of their parents (over 25 percent), seem ill-served by
the traditional basal-reader fare. After carefully exploring their alternatives, these teachers secure funding to change reading instruction
in their classroom through a whole language approach to reading.

Second graders now find themselves engaged in a language arts
curriculum of their own making. All reading and writing focus on
themes that they have chosen—from gardens to dinosaurs. They
choose either trade books ("real" books, as the teachers call them
when comparing them to basals) or their own writing as the reading
"text." They are not ability grouped; they gather for reading groups
by interest. They all read frequently during the day, and much of the
rest of the curriculum—the arts, math, social studies, and science—
flows from this collaboratively directed reading program. The classroom walls are covered with print and art, not copied from books
but originals from the children.

RESISTANCE AND EMPOWERMENT IN CURRICULUM REFORM

Running through the work of these teachers are two themes, resistance
and empowerment. They resist the current trends in school reform that are
designed without reference to the democratic mission of schools. They are
empowered in ways that enable them to embrace a curriculum and practice
that recapture this democratic mission.

Resistance

The current talk about school reform in "official" centers of educational
authority—state legislatures, the U.S. Department of Education, and national
commissions—is dominated by a preoccupation with students as future
workers (Education Commission of the States, 1983; National Commission
on Excellence in Education, 1983; National Science Board, 1983). We are to
ignore problems with the balance of trade, our aging industrial plants, in-
sider trading, programmed trading, and leveraged buyouts and instead
blame the schools for our lack of industrial productivity.

In concert with the focus on children as future workers is a sense that
teachers are merely workers as well. Such an agenda shows up in a variety
of ways. First, there is the nearly total absence of teachers' voices from the
reform reports. This absence is reflected in the reports themselves, which

show no awareness of the daily realities of teaching. It is assumed that simply insisting on more years of exposure to the curriculum in math, reading, science, and so forth will yield higher test scores. Not so, as any good teacher knows who has been faced with overcrowded classrooms, little room to innovate, and the many needs and concerns children bring with them to school.

Curriculum reform has been dominated by an attempt to further "teacher-proof" materials (Apple, 1982; Aronowitz & Giroux, 1985). Curriculum packages abound, and pronouncements come from Washington as to what is to be taught in every subject at every grade level. Curriculum success is to be determined by scores on standardized tests written, normed, and approved by professional test makers, not educators. The clear intent is a continuation of attempts to separate the conception and execution of curriculum—to disempower teachers.

The consequences of such a trend for the civic mission of the school are devastating. Turning our attention to preparing workers comes at the expense of preparing democratic citizens (Wood, 1988). The goals of schooling for work often stress conformity and obedience, encourage rote memorization of correct answers, and are primarily utilitarian in their intent. These goals most certainly conflict with a pedagogy for democracy, the goal of which is to prepare independent thinkers who are committed to the public good and willing to act on their own initiative.

There is a further consequence of schooling for work that is closely linked to the abandonment of the school's civic mission. It is the degrading of the work of the teacher. If the task of the school is only to produce those attributes that industry values, the role of the teacher becomes nothing more than that of a teaching machine. Curricular decisions are made from above, mandated exams dictate the material covered, and the teacher is seen as merely a transmitter of a set body of knowledge. The model is of the teacher as assembly line worker. Responsible for only one fragment of a child's school life and bound to administer only one set treatment (curriculum), teaching becomes a repetitive, mechanical, and even dehumanizing task (Wirth, 1983).

The teachers in the classrooms described at the beginning of this chapter have all resisted this antidemocratic wave of school reform. They have resisted by refusing to allow curriculum mandates to override their vision of a curriculum for the democratic empowerment of their students. Such a curriculum nurtures in students the self-confidence each citizen requires to explore collectively the choices we face and the courage to act upon these choices in the best interests of the many communities to which we belong. It is the way in which these teachers have gathered the courage to resist to which we now turn.

Empowerment

To engage in such resistance, these teachers, along with many others, have formed the Institute for Democracy in Education. The teachers, parents, university faculty, students, and community members involved in the Institute have built their work around five principles that constitute education for democratic empowerment. They believe the school should be a site where students, through experience, come to

1. Believe in the individual's right and responsibility to participate publicly
2. Have a sense of political efficacy, that is, the knowledge that one's contributions to community life are important
3. Value the principles of democratic life—equality, liberty, community
4. Know that alternative arrangements to the status quo exist and are worthwhile
5. Gain the requisite intellectual skills to participate in public discourse

The Institute has evolved through the collaboration of teachers, including myself, over the past six years. It began with a group of classroom teachers, concerned with the top-down nature of much of the recent school reform literature, meeting on their own to discuss alternatives. As a faculty member at the local university, I was invited to attend one of their study sessions and talk about democracy and education. The participants, feeling that there had to be more teachers in the area concerned about the antidemocratic nature of current school reform, set plans for a summer gathering of democratic educators.

The 1983 summer meeting lasted for two weeks. During that time the teachers voiced their frustrations and concerns, hopes and dreams. My role as group facilitator developed in two ways. The first was to help locate their work in a historical context, so we could all understand the roots of antidemocratic school reform as explained by writers like Kliebard (1986), Wirth (1983), Bastian, et al. (1985), and Tyack and Hansot (1982). The second was to help find examples, in works by Dewey (1900), Raywid, et al. (1984), Littky and Freid (1988), and Wigginton (1985), among others, of teachers and schools resisting such reform.

Through building on both of these areas, these teachers became empowered in the way Freire (1968) suggests when discussing education as a process of posing problems. First, they transcended a belief that the system of schooling is neutral (Freire's magical-conforming stage) as they saw the roots of modern school reform embedded in the industrial efficiency movement. Second, they went beyond blaming themselves for their failures in overcoming the corporate agenda for schools (naive-reforming stage) as they saw that other teachers shared their problems. Finally, they arrived at a belief that they can change schools to be more democratic (critical-transforming stage) as they worked together to build for such change, drawing from current and historical examples.

Recognizing that self-transformation is an ongoing process, these teachers established the Institute, which now publishes a journal, holds monthly round tables to discuss issues of interest to participants, presents workshops and conferences, and maintains a curriculum library. The key to all of this is that everything is done at the request of and by practicing teachers.

A CURRICULUM FOR DEMOCRATIC EMPOWERMENT

The curriculum for democratic empowerment that has emerged from the work of the teachers in the Institute is exemplified by the three major motifs of "choice and control," "equity," and "community."

Choice and Control

Fundamental to a sense of democratic empowerment are notions of efficacy and participation. Virtually all of the literature on democracy points out the connection between the individual's experience in decision making and an increased involvement in social affairs. Further, experiencing the power of actually having one's voice be heard and count in the process of decision making engenders the confidence required for future social and political engagement (Pateman, 1970).

Unfortunately, most schooling operates to limit, as opposed to expand, the range of experiences students have with decision making. Simplistic choices, such as of the colors or theme for the prom or the speaker for graduation, do little to enhance efficacy. We develop cynics, not citizens, when students see through this charade.

A curriculum for democratic empowerment engages students in choices about and control over the most central element of their school experience—the curriculum itself. In Bill Elasky's class, for example, students chose the topic, water quality, that would guide the bulk of their future work. After choosing the topic, it was up to the students to decide who took on what responsibility, how to test, how to report results, whom to consult, and so forth. Perhaps the students, in an article based on their experiences, put it best.

> Mr. Elasky helps a lot, but we do the tests and organize things. He helps us, but we make decisions by brainstorming and choosing the best ideas. We have taken over some of the teaching Mr. Elasky once did. (Tweedy, et al., 1988, p. 7)

Nancy Corbett (1988) relinquished control and choice after her own ideas for a class project, involving a slide show on a local organization devoted to assisting disabled citizens, were rejected.

> My students were courteous about, but they really were not interested in my slide presentation. What an ego blow. I wasn't certain I liked democracy in the classroom. I rather enjoyed the dictator role. So, what were their bright ideas? Two words emerged above all others—teen pregnancy. Oh no, I thought, what would their mothers say? (p. 7)

Nancy overcame her initial hesitancy as she realized that the students were not rejecting her, just her agenda. Democratic participation requires that option; that community transcends ego. Genuine participation includes the right to make, not just influence, decisions.

Joyce Hannenberg is one of the second grade teachers referred to above. In Joyce's class, choice is a theme that is always at the forefront.

> In my classroom I try to have children make choices whenever it is possible. We make academic choices: They are always choosing what book they want to read, and choosing what they want to write ... and they choose the project they want to work on. ... I feel [that] the children in my classroom do feel powerful, because they make choices about what they want to learn or choices about something that is going on in the room.[1]

Feeling powerful is precisely the issue. The conviction that students can control their world can be engendered in them only from experiences in which they *are* in control. As another of the second grade teachers, Charlotte Arbuthnot, argues: "I have never believed that my agenda is more important than [the students']. I will go with anything they are really interested in."

This concern with students having choice and control over the curriculum generates a number of crucial ingredients for democratic life. First, children come to see themselves as having control over knowledge and information: They produce rather than memorize knowledge. Second, students gain a sense of their own wisdom—their own ability to think, make judgments, and act. Third, they come to believe that they have the right to order their own world. Students so engaged in choosing and directing the curriculum may come to see themselves as citizens with the right and responsibility, as well as the skill, to participate in democratic governance.

---

[1] All unreferenced teacher comments come from notes and tapes of Institute meetings, 1983–1988. The teachers' real names are used, with their permission, out of respect for their work.

Equity

In each of these classrooms the curriculum is not parceled out differentially. All children have equal access to the curriculum because the teachers involved refuse to group by ability for instruction, research, or project work.

For Joyce this has meant moving away from the traditional strategy of ability-based reading groups. Instead, she gathers children together to read based on interest.

> I don't use reading groups.... Children recognize that they are in the smart group and the dumb group, and they realize that all themselves. Now, that's not even apparent. I mean, everyone is just reading. We read a lot of the same things, we are exposed to the same things, and we are not ability grouping. I feel better about it and I know they do.

In the writing projects that Nancy and Bill carry out, students group themselves by interest, as opposed to ability. Students often find themselves in groups in which traditional notions of who is "high ability" are turned on their head. As the range of valuable skills in the classroom expands, so does the number of students possessing those skills. The students are perhaps the most articulate about this agenda. Here are two twelve-year-olds in Bill's class.

TONY: It used to be that there were two kinds, you know, groups in our grade. Yeah, the tough kids and the smart kids. And we sat in different parts of the room and didn't do anything together . . .

FRED: Like even on the playground we didn't play together, we mostly, well, you know, when we were together we fought.

TONY: But not this year. . . .

FRED: Right, we play together and everything.

TONY: 'Cause in class we are all working together on projects and helping each other and you can't tell who's smart or tough or whatever, you know.

FRED: Yeah, we're like a real team, you know.

Unfortunately, much of what goes on in schools today seems designed to guarantee a stratified curriculum. Such differentiation through ability grouping and gender or racial stereotyping destroys students' notions of self, preparing them for differentiated positions in the world of work, and builds a deep sense of class and political division into American life.

However, if democracy is to have a future it must be based on a shared vision of the equal contribution we all make to public life. The classrooms we are visiting here provide children with that vision through actual curricular experiences. Beyond that, every child in these rooms gains a sense that he or she counts; each has an important contribution to make to the welfare of the group. Equity and efficacy work hand-in-hand in these rooms as children come to see the strength of the collaborative action of equals.

Community

Finally, each of these classrooms is filled with an abiding spirit of community. This emphasis on community flows from the classroom into the surrounding community.

In the classroom it seems clear that each of these teachers and their students are building a commitment to one another. As Marcia Burchby, a first grade teacher involved in the Institute, puts it, "I also want kids to think socially and act socially, so I stress cooperative activities as opposed to competitive activities." Above, we gained a sense of how this works in avoiding ability grouping. Here, the question is how these teachers move beyond preventing inequity to building community.

The main generator of this sense of community is the cooperative nature of these classrooms. As noted earlier, students collaborate in setting the curriculum. Additionally, all classroom rules and procedures evolve out of the perceived needs of the class. Problems and possibilities that arise are dealt with by the group. While it may take a little longer, teachers and students alike accept ownership of the classroom environment.

In Bill's and Nancy's classes students decide as a team how to approach issues and manage the class. In many respects the responsibility for making the classroom "work" is assumed by the students. Bill puts it this way.

> I don't worry about motivating students, managing the classroom, cleaning up after them. They [the students] handle all that because they have a commitment to one another and to the job at hand. [Their work] has to be good, because their names are on it, not mine.

These teachers possess a clear, up front agenda of community building in their rooms. Joyce discusses it as follows:

> We have something that we call forum, and every Monday morning one first grade class and all the second grade classes gather together in the TV room. . . . We are trying to emulate a community. We'll raise a question or ask the children their concerns about current issues. Like this week we have had parent/teacher conferences, and so we asked the children, "What are your concerns about parent/teacher conferences?" And when any child wanted to speak, they would come to the front of the room where

they would feel more comfortable sitting, and then we would have a discussion about that. And I think the previous week we were asking, "What do you think is going well this year? What do you think is really hard this year? What do you think you need to improve on?" It's amazing. This is the second year we have done this. I really see a change in the children. They're much more verbal, and I think they're being more responsible. I think they know that we are really listening and we're in this together as a community. I think it's wonderful . . .

The sense of community inside the school flows to the community outside the school as well. The writing projects in Bill's and Nancy's rooms are perhaps the most graphic examples of this. With the careful advice and encouragement of their teachers, these children identified a way they could make a difference in their communities. Their research and writing were designed to change the world around them. Through such purposeful work they have come to see themselves as members of a community, not passive observers of life.

It is not enough for the curriculum to extol the virtues of community and service. These are shallow maxims when they amount to little more than an add-on to the "real" curriculum of a walk-, read-, bike-, or whatever-a-thon. If the young are to develop a deep, abiding impulse to share in the collective development of the communities within which they live, they must experience the richness of that life as early as possible. A curriculum for democratic empowerment is based on precisely such an experience.

TEACHERS AS CURRICULUM WORKERS

I have tried to describe one process by which teachers become empowered as curriculum workers. In one sense, the Institute for Democracy in Education is curriculum itself—the process through which lived experience is translated into an educative act. The Institute, as curriculum, becomes a way to turn the daily heroism of teachers educating for democratic empowerment into an educational program that in turn empowers other teachers.

My work with these teachers continues on the level of collaborator. My primary task is to help dig out resources and open up new avenues of theory to them. However, all of my work is done at their request and to meet their agenda. In this way, I learn about the daily realities that must be faced by teachers working for democratic school reform. From this experience I have learned several important things about engaging teachers in learning about curriculum.

First, talk about empowering teachers as curriculum workers needs to be rethought. To empower teachers is not enough: We must ask to what end, to what shared agenda? Only by linking democracy to empowerment, that is, working for the democratic empowerment of *students,* will teachers find a genuine sense of empowerment themselves (Dewey, 1903). Any other mission, whether it is preparing workers, soldiers, or just controlling children, only reinforces the disempowerment of teachers. The issue is to break this antidemocratic hold on curriculum, not merely to give teachers more control over it.

The Institute provides such a curricular orientation. Its teachers are clear about their agenda and their work for democracy. Everything they do is linked to that agenda, and all of their work is measured against that sense of purpose. The Institute as curriculum generates a heroic vision of teachers building a democratic future. It is this vision, not merely technical control of books, materials, and timetables, that empowers teachers.

Second, teachers must have a historic sense of the roots of antidemocratic trends in curriculum. At the Institute we work together to uncover these roots both in general—in the industrial model for schools—and in the particulars of their own work environments. Further, Institute teachers have reclaimed the legacy of progressive educational change, demystified curriculum, and recognized themselves as part of a continuing educational struggle. In short, they have named their oppressors and are able, therefore, to challenge them.

Third, teachers need examples of the possibility of change. Through workshops, readings, visits to one another's classrooms, and shared writings, teachers in the Institute continually see actual examples of democratic school change. The teachers described here have found models, both historic and contemporary, from which they draw the possibility for their own actions. In turn, they have become models for other teachers; they have provided inspiration for other teachers to join in working for schooling that democratically empowers children.

Finally, teachers need to see curriculum as a shared process—not as something that teachers dispense the way physicians prescribe medicine. Curriculum is a process in which teachers and students engage to order and make sense of the world. As such, it requires that teachers have a deep respect for the work of children, a respect captured by Marcia this way:

Something that is mandatory for all of us to really work on is to have respect for the child and faith in that child. I need to have respect for their own thoughts, experiences, their own cultural background, as well as their end product. That end product may not look like anything that the teacher may have seen, but it is valuable as it comes from them. A term we use a lot is that we want the children to be risk takers, we want them to be tryers. We don't want them to be afraid of failure, but to have confidence in themselves.

TEACHING CURRICULUM FOR DEMOCRATIC EMPOWERMENT

My own teaching has changed because of my involvement with the Institute. I have come to realize that my own efforts should be exemplars of the democratic curriculum I advocate. As such, the genuine, shared problems of classroom teachers become the curriculum of my classes. We trace the roots of these problems and find that they come from choices made, not inevitabilities. Things can be different—and often should be—if we take seriously the democratic mission of schools.

But can we make things different? The agenda in class is not merely to study curricular forms but to make curriculum. We engage in building democratic alternatives that teachers can actually use in their classrooms. And many teachers commit to continuing work on such democratic alternatives, either with other teachers in their buildings or through participation in the Institute.

Through my involvement with democratic educators, I have changed my orientation to college teaching. I realize that I cannot violate in practice the democratic theory I espouse when teaching the very people with whom the real hope for democratic education rests—classroom teachers. Our work must be not to impose a curricular orientation, but to work toward the democratic empowerment of every teacher. When I try to do this, I learn over and over again that, as one teacher at an Institute meeting put it, "the curriculum is what the kids and I say it is!"

REFERENCES

Apple, M. W. (1982). Curricular form and the logic of technical control. In M. W. Apple (Ed.), *Curricular and Economic Reproduction in Education.* Boston: Routledge & Kegan Paul.

Aronowitz, S., & Giroux, H. A. (1985). *Education Under Siege.* South Hadley, MA: Bergin & Garvey.

Bastian, A., et al. (1985). *Choosing Equality.* Philadelphia: Temple University Press.

Corbett, N. (1988). A Hazen Fellowship and democracy in education. *Democracy and Education, 2*(6), 7–9.

Dewey, J. (1900). *The School and Society.* Chicago: University of Chicago Press.

Dewey, J. (1903). Democracy in education. *The Elementary School Teacher, 4*(4), 193–204.

Education Commission of the States. (1983). *Action for Excellence.* Washington, DC: Education Commission of the States.

Freire, P. (1968). *Pedagogy of the Oppressed.* New York: Seabury.

Kliebard, H. M. (1986). *The Struggle for the American Curriculum, 1893–1958.* Boston: Routledge & Kegan Paul.

Littky, D., & Freid, R. (1988). The challenge to make good schools great. *NEA Today,* January, 4–8.

National Commission on Excellence in Education. (1983). *A Nation at Risk.* Washington, DC: U.S. Government Printing Office.

National Science Board. (1983). *Educating Americans for the 21st Century.* Washington, DC: National Science Foundation.

Pateman, C. (1970). *Participation and Democratic Theory.* Cambridge, England: Cambridge University Press.

Raywid, M. A., Tesconi, C., & Warren, D. (1984). *Pride and Promise.* Westbury, CT: American Educational Studies Association.

Tweedy, F., et al. (1988). Students writing about community affairs. *Democracy and Education, 2*(7), 6–7.

Tyack, D., & Hansot, E. (1982). *Managers of Virtue.* New York: Basic Books.

Wigginton, B. E. (1985). *Sometimes a Shining Moment.* Garden City, NY: Anchor Press.

Wirth, A. G. (1983). *Productive Work—In Industry and Schools.* New York: University Press of America.

Wood, G. H. (1988). The hope for civic education. *Theory Into Practice, 27,* 296–302.

Contestaire

TED T. AOKI

University of Alberta

Themes of Teaching Curriculum

For me, whose initiatory experiences in curriculum studies as a graduate student some years ago were a not too nourishing diet of one curriculum model after another—all, I later came to know, modifications of strictly ends–means systems schema—the chapters by Janet Miller and George Wood point to an inspired world of teaching textually alive to curriculum. I find in Janet Miller's "Teachers as Curriculum Creators" a regard for a deepened presence of students-in-self-transformation; in George Wood's "Teachers as Curriculum Workers" a call for a situated praxical aliveness. These chapters inspire me to open myself to three themes that concern teaching and curriculum.

Theme I:
Our teachers of curriculum embody a deep sense of curriculum-as-lived.

Teachers in the classroom are often described in terms of roles that they play, of the activities they conduct, or of effectiveness in reaching set goals. These descriptions reflect sociological, anthropological, or technological understandings of teaching and, as such, provide us with measures of "disciplined" understandings that are correct sociologically, anthropologically, or technologically. But, by espousing somewhat distanced seeings—distanced from the lived experiences of teachers and students—these understandings neglect meanings embedded in lived experiences. What seems to be forgotten is that teachers' true vocation calls for a transformation of the sociological, anthropological, and technological environment into a pedagogical situation within which teachers and students experience life. For when a teacher begins to indwell with students, the environment ceases to be environment, and in its place comes into being a lived pedagogical situation pregnantly alive with possibilities in the presence of people.

This is the world of curriculum-as-lived that our teachers and students experience. For George Wood, it is the face-to-face living with the concrete experiences of Bill Elasky, Nancy Corbett, and others, all using their real names, each a unique human being. George knows that their uniqueness disappears into the shadow when they are spoken of in the prosaically abstract language of external curriculum planners who are, in a sense, condemned to plan for faceless people who become generalized entities often defined abstractly in terms of performance roles, activities, and techniques. For Janet Miller, it is the experiences of curricula and remembrances of curricula experienced that students are asked to journalize. It is the thoughtfully reflective dialogue she engages with Ben, an English teacher, as together they constitute their own curriculum.

Theme II:
Curriculum teaching as an invitation to indwell in tensionality.

"My teaching of curriculum is . . . about the difficulties I experience when I try to see the world in new ways. . . . [It] also is about the tensions I feel."   —Janet Miller

"The teachers . . . resisted by refusing to allow curriculum mandates to override their vision of . . . curriculum."   —George Wood

For me what is notable about these remarks is the way in which they point to the place of indwelling for these curriculum teachers. It is, as we can see, a place of tension marked by differences and difficulties. It is a place between curriculum worlds—for Janet, between the world that is and the world yet to be; for George, between the world of the mandated curriculum and the students' own vision of curriculum.

Such a realm of the between is a situated place where difficulty resides. In such a situation many of us tend to problematize the difficulty and seek solutions that offer closure. To be so oriented to difficulty reflects a reductive understanding of it, for which technical rationality may be the most appropriate means of resolution. In being so oriented, is there not a risk of foreclosing too hurriedly other ways of understanding difficulty? Is it not possible that certain difficulties are openings granted to us, calling upon us to struggle in and through the difficulties, thereby yielding fresh possibilities?

> Here, I am reminded of Daisetz Suzuki, a Zen master, who said: It is not a sense of identity nor tranquility that Zen sees and loves in nature. Nature is always in motion, never at a standstill; if nature is to be loved, it must be caught while moving and in this way its aesthetic value must be appraised. To seek tranquility is to kill nature, to stop its pulsation, and to embrace the dead corpse that is left behind. Advocates of tranquility are worshippers of abstraction and death. (Beny, 1967, p. 8)

I feel that these authors as teachers of curriculum show a deference for tensionality in difficulty and difference. They seem to have knowingly chosen to indwell in difficulty, seeking not a way of ease but rather a way, though difficult, that may grant an opening to new possibilities. And in the lived tensionality that marks such difficulty and difference, they seem to be within reach of a quality of tautness—like that of a properly attuned violin string—that allows a sounding and resounding that resonate vitally.

Could it be, I now ask, that a good teacher of curriculum keeps a watchful eye for ruptures and differences between curriculum worlds that promise edifying experiences? Could it be that ruptures and differences are encountered in curriculum teaching that allow a revealing of life's truths? Could it be that this is the sort of questioning that John Caputo (1987) speaks of when he talks of restoring life to its original difficulty?

I feel that the authors show a commitment to difficulty and differences in life by situating themselves in that opening I have called "the between" and by facing up to the tensionality within difference and difficulty. By their commitment, I feel that they are calling upon us to indwell authentically in the life of difficulty, not to betray it with easier technical solutions.

Theme III:
The curriculum teacher is fundamentally an educated person.

"I'm trying. For me it's been a process of becoming more involved with the roots of my work."   —Ben, in Janet Miller's chapter

"Teachers . . . have a historic sense of the roots of . . . trends in curriculum. We work together to uncover the roots."

—George Wood

In the chapters before us, I am stirred by the sense of curriculum teaching that decries curriculum standpoints that diminish the teacher's authenticity as person and educator. These authors, in speaking of teaching teachers for democracy, and of teaching teachers to be reflective curriculum creators, seem to converge in their search for some deepened understanding of what it means to be an educated person who teaches curriculum. I hear their voices inviting us to join in the search for who an educated person is. I join the search and offer a reply.

An educated person, first and foremost, understands that one's way of knowing, thinking, and doing flow from who one is. Such a person knows that an authentic person is no mere individual, an island unto himself or herself, but a being-in-relation with others and hence is, at core, an ethical being. Such a person knows that being an educated person is more than possessing knowledge or acquiring intellectual or managerial skills, and that being an educated person is more a dwelling aright in thoughtful living with others.

An educated person, thus, not only guards against disembodied forms of knowing, thinking, and doing that reduce self and others to things, but also strives, guided by the authority of the good in pedagogical situations, for embodied thoughtfulness that makes possible living as human beings.

Moreover, an educated person speaks and acts from a deep sense of humility. He or she is conscious of the limits set by human finitude and mortality, and acknowledges the grace by which educator and educated are allowed to dwell in a present that embraces past experiences and is open to possibilities yet to be.

Thus, to be educated is to be ever open to the call of what it is to be deeply human and, heeding that call, to walk with others in life's ventures.

REFERENCES

Beny, R. (1967). *Japan in colour.* London: Thames & Hudson.
Caputo, J. (1987). *Radical hermeneutics: Repetition, deconstruction, and the hermeneutic project.* Bloomington: Indiana University Press.

Conversation parmi animateurs

O. L. DAVIS, JR.
University of Texas at Austin

PAUL KLOHR
Ohio State University

NORM OVERLY
Indiana University

DAVIS: These chapters prompted thoughts about action research. There is a story that Wells Foshay tells far better than I. When
he was director of the Bureau of Educational Research at Ohio State,
he asked a kindergarten teacher the question: "Tell me why you did
what you did?" It was a question to which she couldn't reply. Indeed, it
was almost an obscene question. She simply didn't know. But, when
Wells asked her to tell *her story* she could do that with brilliance. She
could tell her story, but she couldn't take it apart. She was not, herself,
the analyst; she was intensely enmeshed in the fabric of the experience
itself.

I think that that's what most of us find ourselves doing. It's helpful
to have another person, like Janet Miller or George Wood, hear what
we've said. That is, hear our story. And, it's helpful to have someone
else help to make sense of our story. Or, with us, to help us make sense
of it in a way that this sense can be communicated to others. That's a
notion of action research that is tremendously impressive.

KLOHR: Janet is trying to work with teachers so that they become
producers—in contrast to consumers—of knowledge. You see what a
tremendous thrust that gives to the development of self, if you can say,
"What I'm doing is significant because I am answering my own important questions as I'm caught up in it." How do you use yourself as a
main resource in the teaching act? That's the problem for curriculum

students. As curriculum teachers, we can start with that question and struggle toward some solution.

DAVIS: This discussion reminds me of how Hilda Taba and Ralph Tyler came into East High School in Denver and talked with the teachers in the Eight Year Study. The way they got the teachers to talk about what they were doing and what they liked to do was not to ask, "What are your objectives?" but to ask them to describe what it was that they were doing. That doesn't sound like the linear system that Tyler wrote about years later and that serves as a kind of foil for a lot of the writings in this volume. According to the story, that was not the way Taba and Tyler worked with teachers. They saw that teachers had choice; they saw that teachers were in control. And, as teachers saw their ideas developing, they would have options for choice.

KLOHR: To my mind, O.L., the historical precedent that comes closest to action research is a movement that was underway even back in the 1950s. It wasn't the sophisticated movement we have now with ethnographic kinds of procedures for research. But, it was good. Wells Foshay's work with Kenneth Wann on children's social values is a good example. This whole effort in the field of curriculum was accentuated a great deal by what was happening in the ASCD right after World War II. People like Kenneth Benne and Herb Thelen began to focus on the importance of group process. ASCD began to offer sessions where people would actually respond to what was being said. You'd have to appreciate what a tremendous difference this meant; for example, to go to a national conference and be able to sit in a group where what you said made some difference. This all sounds common now, but when tied into action research, these movements resulted in our seeing the teacher as curriculum developer—a very different role from what it had previously been. In contemporary curriculum thought, reflected by George Wood and Janet Miller, teachers are integral to the curriculum process.

OVERLY: I don't know about you two, but my sense is that within the last five years teachers *have* begun to see themselves as curriculum makers. When I first started teaching curriculum in the 1960s, I found it very difficult to get teachers to think of themselves as being responsible for making curriculum beyond simply teaching what they were supposed to teach. Now, I am finding teachers, even administrators, saying teachers must take charge of the curriculum. I think that's been a change within American education. Teachers are being given more responsibility for curriculum and for curriculum decisions—at the very least in the classroom. And, of course, when they close the classroom door, they're really in charge of the curriculum.

DAVIS: But, you'll recall, Norm, that there have been instances in the past when teachers didn't have to close their doors. Stories like Wood's about teachers working with students can be found throughout curriculum history. One example took place at Skokie Junior High School in Illinois. There is a marvellous series of historical anecdotes from that school about students forming an insurance company and organizing a union of pupil-cafeteria workers. As an outcome of their involvement in studying particular events in social studies, the students negotiated with the school people and got higher salaries for the workers. It wasn't just kids playing at this stuff; they really *did* it!

KLOHR: The point in all of this is that classroom teachers are really an integral part of the curriculum development process; teachers of curriculum, like curriculum specialists in the school district, serve in an advisory role. In my own work, instead of developing great masses of syllabi and course descriptions, I was very interested in developing what Alberty called "resource units." Again, you see this was quite a shift in the development of curriculum materials because it assumed that teachers could develop their own, or a great part of their own, curriculum materials. This was an evolving process. You began with a core of materials, and a small group of teachers would continue to develop it. They would identify a very wide range of potential educational experiences within the problem area of the resource unit. It was a very broad organization of curriculum materials. I see this as a kind of manifestation, during that period of time, of putting to work both the notion of self and also this shift to working with other people in groups. Keeping track of it was the action research part. The teachers did it themselves rather than depending on some expert.

DAVIS: You make an important point, Paul, and that is that these teachers worked *together* on these units. Sometimes, I'm afraid that curriculum teaching in the university is understood to be much larger than most of us would recognize. It has grown apart from the structures of schools to which it would relate. We work with our students, whether they're undergraduates, teachers, or people working on additional certificates or advanced degrees, as *single* persons to be sent out, like monks from a monastery, into the world to carry the message to their workplaces without much local institutional support. It's important work to be done, but I'm convinced that we need to be less personalistic, or at least that shouldn't be our exclusive goal. We must recognize not only that individuals must be empowered but that empowerment must be sustained. The development of the ethos within the school is far more important than having an "effective" school principal. That's how empowerment can be sustained.

OVERLY: I'm becoming a little more sensitive to the contexts within which teachers work. I see myself as one who thinks that you can do anything, anywhere—or at least you can try. I was not sensitive enough to the extreme difficulty that teachers face. Empowerment involves helping teachers transcend the difficulties.

DAVIS: In some respects this may be a fruitless discussion, gentlemen. People need to be empowered, sure enough. And when individuals are better in their classrooms, whole departments are improved. I guess I'm one of the few people who think that whole institutions don't have to change for there to be important curriculum strides forward. But, I do believe that we need to expand our concerns for and interests in curriculum relationships from single individuals to groups of teachers working within the context of the school. It may be that for a university professor, however, that's not even viable.

OVERLY: I don't know, O.L.—I may have seen it. I had what was a very good experience last semester in a practicum with doctoral majors in curriculum. I loved it. I think the students did too. We spent most of our time in one school working with teachers. The thing that I found interesting was that I had to try to get the students to be more accepting and appreciative of the constraints of the school system. They were so horribly critical of the school setting and what was going on that it seemed they just couldn't wait to get together to tear it apart! It took a lot of effort to get them to see that just being critical from only the analytical stance wasn't going to do anything for the teachers who were in that situation; that they really had to engage those teachers in the change process and that that was going to take some time.

KLOHR: It sounds as though your students had to struggle mightily to put aside their taken-for-granted image of the role of the teacher in the curriculum development process as well as their own role as educational midwives. As Ross Mooney eloquently argued, it is the teacher, himself or herself, who is the researcher. Reading his essay, though, is quite different from experiencing such an assertion. To appreciate this, you need to shift your image of a teacher from that of a consumer of information to that of a producer of knowledge. In his classic essay, Mooney listed a series of questions to help persons undergo this conceptual shift. The earliest and most effective practitioner of this approach, I think, was Hilda Taba. In her years of work with teachers, she put this concept of teacher-as-researcher-and-curriculum-developer into practice. She was also one of the first to employ group observers and recorders in the curriculum development process. That sounds so common now, but group process tied to action research profoundly changes the role of teacher-as-curriculum-developer.

DAVIS: You know, Paul, Caswell's pioneering curriculum development work in Florida and Virginia began with teachers studying and conversing—not just talking—about matters that were important to them and that they believed should be continued. Interestingly, the idea for this process came after his work in Alabama and Mississippi in which he just went in and helped create the courses of study and, afterwards, teachers ignored the documents.

OVERLY: Well, we didn't experience a debacle. I think these students were really successful. I had arranged for the students to evaluate four new programs that the school had started. To determine the extent to which they were effective. They each had the added task of working with an individual teacher to try to meet whatever needs that teacher could articulate. Of course, helping the teachers articulate a particular need was a big problem. They weren't used to having someone come in and say, "Oh, we'll help you do whatever you would like to do." That task presented a further challenge for my students because some of the things that teachers wanted to do were not seen by the students as particularly wise. So, the students then had the additional task of helping these teachers reevaluate the desirability of those things. At the end of the semester, the teachers and administrators at the school really wanted us to continue.

DAVIS: You know, I'm glad you didn't say your students or the school administration "allowed things to happen." It's not that we allow people to have ideas but that we encourage or restrict them. They're going to have them. Their ideas are not ours to allow.

OVERLY: Well, my goal for this curriculum course was that my students attempt to empower those teachers so that they would become better teachers, critically evaluate what they were doing, not feel threatened by having someone with them, and ultimately improve education for the kids. In the process, I hope that I also opened up spaces for my students.

PART III

TEACHING FROM THE PERSPECTIVE OF COMMUNITY

Communities bond individuals and families to human networks of parallel and, at times, conflicting interests. The integral relationship between schools and a variety of communities has been discussed by such influential and diverse thinkers as Plato, Aquinas, Durkheim, Dewey, and Jefferson. The differing conceptions of community are also reflected in the chapters in this part. Each author, however, starts with community as the perspective through which issues relating to content and pedagogy in the teaching of curriculum are viewed.

In Chapter 8 Landon Beyer, following his critique of the technical/procedural model of curriculum decision making, argues that all curriculum deliberation is, at its root, normative. Further, Beyer notes that such normative decision making is conducted within a wider social, economic, and political framework. Bringing this perspective to bear in his curriculum teaching, Beyer asks his students to develop "normative plans of action" as they contemplate their teaching assignments. The impact of this approach to teaching curriculum with preservice elementary teachers is explored through a case study of one of his students.

Sharing Beyer's concern for educators to critically examine the taken-for-grantedness of their culture, William Pink discusses the empowerment of veteran teachers/doctoral students through curriculum studies. In Chapter 9 Pink outlines nine barriers to teacher empowerment that reflect the powerful influences of our shared culture. Using extensive readings and class discussions, Pink challenges these teachers to make problematic "the commonplace in schools." Using the metaphor of an airline flight, he analyzes student reactions to his approach to teaching and thinking about curriculum. Pink concludes by noting the implications that such an approach has for the university and the schools.

Robert Donmoyer, in Chapter 10, is also concerned about the relationships among curriculum, community, and culture. His conception of community and culture, however, differs significantly from those of Beyer and Pink. Beginning his chapter with a discussion of the educational experiences of Aborigine males in Western Australia, Donmoyer asserts that to understand curriculum we must first understand the community's culture and its efforts to reproduce itself through educational institutions. Three complementary conceptions of politics, he argues, are essential to teaching and thinking about curriculum. Donmoyer concludes with a description of approaches and strategies he uses to teach about curriculum from a community orientation.

The importance of developing a caring community within the contexts of the college classroom and the elementary school is the theme explored by Jean Erdman in Chapter 11. Feminist scholarship and principles are the foundation of Erdman's teaching of an elementary curriculum course that forges and supports a community of shared interests. Arguing for "gender-sensitive curriculum teaching," she outlines classroom approaches to raise students' consciousness, broaden the range of classroom voices heard and valued, reduce the distance between teacher and student, and model the ethics of caring. Erdman concludes by examining how socioeconomic, linguistic, and cultural contexts, reflect and reproduce patriarchal communities.

8

Curriculum Deliberation

Value Choices
and Political Possibilities

LANDON E. BEYER
Knox College

*My doctoral studies in education were completed at the University of
Wisconsin-Madison, with previous doctoral work at the University of Illinois at Urbana-Champaign. At Wisconsin, Mike Apple was my advisor,
while at Illinois I studied extensively with Walter Feinberg. Mike graduated from Teachers College, where his mentor had been Dwayne Huebner.*

*I began my undergraduate course work with a desire to teach high
school English. Along the way I got corrupted by an interest in philosophy,
especially aesthetics. In my senior year I decided to get a secondary degree
with a major in philosophy, and for a brief time I taught high school philosophy. Subsequently I completed graduate work in philosophy and a
second undergraduate degree, this one in elementary education. I taught
fourth-fifth grade in a suburban, mostly white middle class school, and
seventh grade on a remote Indian reservation. I recall incidents from both
positions almost daily.*

*Among the most important influences on my teaching have been one
or two high school teachers who helped me to see the possibilities of intellectual engagement, several undergraduate professors, and, at the graduate level (besides Apple and Feinberg), Donald W. Crawford, Clarence J.
Karier, and Herbert M. Kliebard. My supervision of student teachers at Wisconsin also proved to be of long-lasting benefit.*

*I had decided somewhere in the recesses of my consciousness to pur-
sue a doctorate and college level teaching relatively early in my education
(though that always seemed a bit presumptuous to me). It seemed the best*

way to combine my fondness for teaching and my commitment to writing. It still seems that way to me, at least most of the time.

The contours of curriculum decision making have often outlined a domain within which technical, procedural, and pragmatic questions are primary. In treating curriculum decisions as procedural questions that often take for granted the ends or aims of education, teachers and others become surrounded by a technical mode of rationality. As outlined by Schön (1983), this way of thinking assumes that "professional activity consists in instrumental problem solving made rigorous by the application of scientific theory and technique. [On this view] only the professions practice rigorously technical problem solving based on specialized scientific knowledge" (pp. 21–22). A science of education is thus predicated on articulating general principles, rules, or methods that can be applied systematically to specific questions and settings, in the process resolving whatever problematic situation has arisen.

There are two general shortcomings to this approach to curriculum that need to be noted. First, a technical/procedural model overlooks the fact that curriculum deliberation takes place "on the spot," in response to classroom conditions that often cannot be anticipated (Smyth, 1987). Second, a technical view of curriculum overlooks an important range of social and political questions that are inevitably involved in education. As a number of writers have demonstrated, decisions about what content is to be included in the curriculum, how it is to be organized and implemented, what means should be employed to evaluate it, and so on, all involve a broad range of normative questions that necessitate not only a technical approach to curriculum but one responsive to political, ethical, and social issues (Apple & Weis, 1983; Beyer & Apple, 1988; Pinar, 1988; Whitty & Young, 1976; Young, 1971).

This perspective is not new. People like Dwayne Huebner (1975), Maxine Greene (1979), James Macdonald (1975), Joseph Schwab (1970), and others have helped articulate the major questions—at once political, personal, practical, and theoretical in character and origin—that constitute curriculum inquiry as a normative field. For example, in concluding his essay on "Curriculum and Human Interests," Macdonald (1975) states the importance of work in our field in clearly normative terms.

> I suspect that in many ways all curriculum design and development is political in nature; that is, it is an attempt to facilitate someone else's idea of the good life by creating social processes and structuring an environment for learning.

Curriculum design is thus a form of "utopianism," a form of political and social philosophizing and theorizing. If we recognize this, it may help us sort out our own thinking and perhaps increase our ability to communicate with each other. (p. 293)

Maxine Greene (1979) has eloquently addressed the intellectual, political, and emotional work that is required to generate different linguistic and social possibilities for the curriculum developer. As she says, one of the biggest obstacles to the creation of alternatives is the presentation of the world around us "as *given,* probably unchangeable and predefined" (p. 56). To the extent that we see the world as given or found, rather than constructed, we condemn ourselves and our students to the obvious inadequacies (political, ethical, and educational) that it now embodies.

The realization that all curriculum deliberation has a normative face is especially pertinent within the current climate of educational criticism and reform. Contemporary discussions surrounding the need for greater standardization of educational outcomes and procedures, more stringent standards for practicing and prospective teachers, increased emphasis on technology and a specious pseudo-science, differentiated staffing that enhances career opportunities for professional teachers, and so on, all serve to militate against the realization that curricular decisions contain crucial normative components. Indeed the most disturbing quality of current debates about "educational excellence" is the frequent substitution of technical, managerial, competency-based, and positivistic language for discourse embedded in those political, social, and ideological decisions that await curriculum workers, especially teachers, at every turn.

CURRICULUM THEORY AND SCHOOL PRACTICE

Teachers at all levels are confronted by a range of decisions and questions that virtually constitute the curriculum field. For teaching to take place:

1. There must be some idea, value, information, or skill that can be communicated to another person or group.
2. A language or other symbol system must be utilized with which these ideas or values can be communicated.
3. Certain "ground rules" for the relationships among the people involved must be agreed on to facilitate the communication that ensues.

4. Some means of placing value on the activities that are generated must be created, so that we can tell if redirections are desirable.

Couching curriculum deliberation in these terms is a useful way to begin to unpack the complexity of decision making. A crucial question is how to judge what ideas or values are most worthy of being communicated through the curriculum. The problems here are twofold. First, we must somehow cull from the universe of possibilities those ideas that are most compelling. Hence, the process of developing curricula is always a *selective* one, requiring judgment and an awareness of the range of possibilities that might be considered. Such selectivity calls upon our best thinking about issues in epistemology, value theory, and history, among other areas. Second, the processes of inclusion and exclusion frequently reflect patterns and realities that have nonintellectual origins and consequences. The selectivity involved here is both philosophical and ideological, affecting not only which subjects will be included in the curriculum, but the perspective that will be taken on those subject areas.

Making these connections clear and manageable is a major aim of my own teaching efforts.[1] To accomplish this, I take seriously two claims made earlier: that all curriculum development is a form of political utopianism, and that a major impediment to the creation of alternatives in education is an often only half-conscious sense that the world is predefined and unchangeable. Frequently my students confer upon the world of schooling a taken-for-granted stability, constituting the boundaries within which they are to remain, instead of the contingent parameters of a world in the process of being remade.

In my experiences with teachers and prospective teachers, the two claims above have frequently been illuminated by looking at the history, philosophy, and sociology of education. In looking at the general history of education and of the curriculum field in particular, students see that ideas and perspectives ebb and flow in response not only to educational thought but to larger social, economic, and political influences. As an area of study, the curriculum field reveals both constancy and change. Competing groups have sought to exert a directive influence on the substance and form of the curriculum in the process of maintaining their influence. This can be seen clearly in the frequently heated debates over censorship of curriculum materials. Less dramatic but more common is the often implicit question of whether the curriculum should aim at some form of social adaptation or transformation (Wood, 1984). These competing points of view make up the

---

[1] The experiences and anecdotes reported here took place during my employment at Cornell College in Mt. Vernon, Iowa, from 1986 to 1988.

struggle between the proponents of social efficiency and those of social meliorism/reconstructionism (Eisner, 1985; Kliebard, 1986). As outlined by Donmoyer in Chapter 10, issues from curriculum history can illuminate contemporary classroom problems. Students then come to see curriculum as less fixed and the educational world generally as created rather than discovered.

Of course not all students respond enthusiastically to the larger context for curriculum deliberation sketched here. Some resist such an expanded contour of analysis. They revert to the "safer" world of the isolated classroom they believe to be given and, if not unchangeable, at least not to be disrupted—certainly not by the beginning teacher. One such student, whom I shall refer to as Helen (not her real name), recently reflected the perspective of Pink's "resistant flier" (Chapter 9). Helen had a deep-seated, child-centered, romantic ideology that she regarded as beyond analysis or critique. Classroom discussions, private meetings I attempted to set up, and sensitive, caring comments from other students were equally ineffective. One individual meeting with Helen ended abruptly when she screamed, "I'm tired of having to justify everything!" and stomped out of my office. For Helen the journey during which a critical analysis of curriculum and teaching could at least begin never got off the ground, much to my (and other students') frustration.

As a teacher of curriculum, I have also introduced issues in the philosophy and sociology of education, connecting these to the particularities of curriculum decision making. Discussing the wide variety of philosophical positions writers have taken on educational questions exposes students to an array of educational principles and modes of analysis. Through such writings, they acquire a sensitivity to educational questions and a set of intellectual tools that provide a variety of ways to analyze these questions.

Less abstract are questions dealing with the relationship between school practice and the recreation of social inequalities. A frequent perspective of students, again fostered by the common sense of U.S. social and educational thought at least since Horace Mann, is that education is the gateway to opportunity. Schooling, in this view, provides a foothold on the ladder with which all may climb to socially mobile lives within an open, meritocratic, individualistic socioeconomic order. Prospective teaches who hold this view visualize teaching and curriculum as politically and socially neutral phenomena, within which students can, through "native ability" and hard work, develop to their highest potential. As the engines for equal opportunity, so the story goes, schools sort and select students on the basis of merit, and help allocate scarce social and economic goods.

In countering these presuppositions, I have found two sorts of analyses to be helpful. First, as sociologists have shown, schools and other segments of U.S. society are less meritocratic than we like to think. At a variety of levels, schools seem to legitimate and reproduce inequalities by race, gender, social class, ethnicity, and age (Apple, 1979; Apple & Weis, 1983; Bowles & Gintis, 1976; Feinberg, 1983; Jencks, et al., 1979). Second, these inequalities are furthered by other social policies and institutions (Castells, 1980; Children's Defense Fund, 1984; Navarro, 1976). This literature provides a background for the more specific questions of social maintenance/reconstruction noted above with respect to curriculum deliberation. For instance, the dominant way of thinking about the curriculum since the second decade of this century has been shaped by the forces of industrialization, urbanization, and immigration, as administrative and business interests allied in an attempt to use the schools as an agent of social cohesion (Apple, 1979; Callahan, 1962; Franklin, 1986). Efforts to stratify, divide, and increase the efficiency of workers were transported into the schools, where predictability would be emphasized, waste eliminated, and the "proper" American values instilled.

In many respects my students have already experienced such educational policies and ideas in their own schooling experiences. There is a tendency, therefore, for many students to see these experiences, and the values on which they are based, as unproblematic. The critical literature that examines these values often results in a re-examination of students' experiences in the public schools and of the classroom activities in which they are involved during my courses. Yet this is not universally so. Especially when, as Pink reminds us in Chapter 9, the perspective advocated in critically oriented courses is only a small fraction of students' college course work, students sometimes resist the analysis of curriculum discussed here. Recently one student of mine rejected this approach because of its conceptual difficulties; another, out of a desire to "fit in" to the existing realities of a local high school in which she was observing. Such results, though they represent a relatively small fraction of the student population, are among the most frustrating aspects of my college teaching experiences.

The wide range of issues and ideas summarized here illustrates at least three things.

1. The educational world, and society in general, have been created by individuals and groups with particular interests and values, and have not simply appeared by some natural or supernatural process.
2. Educational ideas and practices are often quite closely linked to phenomena outside of schools; an isolated focus on classroom interchanges and technical rationality is simply an inadequate way to conceptualize curricular decisions.
3. The educator cannot be a neutral bystander, dispensing objective val-

ues and forms of knowledge to individual students who must make their way in an open, meritocratic system.

As students realize the contours and responsibilities of curriculum deliberation, the normative dimensions of such deliberation become powerful catalysts for reflection.

Yet such reflection, aided by important critical analyses in education, can lead to a kind of paralysis. Prospective teachers must develop concrete ways to deal with the range of complex ethical and political questions confronting them as curriculum developers. Otherwise, the normative dimensions of curriculum deliberation are apt to be daunting. In response, students may go back to "business as usual," denying the legitimacy of the issues raised in this approach to curriculum.

CURRICULUM DELIBERATION AND NORMATIVE ACTION

Following course work in which I seek to incorporate the sort of critical, foundational questions raised above (in the history, philosophy, and sociology of education and curriculum), my students are engaged in a series of courses designed to acquaint them with curriculum inquiry and development in content areas. The discussion here will center on the efforts of students in the elementary education programs with which I have been associated.

The construction of a "platform" on which to build curriculum is an initial step in the generation of curriculum projects in my courses (Barone, 1988; Walker, 1971). This platform is the most visionary or utopian aspect of curriculum design. It articulates a vision of the values and ideas that society ought to conform to, and a view of the educational ideas and strategies that are consistent with that vision (Bunch, 1983). This approximation of social and educational ideals is often tentative and fragmentary, of course, and open to further study and enactment. Yet this platform serves as a reminder to students that they must think carefully and deeply about the values and perspectives that animate their teaching and about the sort of social vision that springs from those presumptions.

We spend a good deal of time in such courses attempting to articulate an approach to curriculum deliberation that is democratic in spirit and outcome. While the nature of democratic ideals and practices is itself a contentious and complicated issue, consideration of current practices frequently reveals their antidemocratic tendencies (Beyer & Wood, 1986). The nature of democratic classrooms then becomes a focal topic of concern.

In addition to articulating a vision of education and its social outcomes, students analyze and develop their own approach to curriculum design that embodies that vision and can guide classroom activities. The various competing interest groups—the humanists, developmentalists, social efficiency advocates, and social reconstructionists (Kliebard, 1986)—are discussed in terms of their tendencies and inconsistencies as well as their compatibility with students' platforms. Consider, for example, students who advocate educational and social practices that emphasize equality, democratic social relations and decision making, and cooperation (frequently specified elements of students' visions). Given the foundational questions enumerated above, it is clear that in many respects contemporary U.S. society is inconsistent with such visions. Accordingly, some form of social meliorism/reconstructionism becomes appropriate, as students seek historical precedents for their own projects.

The development of a curriculum project is facilitated by issues and perspectives such as these. Yet, as important as the discussion of such issues is, by themselves they lack the specificity of concrete "normative plans of action" that are required for aspiring teachers. Course work also requires, therefore, that students plan a curriculum unit, spanning at least two weeks, in a content area emphasized in succeeding courses. Activities, materials, classroom organization, and other aspects of curriculum implementation are identified in this unit. These vary in complexity and depth, depending on the students' platform, curriculum approach, and subject area concentration. But these projects must be complete enough to serve as at least first attempts at implementing ideas, values, principles, and actions that are well thought out, normatively guided, and responsive.

The most difficult aspect of this project, understandably, is making sure there is some consistency among platform, curriculum approach, and specific classroom activities. In view of the complex dynamics of each of these areas, it is all too easy to conceive of them as relatively independent aspects of educational inquiry. Some students tend to focus on curricular ideas and issues, others on classroom interactions. To help ensure an integration of these areas, students are required to (1) teach at least a portion of the ideas they develop in practica that accompany the courses; and/or (2) analyze the difficulties they are likely to experience, based on their own classroom observations, in convincing a reluctant administrator or colleague of the desirability of these ideas.

To illustrate the sort of student projects that result from an approach to curriculum deliberation as a normative enterprise, I have selected the work of one recent student, Kathleen Poduska. She was a continuing education student who enrolled in a program in elementary education after having received a bachelor's degree in music education from another institution. Although she taught music for a time, Poduska had spent the preceding several years raising a family. Excerpts from her work are taken from three separate courses she took with me; they provide a case study for the views outlined in this chapter.

Philosophy of Education

The first course Poduska took in the elementary education program was entitled Educational Philosophies. During that course we read works by a number of authors, including Plato, Rousseau, Dewey, Murdoch (1970), and Feinberg (1983). One of the options for the final paper was to write a response to an imaginary student, Sandy, who resisted taking the ideas of the course seriously, wanting "only to be a schoolteacher."

Poduska created what is in many ways a model analysis of Sandy's inclinations, in the form of a dialogue among the authors we had read. The authors included in her script not only "recounted" their own views but also "spoke" with each other about similarities and differences among views, creating an imaginative and accurate rendering of several key issues. In her analysis of this dialogue, and of the ideas and issues encountered in the course generally, Poduska presented an insightful, introspective look at her own experiences in the course.

> When I was first introduced to these new ideas, my reaction was "Don't confuse me—I have this already worked out." Two passages from Plato helped me to confront this:
>
> "For this is the worst of ignorance, that one who is neither beautiful and good nor intelligent should think himself good enough, so he does not desire [wisdom], because he does not think he is lacking in what he does not think he needs" [Warmington & Rouse, 1956, p. 99]. I was and still am challenged in my assumptions and judgments. But I am beginning to see a new understanding come forth which is more complete since it has been dissected, examined, and reassembled into a different form. The new form has elements of the old transformed by the new.
>
> I realize now that my previous selection of the best teaching methods had been narrow in scope and limited in effectiveness. Consideration of each of the concepts of "the good" has drawn me out of my own limited viewpoint to consider something beyond myself.
>
> The temptation is to view education in my own sphere as a particular grade teacher and to focus my energies in that direction. By viewing education as EDUCATION, I am allowing the process to become a growing experience for me as well as for my students.
>
> In conclusion, I have reached the decision, unlike Sandy, the hypothetical student, that educational philosophy is not a "waste of my time." The process this course has evoked in me can best be described by utilizing Iris Murdoch [1970, p. 91]:

"The love which brings the right answer is an exercise of justice and realism and really *looking*. The difficulty is to keep the attention fixed upon the real situation and to prevent it from returning surreptitiously to the self with consolations of self-pity, resentment, fantasy, and despair." (Poduska, 1987, pp. 15–25)

School and Society

The next course Poduska took from me was Schooling in American Society. The theme of this course revolved around the effects of social inequality in schools and other institutions. We read about and discussed issues regarding the reproduction of inequality by race, social class, gender, ethnicity, and age, and related demographic shifts (Apple, 1982; Bowles & Gintis, 1976; Hodgkinson, 1985). A central component of this course was a one-week, full-time experience working on a community service project, mostly in a nearby medium-sized city. Poduska chose to work with other students in a preschool setting for low-income, mostly minority students. For her as well as almost all my students, this proved to be a very important, eye-opening experience. In addition to dealing with inequality as a sociological issue, this course was designed to give students a "first hand" look at, and feel for, the real, human consequences of inequality in American life.

We explored at length in this course the need to develop an extra-individualistic sensitivity to communities, which included a discussion of how some groups historically have been excluded from such communities, as Erdman argues in Chapter 11. One of the assignments for this course was to write a paper discussing the tension between "self-reliant competitive enterprise and a sense of public solidarity," as outlined by Bellah, Madsen, Sullivan, Swidler, and Tipton (1985, p. 256). Additionally, students were asked to specify what values, social practices, and perspectives they would support in dealing with the split between self-reliance and public solidarity, and the implications of these values for schooling and teaching. One of the central thrusts of Poduska's paper (1988a) was an emphasis on teaching students a vision of "the good society" that underscores "the dignity, worth, and autonomy of the individual in a democratic context" (pp. 10–11). She recognized and discussed in detail the political nature of this process, involving the development of character traits such as civic courage, cooperation, tenacity, honesty, an attitude of shared authority, and the linking of the self with the common good. She regarded such character traits as essential for both her professional and private lives.

Curriculum Development: Reading and Language Arts

The next course in the sequence leading to elementary certification was Teaching of Reading and Language Arts. During this course we read about the various interest groups represented by approaches to curriculum and discussed theoretical and practical issues in curriculum design and development. Students participated in practica in local schools and were involved in creating a curriculum project in reading and language arts. This course, like others in the program, was founded on a conception of *praxis* in which the personal, the political, and the theoretical are fused (Beyer, 1988). The final assignment consisted of a curriculum project in reading and language arts that included students' platforms; approaches to curriculum; a two-week, day-by-day set of activities in the language arts; and an analysis of the differences between the students' preferences in these areas and the actual activities they had been observing. Poduska's (1988b) project included the following ideas and activities:

The act of teaching involves the operation of influential acts in a system which, by description, involves moral and political actions. The school itself is a "mechanism of cultural and economic preservation and distribution" [Apple, 1982, p. 3]. Teaching then becomes a choice between fitting children into the system or helping the children to remake the system to fit them.

The challenge I see in this choice is reclaiming and teaching to my students a vision of the good society. The vision includes the dignity, worth and autonomy of the individual in a democratic context. Inherent in this process is the politicization of myself as a teacher as an autonomous, critically conscious individual. Such a teacher situates herself into the social context in which her teaching, her students and the school itself reside.

The democratic teacher views teaching itself as a continuous and interactive process with the following elements: (1) teaching as dialectic; (2) teaching as political; (3) teaching as nurturing; (4) teaching as moral.

A democratic teacher . . . would have as a primary curriculum orientation that of a social meliorist. Such an orientation views the school as a major force for social justice. This force involves the politicization of the teacher herself and her guidance in empowering her students toward politicization. Central to this direction is the knowledge that "the power to change things for the better lies in our hands and in the social institutions we create" [Kliebard, 1982, p. 23]. This power is released through the dialectic, through the communication of ideas, through the establishment of shared common experiences. This process nurtures both the students and the teacher in a moral, social context.

Social melioration, influenced by other orientations ["the development of cognitive processes" and "personal relevance"], and enhanced through the social, moral, dialectic and nurturing processes of the democratic teacher's platform, can provide for "honest, controversial, racially, sexually, and economically progressive materials" [Apple, 1982, p. 88]. Such materials view the learning process as a work process; as "experience

that contributes to self-development and identity formation and that contributes to the 'making' of culture" [Carlson, 1988, p. 111]. This experience is "personalizing": the students sense that the educational system
basically serves their interests. It implies a curriculum that is
1. Not pre-determined
2. Open to modification in classroom practices
3. More concerned with the development of high-order critical thinking skills than with the acquisition of basic skills (pp. 2–6)

Poduska's curriculum project for the reading and language arts course
incorporated materials from several Dr. Seuss books and was intended for
students in the primary grades. This curriculum was motivated by a desire
for students to understand language as descriptive, communicative, and persuasive (in the sense of raising consciousness regarding important issues).
The materials and activities in this curriculum were designed to foster creative expression and:

1. A community of memory [Bellah, Madsen, Sullivan, Swidler, and Tipton, 1985] through shared group experiences.
2. A common moral language through dialectical discussion of social
   issues in several Dr. Seuss books.
3. A political vision through the connection of the dialectical discussions to larger social contexts: the community of the school and the
   outside community.
   Meaning for children will be a move from personal relevance to social melioration; a move from self to the larger social context in which
each child resides. The development of this awareness will be a three-step
process using Dr. Seuss books in progressively larger social perspectives
[from the individual alone, to the individual in relation to others, to the
individual in relation to society]. (p. 8)

To illustrate her selection of specific teaching activities, I include Poduska's plans for the final day of her two-week curriculum unit.

"Language as Persuasion" (Consciousness); the individual in relation to
society
MATERIALS: *The Butter Battle Book*
AIM: To discuss alternatives to aggressive forms of conflict resolution
NEEDS: 1) Children must begin to realize that differences of opinion can be
settled in peaceful ways; 2) teacher must relate the story to social context
of children
EXPERIENCES:
Introduction to the book. There is another way to solve a conflict. Listen
to this story to find out. Is this a good way or a bad way? Read *The Butter*

Battle Book. Discussion questions: How do you think this should end? Why? What would happen? Would that solve the conflict? Why or why not? Do we have such a conflict in our school? Do we have such a conflict in our world? Who is involved in it? If you were the President, what would you do? How do you feel about this? Have you talked about this before? Why or why not? Is this the best solution? What other things could we do? Evaluation. Have the students describe "their trip through the enchanted forest of Dr. Seuss" these past two weeks. What did they see, hear, and learn about? What was most interesting? What was most difficult? What activities would they like to do again? (p. 20)

The curriculum project Poduska created articulated a comprehensive plan that incorporated several important works of children's literature within the framework of the language arts. More generally, tied to that plan were the development of a curriculum platform containing a vision of educational and social life, and the creation of a curricular approach that approximated that vision. In terms of the political and moral contours of a language arts curriculum unit, Poduska's work illustrates the sort of normative reflection that must accompany curriculum deliberation in the process joining educational with social, technical, political, personal, and moral judgments. Such integration forms the core of the approach to curriculum advocated in this chapter.

REFERENCES

Apple, Michael W. (1979). *Ideology and curriculum.* Boston: Routledge & Kegan Paul.

Apple, Michael W. (1982). *Education and power.* Boston: Routledge & Kegan Paul.

Apple, Michael W., & Weis, Lois. (1983). *Ideology and practice in schooling.* Philadelphia: Temple University Press.

Barone, Thomas E. (1988). "Curriculum platforms and literature." In Landon E. Beyer & Michael W. Apple (Eds.), *The curriculum: Problems, politics, and possibilities.* Albany: State University of New York Press.

Bellah, Robert N.; Madsen, Richard; Sullivan, William; Swidler, Ann; & Tipton, Steven M. (1985). *Habits of the heart: Individualism and Commitment in American Life.* Berkeley, CA: University of California Press.

Beyer, Landon E. (1988). *Knowing and acting: Inquiry, ideology, and educational studies.* London: Falmer Press.

Beyer, Landon E., & Apple, Michael W. (1988). *The curriculum: Problems, politics, and possibilities.* Albany: State University of New York Press.

Beyer, Landon E., & Wood, George H. (1986). "Critical inquiry and moral action in education." *Educational Theory, 36*(1), 1–14.

Bowles, Samuel, & Gintis, Herbert. (1976). *Schooling in capitalist America.* New York: Basic Books.

Bunch, Charlotte. (1983). *Learning our way.* Trumansburg, NY: Crossing Press.

Callahan, Raymond E. (1962). *Education and the cult of efficiency.* Chicago: University of Chicago Press.

Carlson, Dennis L. (1988). "Curriculum planning and the state: The dynamics of control in education." In Landon E. Beyer & Michael W. Apple (Eds.), *The curriculum: Problems, politics, and possibilities.* Albany: State University of New York Press.

Castells, Manuel. (1980). *The economic crisis and American society.* Princeton: Princeton University Press.

Children's Defense Fund. (1984). *American children in poverty.* Washington, DC: Children's Defense Fund.

Eisner, Elliot W. (1979/1985). *The educational imagination: On the design and evaluation of school programs.* New York: Macmillan.

Feinberg, Walter. (1983). *Understanding education.* New York: Cambridge University Press.

Franklin, Barry F. (1986). *Building the American community.* London: Falmer Press.

Greene, Maxine. (1979). *Landscapes of learning.* New York: Teachers College Press.

Hodgkinson, Harold A. (1985). *All one system.* Washington, DC: Institute for Educational Leadership.

Huebner, Dwayne. (1975). "Curricular language and classroom meanings." In William Pinar (Ed.), *Curriculum theorizing: The reconceptualists.* Berkeley, CA: McCutchan.

Jencks, Christopher, et al. (1979). *Who gets ahead?* New York: Basic Books.

Kliebard, Herbert M. (1982). "Education at the turn of the century: A crucible for curriculum change," *Educational researcher, 11*(1), 16–24.

Kliebard, Herbert M. (1986). *The struggle for the American curriculum 1893–1958.* New York: Routledge & Kegan Paul.

Macdonald, James B. (1975). "Curriculum and human interests." In William Pinar (Ed.), *Curriculum theorizing: The reconceptualists.* Berkeley, CA: McCutchan.

Murdoch, Iris. (1970). *The sovereignty of good.* Boston: Ark Paperbacks.

Navarro, Vicente. (1976). *Medicine under capitalism.* New York: Neale Watson Academic Publications.

Pinar, William F. (1988). *Contemporary curriculum discourses.* Scottsdale, AZ: Gorsuch Scarisbrick.

Poduska, Kathleen. (1987). "A justification for educational philosophy." Unpublished paper, Cornell College.

Poduska, Kathleen. (1988a). "Teaching democratically in an undemocratic society." Unpublished paper, Cornell College.

Poduska, Kathleen. (1988b). "Dr. Seuss: A curriculum of language experiences." Unpublished paper, Cornell College.

Rosenbaum, James. (1976). *Making inequality: The hidden curriculum of high school tracking.* New York: John Wiley.

Schön, Donald. (1983). *The reflective practitioner: How professionals think in action.* New York: Basic Books.

Schwab, Joseph J. (1970). *The practical: A language for curriculum.* Washington, DC: National Education Association.

Smyth, John. (1987). *Educating teachers: Changing the nature of pedagogical knowledge.* London: Falmer Press.

Walker, Decker. (1971). "A naturalistic model for curriculum development." *School Review, 80*(1), 51–65.

Warmington, Eric H., & Rouse, Philip G. (1956). *Great dialogues of Plato.* New York: The New American Library.

Whitty, Geoff, & Young, Michael F. D. (1976). *Explorations in the politics of school knowledge.* Nafferton, Driffield, England: Nafferton Books.

Wood, George H. (1984). "Education in a democracy: Transformation or reproduction?" *Educational Theory, 34*(3), 219–239.

Young, Michael F. D. (1971). *Knowledge and control.* London: Collier-Macmillan.

9

Implementing
Curriculum Inquiry

Theoretical and Practical
Implications

WILLIAM T. PINK
National College of Education

*I received my Ph.D. in social foundations of education from the University
of Oregon in 1972 and worked most closely with Grace Graham (social
foundations), C. A. Bowers (educational history, philosophy, and curriculum theory) and Ken Polk (delinquency, deviance, and sociology of education).*

*Born in England during World War II, I was socialized into a highly
stratified class-conscious society. My initial education was in the elitist
State school system that differentiated students according to their presumed academic ability, based primarily on the national level eleven-
plus and General Certificate of Education examinations, and their social
class status. While I could recognize the privilege of status, that is, high
social class lineage, grammar or preferably public school attendance,
graduation from Oxbridge, I was unable to analyze how and why the system worked the way it did. Subsequently, I learned that this analytic short-
coming was a function of cultural hegemony. Simply, I had been socialized to believe that everything was as it was "ordained to be."*

*As a Fulbright Scholar, I found critical reflective distance by stepping
out of my culture and going west to the University of Oregon. Beginning
with my study of deviance and delinquency, I developed insight into my
own educational and social history by understanding how personal identity and access to knowledge (and thus status) are manipulated by the*

educational experience. This awareness has fueled a passion for issues
such as equity and social justice, as well as a belief in the need to em-
power individuals in order to change existing practices and beliefs. Since
that time I have been working to (1) better understand how the educa-
tional system works to disadvantage students based on factors such as
their presumed educability, class, race, and gender, and (2) develop a
theory about and structure for school change that will remediate these
inequities by working with *students and teachers to analyze both the ori-*
gins and the implications of their taken-for-granted beliefs, values, as-
sumptions, and practices.

> The goal of anyone who sets out to teach teachers is to enable these
> teachers to become students of their teaching. Having become students
> of their work, they may then, by their manner, enable those in their cus-
> tody to become students themselves. (Fenstermacher, 1986, p. 48)

I believe that the major purpose of education should be to empower students to think critically about their culture and their place in it. To achieve
this end, teachers need to make the commonplace problematic for students
by raising to the level of consciousness the taken-for-granted assumptions,
beliefs, values, and practices of the culture. In short, teachers should explore
the culture by examining how it was initially conceptualized, subsequently
developed, and is presently sustained. Such an investigation would involve,
of course, examining such key concepts as socialization, language, work,
capitalism, and schooling. These concepts are so deeply embedded in the
lived culture that they are typically inaccessible in daily discourse.

Engaging students in such an investigation is a necessary (although not
sufficient) step in empowering students to become *active,* as contrasted
with passive, players in a democracy. Raising critical consciousness by de-
mythologizing the taken-for-grantedness of culture, analogous to taking students behind the theatrical scenery to show them how the strings are manipulated in a marionette show, requires us to conceptualize education as
something other than the simple transmission of a predefined and prepackaged body of "essential knowledge."

To influence the form and content of the education experienced by
students, to reconceptualize the schooling experience for students, we must
go through teachers. Teachers are the key actors in the teaching act. Not
only do they both create and sustain the lived culture of the school, but they
are also the key actors in interpreting (some argue reflecting) the larger out-
of-school culture. Thus, because teachers direct both what is taught and

how it is taught in schools, it is essential to empower teachers to think critically about the culture and their place in it *before* they can begin to empower students.

BARRIERS TO CURRICULUM INQUIRY

Sadly, discussion aimed at developing fundamental, as contrasted with simple cosmetic, changes to the organization of schools and what is taught in schools is noticeably missing from the many recent national foundation and commission reports (Carnegie Corporation of New York, 1983; Committee on Economic Development, 1985; National Commission on Excellence in Education, 1983; Task Force on Education for Economic Growth, 1983). Several have argued that this silence, intended or not, reflects the fact that representatives of the capitalistic economic system were the primary authors of the reports. Thus, not unexpectedly, the reports propose reforms that, even if adopted, would leave schools essentially unchanged. Without systemic changes, they argue, schools will continue to function to protect the vested interests of the authors of these reports (Apple, 1987; Berman, 1986; Brosio, 1987). What is *not* examined and discussed in these influential reports becomes taken-for-granted by both educators and the public. Erdman (Chapter 11) provides a good illustration of the way in which the taken-for-granted assumptions about the inferiority of women and "female traits" is embedded in the language. Yet, it is this tacit and unexamined knowledge that works to restrict the discovery and subsequent development of alternative ways of organizing schooling and the curriculum.

Several of the most popular proposals in the emergent reform agenda have been counterproductive to an analysis of these taken-for-granted practices and beliefs (for example, tracking and ability grouping, and the presumed connection between race and I.Q.). Instead of acting as a catalyst for rethinking schooling, the reports have proposed reforms that have done little but narrow the focus to the more efficient implementation of existing practices.

A number of factors are equally damaging to the emergence of an ambience in schools that would facilitate the development of the critical consciousness of students by empowered teachers. These factors, individually and collectively, function as barriers to teacher empowerment (Pink, 1988).

1. State reform mandates (such as effective school programs that emphasize basic skills acquisition and the use of direct instruction) that limit teacher decision making.
2. Standardized tests mandated by the state or district, especially in urban

districts, which frequently narrow instruction to areas covered by the tests. As a result, the curriculum becomes driven by the tests.

3. District curriculum guides developed by a committee that prescribe the content of the curriculum and discourage teacher decision making.

4. Required texts, such as district or state adoptions, which limit teacher choice about curriculum materials and control what knowledge students have access to.

5. Uniform instructional pacing requirements at the district or state level that not only commodify education into discrete units for presentation to students, but also remove teachers from decision making about the appropriate materials for instruction and the specific needs of individual students.

6. The absence of an adequate staff development program in many school districts, which reflects the fact that districts infrequently invest in the long-term professional development of teachers and administrators. Staff development programs are typically designed to tell teachers about new content or instructional methods identified as important by central office staff—for example, assertive discipline or the Madeline Hunter (1984, 1985) technique.

7. The current organization of schools (the six- or seven-period day, tracking, ability grouping, and differential expectations of students based on race, social class, and gender), together with the belief system that supports it, functions to systematically limit teachers' discussion of the factors critical to curriculum inquiry and reform.

8. Teacher evaluation models that define teaching as the slavish modeling of prescribed "effective teacher" components (such as direct instruction, Hunter's "seven steps"), thus eliminating teacher spontaneity and experimentation.

9. The professional preparation of teachers and administrators (including preservice, induction, and professional development activities), which typically involves limited exposure to critical issues in curriculum theory, social foundations, and organizational/school change. Instead of providing experiences in critical inquiry, such programs usually emphasize the mastery of technique over analysis.

These nine factors exert a powerful influence over the way in which schools operate and on what is taught in schools. In simple terms, these factors centralize decision making and regulate both what teachers can teach and how they can teach it. Thus, they function to deskill and deprofessionalize teachers by further insulating them from decisions about the form and content of instruction. Such tight regulation is counterproductive to thinking and requires that teachers act mechanistically to deliver a predefined curriculum. Because these factors control the lived life in school for both teachers and students, they must be confronted in any strategy for improving schools (Apple, 1983; Giroux & McClaren, 1986; Whitty, 1985).

Asking teachers to confront these factors becomes problematic, however, because there is typically little opportunity in the professional lives of teachers and administrators to systematically engage in reflective thinking about what they do, nor would the effort be rewarded. Moreover, because research is incomplete on the impact of several of the barriers outlined above, and a critical analysis of these barriers is frequently characterized as a radical or subversive activity, raising the critical consciousness of teachers about these issues is difficult, even in the best of circumstances. These problems notwithstanding, I would submit that *without* such a critical analysis, curriculum reform, as contrasted with curriculum revision (tinkering with the content and delivery of the curriculum without really disturbing its message and impact on students) is unlikely to occur. The question we curriculum teachers must address is how best to involve teachers in critical inquiry concerning their taken-for-granted assumptions, beliefs, values, and practices.

CREATING SPACE FOR THINKING ABOUT CURRICULUM

One way to engage teachers in critical thinking about curriculum issues is to include such an activity in their professional preparation at the university level. I do this by working *with* teachers and administrators enrolled in my classes to examine the normative practices and belief systems at work in schools and the culture. I raise critical questions in four areas.

1. The content and the meaning of the curriculum in use in schools
2. The instructional strategies used in schools and the research on instruction
3. The organizational structure of schools
4. The varied outcomes of schooling using race, social class, and gender as analytic categories

In a recent doctoral class, I selected as required reading several chapters (for example, those by Brophy & Good, Doyle, Erickson, Feiman-Nemser & Floden, Fenstermacher, Shulman, Walberg) in the latest *Handbook of Research on Teaching* (Wittrock, 1986), as well as the work of several other authors (Apple, 1987; Berman, 1986; Bowers, 1984; Carroll, 1963, 1985; Cuban, 1982; Oakes, 1985; Pink & Leibert, 1985; Rist, 1970; Whitford & Hovda, 1986; Wilcox, 1982). In conducting the class as a seminar (a requirement was to write a reaction log containing a critical review of each reading), my intent was to explore with the students the meaning and implications of a wide range of research and theorizing about teaching. Thus, we talked about different conceptions of teaching (especially varying definitions of "effective instruction"); alternative research paradigms; the covert curriculum; the social, political, and economic factors that historically and presently have shaped schools *and* the knowledge that is transmitted in schools; and how factors such as race, social class, and gender play out in a variety of context-specific settings.

I used a sociology of knowledge perspective (Bowers, 1984; Berger & Luckmann, 1967) to detail how the individual is socialized into a normative world view, primarily by significant others who use a language and symbol system that both creates and sustains taken-for-granted assumptions, values, and beliefs. This same perspective illuminates the teacher's roles in creating learning settings and transmitting knowledge that function to disenfranchise, instead of empower, students to think critically about the constructed world in which they play out their daily existence.

Specifically, I attempted to examine three things *with* the students.

1. The implications for both teachers and school organization of viewing social reality as socially constructed and thus capable of being reconstructed.
2. How social reality develops and sustains its normative aspects.
3. The ways in which schools play a major role in defining not only the self (for both students and teachers) but also the parameters within which questions about meaning, truth, reality, and the like can be raised and answered.

By problematizing the commonplace in schools *with* rather than *for* this group of doctoral students, my intent was to empower them through evaluating anew what they teach, why they teach it, and how they teach it. In Erdman's terms, we worked on "joint constructions of meaning" about their teaching experiences (see Chapter 11). I also hoped that such an examination might result in proposals, if not action, to change current practices and beliefs (to reflect principles generated by concerns for equity, democratic empowerment, and social justice), which would in turn translate into changes in the lived culture in schools for both students and teachers.

Taking a Trip

It is clear that change (in practice and beliefs) must be seen as a process, not an event, and that change involves individuals, not organizations.

Nevertheless, I was unprepared for the range of reactions from the students concerning the issues raised in class. Several factors seem to work against change in practice and beliefs. First, a 10 week quarter is too short to seriously engage important and complex ideas in great depth, or to expect significant growth in a student's sense of efficacy and power to reform the lived culture of the schools. Second, a university classroom is frequently perceived as an inappropriately detached setting in which to examine school-based practices and beliefs; a doctoral class is frequently a collection of bright and highly motivated individuals who are not representative of a typical school faculty but who must address these issues in the "real world" setting of schools. Finally, the pressures of other university classes, and in the majority of cases, full-time jobs, compete for time between class meetings. Clearly, these and other factors tend to work against the effectiveness of instruction.

I began the class by inviting a group of doctoral students to take a trip with me as a co-investigator. The trip required not only that we suspend the traditional practice of information transmission from instructor to student but that we also collaborate in a systematic effort to examine the foundations of our culture and the place of schools in it. Stated differently, I shelved the cookbook or recipe knowledge approach to learning in favor of a critical inquiry approach that emphasizes both the individual and the context. To illustrate the range of problems that surfaced during this 10-week trip, I will characterize the doctoral students in the class as representative of four different kinds of fliers. Reflecting on this class, I was struck by the fact that the students seemed to fall into one of four categories of passengers found on a commercial flight. While I don't wish to suggest that these categories are mutually exclusive, they are a useful heuristic.

1. *Frequent fliers.* Students comfortable with their role in a doctoral class that requires them to do more than memorize facts. They manage uncertainty and the contradictions generated by competing paradigms, that is, delays in flights and the variations in service provided by different carriers. They are avid readers who enjoy wrestling with questions that require them to synthesize diverse material and perhaps develop positions radically different from those currently held. In short, they enjoy flying. They are the travelers who frequently seek out the more challenging routes (for instance, Scandinavia via Australia and Peru) and are often seen socializing with the flight crew.
2. *Infrequent fliers.* Students somewhat less experienced than their frequent flier peers, but who nevertheless enjoy the experience. They are less well read but are willing to entertain ideas not previously encountered. They are somewhat cautious about raising questions in class unless

they have done sufficient reading ("not wishing to sound like an ass if asked to explain something"). They are, however, at ease flying, even when they encounter turbulence caused by some difficult reading or spirited classroom discussion.

3. *First-time fliers.* Students encountering the first class in which they are asked to ignore their previous socialization experience with a cookbook approach to learning, synthesize diverse materials, and think critically about their taken-for-granted assumptions and practices. They are white-knuckle fliers, so caught up in the mechanics of surviving the flight that they are unable to get reflective distance. They do, however, do everything asked of them during the trip. They even eat the food.

4. *Resistant fliers.* Students who would much prefer to stay in the departure lounge but are forced to fly because the class is a program requirement. They find the trip very stressful. Critical inquiry creates so much dissonance for them (a fear of flying?) that they spend much of the trip with their eyes closed and their teeth clenched, resisting both the ideas examined in the course and all invitations to explain their resistance. They will scan the assigned material, but they never actually *read* it. They never eat. They are always the first up to "deplane" even though they are sitting in row 33.

A Closer Look at Two Fliers

Comparing the reactions of two students in the class (their names have been changed) will illuminate several problematics that surface when teachers and administrators engage in critical inquiry.

Christine is a first-year doctoral student in her mid-40s. She has had a wealth of experience in the field of education. She is presently the director of special education for a medium-sized, predominantly white middle class school district adjacent to a large city in the Midwest. She is a frequent flier.

Christine was excited about the class from the moment the syllabus was distributed at the first class meeting. She stayed after the first class to express her excitement about the way the class was structured and to ask me to suggest some readings for the special education teachers she supervised. Throughout the course she was always thoroughly prepared for each session, bringing both insight to our discussions and penetrating questions for us to ponder. Christine demonstrated an eagerness to learn new conceptions about teaching, as well as a consistent desire to translate the issues raised in the class to her own work setting. In short, Christine valued theory as a tool to help her make better sense of the setting in which she worked. Her goal was to create the very best special education program possible by working as a change agent with her teachers.

Christine was looking for ways to improve herself as a teacher/administrator *and* her program. She found many of the insights revealed through the sociology of knowledge perspective intellectually exciting. She read ahead, synthesized other material with the assigned readings, and maintained an ongoing out-of-class dialogue with me. Christine enjoyed flying. Moreover, she had found in this class a way to better understand how education worked, as well as a way to conceptualize changes for her own program. Although she was working full time and taking one other course that quarter, Christine gave whatever time it took for her to understand (or know why she didn't understand) the ideas that emerged from the readings and classroom interactions.

Ron is a first-year doctoral student in his late 30s. He has had extensive and varied experience in the public schools: as a K–2 teacher in several inner city schools ("I was transferred seven times . . . [in] nine years"); as a learning disabilities teacher in a white middle class suburb; and presently as a school psychologist in a predominantly middle class school district adjacent to a large city in the Midwest. He is a resistant flier.

Ron was the first to complain at the initial class meeting about the amount of required reading. He was the first to ask what the page limits for the reaction log were. He was also the first to suggest that school psychologists could do a great job with little knowledge of instruction. As the class progressed, it became apparent that our examination of varying conceptions of teaching and alternative research paradigms (which reach very different conclusions about the best instructional settings for students) was making Ron very uncomfortable. He resisted, for example, the notion that there might be some basic flaws in the logic supporting positivistic research, as well as the observation that several special education categories may have no real meaning vis-à-vis instruction beyond that given to them by school psychologists and special educators.

In contrast to Christine, Ron was not open to the concept of competing views of reality or to the idea that his role as a school psychologist in the sorting function of schooling was in any way problematic. He argued, for example, that students with ability (a term he was unable to define without resorting to the use of standardized test scores in traditional subject areas), independent of race, social class, and type of school, could excel in American schools. He dismissed as irrelevant the contradictory evidence presented by researchers such as Rist (1970) and Wilcox (1982) because "it was based on observational data from small samples." At another time he dismissed the importance of the work highlighting the negative aspects of tracking and the covert curriculum in restricting a student's intellectual development and future career options, saying that in his experience "teachers always did their best to help *all* students achieve up to their measured potential."

Ron demonstrated an unwillingness to take seriously any perspective other than his own. He dismissed much of what he called "only theorizing" in the selected readings by saying that it wasn't practical ("Has this guy ever taught in school?"). He missed entirely, or chose to miss, the challenge to think about how the ideas discussed in class "play" in his own context. He once wrote in his log:

> I left that [urban] district and went to a nice, white, upwardly mobile school district.... I had basically decided that as one individual I could not change the world.... In my new job (as a school psychologist) I discovered two strengths, my diagnostic skills as well as my consultation skills.... Diagnostic and consultation skills require a certain level of process/product mentality.... Process/product research such as Brophy's [Brophy & Good, 1986] summary of teacher behaviors which he believed increased student achievement and Carroll's [1963] time on task hypotheses are all important in working with teachers to develop possible workable interventions within the classroom.

Clearly, much of the substance of the course was ego threatening to Ron. Being asked to confront the conception that reality is socially constructed and that schools manipulate both the academic and social development of students via (1) the academic placements made by teachers, school psychologists, and administrators, and (2) the differential access to knowledge and instruction students experience as a consequence of these different placements, created considerable existential angst for Ron. His resolution of this angst, at least in the time frame of the class, was one of anger, resentment, and resistance. In contrast, Christine used the insight gained to redesign her program and her own role.

One optional (take home) question on the final exam for the class was as follows:

> Detail how this collected set of readings (and anything else you have read this semester) has altered your view of instruction. Be careful to state where you started from and where you are now. Also, if appropriate, give some thought to what changes in practice (personally and/or within your administrative domain) you have made and/or are contemplating as a result of this reading.

Ron's responses were, "It hasn't" and "None." Clearly, Ron has some way to go to graduate from the resistant flier club.

LESSONS LEARNED FOR CURRICULUM INQUIRY

I certainly do not want to argue that from this small-scale investigation I have discovered all there is to know about engaging teachers and adminis-

trators in curriculum inquiry. However, I do believe that there are some implications to be drawn from these data in two important areas.

In the University

Several factors make curriculum inquiry problematic when undertaken
at the university level. Considerable demands are placed on me as instructor
because students like Christine, Ron, and Beyer's Kathleen (1) initially
come to class at different stages of intellectual development and with different expectations of the way in which research and theorizing about curriculum and instruction can be helpful to them in their jobs; (2) display differential ability to read for understanding, synthesize a range of perspectives,
and connect these various positions to the contexts of their own experience
(in part a function of their earlier training and the predominant paradigm
used in their job setting); and (3) require a variety of instructional strategies
because they move, intellectually, at different rates throughout the course.
The problem of engaging in critical inquiry is further compounded because
the kinds of issues raised in class are frequently ignored in the other classes
making up their programs.

Inasmuch as most universities are ill-equipped to resolve the problems
these factors create, it is evident that we must rethink how we teach. Given
the importance of the substance of the class for framing how teachers can
think about curriculum and instruction, four changes seem critical.

1. The class should be no larger than five or six students. A tutorial setting
   would permit each student's perspective to be taken seriously.
2. The class should be team taught in some way, thus removing the perceived, even if nonexistent, bias of a single instructor's ideological and
   methodological leanings from hampering the development of alternative
   conceptions.
3. The class should extend across two or more quarters, thereby providing
   both time for a more thorough examination of key ideas and more opportunities for one-on-one interaction between instructors and students.
4. The class should involve a project, perhaps an action research activity,
   that brings the instructors into the work site of the student. This would
   permit a joint investigation of the barriers to reform, which confront students like Christine and Ron, to become a primary focus of the learning
   process.

Making these changes would ensure not only that all four types of fliers
would enjoy ongoing support as they try to come to terms with the implications of curriculum inquiry in the settings with which they are most fa-

miliar, but that they would also have an opportunity to think about how the issues raised in class connect to ideas presented in other classes.

Understanding the settings with which we are most familiar is frequently the most difficult task we face. Making the familiar strange *is,* however, an essential first step. Donmoyer, in Chapter 10, presents a strong case for using both a cross-cultural and a historical perspective to illuminate how beliefs and practices are nothing less than "cultural artifacts" with human authorship. Students can learn from and support each other if the group works together over an extended period of time to explore the familiar. Some curriculum teachers argue that engaging first-year doctoral students like Christine and Ron in an investigation of their taken-for-granted practices and beliefs is wrongheaded because the focus is ill-timed. I argue the opposite position. An understanding of what we do in schools, why we do it the way we do, and what impact these practices have on students must be the *first stage* in engaging in curriculum reform.

In Schools

A second critical area in which data presented here have some relevance is curriculum inquiry in the schools. As we come to recognize both the importance of the school as the unit of change and the power of bringing decision making about curriculum and instruction close to those who teach (Fullan, 1982, 1985; Levin, 1987; Pink, 1986), the problematics that surfaced in my class become more significant. I suggest that we give attention to six factors as we think about how best to engage in curriculum inquiry and school reform.

1. Curriculum inquiry should be the primary focus of the building level faculty and the major component of a sequenced and planned staff development program designed at the building level. A building-wide emphasis will facilitate collaboration among teachers. It will also empower teachers to think about the meaning and impact of the curriculum-in-place and about their current instructional strategies. Engaging teachers in curriculum inquiry can also lead to a reconstruction of the socialization process in schools. Typically, that process initiates teachers into a system that accepts the barriers outlined earlier in the chapter as "givens" and therefore as outside of the control of teachers.
2. Building administrators should join *with* teachers, in contrast to directing teachers, in planned curriculum inquiry. Such involvement by administrators would legitimate the activity in the school and serve to lay the groundwork for collaboration among *all* professionals in the building. It would also demonstrate to teachers that administrators value their ex-

pertise as colleagues capable of analyzing, designing, and delivering the curriculum-in-place in their own building.

3. The process of curriculum inquiry should be grounded in the context of the individual school. The inquiry process should begin with an examination of the local setting and the problematics created by that setting. The success of this process of curriculum inquiry seems to lie in the connection teachers perceive between the intellectual investment they must make and the subsequent improvements made in the quality of life in school for both teachers and students.

4. Curriculum and instructional reforms generated by the inquiry process should be piloted in the school. Teachers should be directly involved in action research projects and in the evaluation of the reforms that *they* see as important and that *they* have designed. Bringing the responsibility for evaluation to the teachers is an important component of both the conceptualization and the implementation of reform. Not only does it signal that teachers are responsible for the outcomes of their own classroom activity, but it also serves to keep curriculum and instructional issues as priorities at the school level.

5. Curriculum and instructional inquiry must be an ongoing priority for the school. Presently, teachers are frequently asked to attend to many activities during the school year that are managerial rather than instructional. In many cases, the demands these activities place on teachers are also in conflict with each other. As a consequence, fragmentation and stress characterize the lives of many teachers. Deciding on an improvement focus that is sensitive to the local context helps to unite the faculty and maximizes the potential for change at the school level (Pink, 1987a, b; Pink & Wallace, 1984).

6. The process of curriculum inquiry should be facilitated by an outside person. This person would be responsible for raising questions and facilitating discussion of readings such as those I used in my class. This person would also work *with* teachers and administrators throughout the school year to conceptualize and evaluate their action research projects. A person who is not invested in the existing practices and beliefs of the building is critical, I believe, because of the barriers to reform outlined in this and other chapters in this part of the book.

A Last Word

What I am suggesting is a difficult task. Because it opposes current practice, it also becomes a political issue. Nevertheless, my experiences teaching at the university level and working with teachers and administrators in schools have convinced me that Fenstermacher (1986) is right in suggesting that we must enable teachers to become students of their own teaching, before they can help those in their classrooms to become students. Thus, we must redefine the work world of teachers in such a way that curriculum inquiry becomes a major priority in the daily lives of all teachers. We must also work diligently to raise the critical consciousness of preservice and practicing teachers about issues concerning the content and practice of schools. We must recognize that a failure to take these two tasks seriously will mean that school reforms will continue to be driven by proposals as uncritical of the existing conception of schools and schooling as those contained in many of the recent national commission and foundation reports (National Commission on Excellence in Education, 1983; Task Force on Elementary and Secondary Educational Policy, 1983).

REFERENCES

Apple, M. (1983). Curricular form and the logic of technical control: The building of the progressive individual. In M. Apple & L. Weis (Eds.), *Ideology and practice in schooling*. Philadelphia: Temple University Press.

Apple, M. (1987). Producing inequality: Ideology and economy in the national reports on education. *Educational Studies, 18*, 195–220.

Berman, E. (1986). The state's stake in educational reform. *The Urban Review, 18*, 6–18.

Berger, P., & Luckmann, T. (1967). *The social construction of reality*. Garden City, NY: Anchor Books.

Bowers, C. (1984). *The promise of theory: Education and the politics of cultural change*. New York: Teachers College Press.

Brophy, J., & Good, T. (1986). Teacher behavior and student achievement. In M. Wittrock (Ed.), *Handbook of research on teaching* (3rd Ed.). New York: Macmillan.

Brosio, R. (1987). The present economic sea changes and the corresponding consequences for education. *Educational Foundations, 3*, 4–38.

Carnegie Corporation of New York. (1983). *Education and economic progress: Towards a national economic policy*. New York: Carnegie Corporation.

Carroll, J. (1963). A model of school learning. *Teachers College Record, 64*, 723–733.

Carroll, J. (1985). The model of school learning: Progress of an idea. In C. Fisher & D. Berliner (Eds.), *Perspectives on instructional time*. New York: Longman.

Committee on Economic Development. (1985). *Investing in our children: Business and the public schools*. New York: Committee on Economic Development.

Cuban, L. (1982, October). Persistent instruction: The high school classroom 1900–1980. *Phi Delta Kappan*, pp. 113–118.

Doyle, W. (1986). Classroom organization and management. In M. Wittrock (Ed.), *Handbook of research on teaching* (3rd Ed.). New York: Macmillan.

Erickson, F. (1986). Qualitative methods in research on teaching. In M. Wittrock (Ed.), *Handbook of research on teaching* (3rd Ed.). New York: Macmillan.

Feiman-Nemser, S., & Floden, R. (1986). The cultures of teaching. In M. Wittrock (Ed.), *Handbook of research on teaching* (3rd Ed.). New York: Macmillan.

Fenstermacher, G. (1986). Philosophy of research on teaching. In M. Wittrock (Ed.), *Handbook of research on teaching* (3rd Ed.). New York: Macmillan.

Fullan, M. (1982). *The meaning of educational change.* New York: Teachers College Press.

Fullan, M. (1985). Change processes and strategies at the local level. *Elementary School Journal, 85,* 391–421.

Giroux, H., & McClaren, P. (1986). Teacher education and the politics of engagement: The case for democratic schooling. *Harvard Educational Review, 56,* 213–233.

Hunter, M. (1984). Knowing, teaching, and supervising. In Phillip L. Hosford (Ed.), *Using What We Know About Teaching.* Alexandria, VA: Association for Supervision and Curriculum Development.

Hunter, M. (1985). What's wrong with Madeline Hunter? *Educational Leadership, 42,* 57–60.

Levin, H. (1987). Improving productivity through education and technology. In G. Burke & R. Rumberger (Eds.), *The future impact of technology on work and education.* Philadelphia: Falmer Press.

National Commission on Excellence in Education. (1983). *A nation at risk.* Washington, DC: U.S. Government Printing Office.

Oakes, J. (1985). *Keeping track: How schools structure inequality.* New Haven: Yale University Press.

Pink, W. (1986). Facilitating change at the school level: A missing factor in school reform. *The Urban Review, 18,* 19–30.

Pink, W. (1987a). Continuing the struggle to improve urban schools: An effective schools project revisited. *Journal of Negro Education, 56,* 184–202.

Pink, W. (1987b). In search of exemplary junior high schools: A case study. In G. Noblit & W. Pink (Eds.), *Schooling in social context: Qualitative studies.* Norwood, NJ: Ablex.

Pink, W. (1988). Equity and excellence reconsidered: Thinking about empowering children. Paper presented at the Equity and Excellence Conference, Institute for Democracy in Education, Athens, Ohio.

Pink, W., & Leibert, R. (1985). Reading instruction in the elementary school: A proposal for reform. *Elementary School Journal, 87,* 51–67.

Pink, W., & Wallace, D. (1984). Creating effective urban elementary schools: A case study in the implementation of planned change. *Urban Education, 19,* 273–315.

Rist, R. (1970). Student social class and teacher expectations. *Harvard Educational Review, 40,* 411–451.

Shulman, L. (1986). Paradigms and research programs in the study of teaching. In M. Wittrock (Ed.), *Handbook of research on teaching* (3rd Ed.). New York: Macmillan.

Task Force on Education for Economic Growth. (1983). *Action for Excellence.* Denver: Education Commission of the States.

Task Force on Elementary and Secondary Educational Policy. (1983). *Making the grade.* New York: Twentieth Century Fund.

Walberg, H. (1986). Synthesis of research on teaching. In M. Wittrock (Ed.), *Handbook of research on teaching* (3rd Ed.). New York: Macmillan.

Whitford, B., & Hovda, R. (1986). Schools as knowledge work organizations: Perspectives and implications from the new management literature. *The Urban Review, 18,* 52–70.

Whitty, G. (1985). *Sociology and school knowledge.* London: Methuen.

Wilcox, K. (1982). Differential socialization in the classroom. In G. Spindler (Ed.), *Doing the ethnography of schooling.* New York: Holt, Rinehart and Winston.

Wittrock, M. C. (Ed.) (1986). *Handbook of research on teaching* (3rd Ed.). New York: Macmillan.

10

Curriculum, Community, and Culture

Reflections
and Pedagogical Possibilities

ROBERT DONMOYER
Ohio State University

I grew up in Lancaster County, Pennsylvania, in a community that was rural, ethnically homogeneous, and politically conservative. I knew at a fairly young age that this was not my home. I longed to move to a more cosmopolitan place, a place in which, I assumed, people would be far more enlightened and much less narrow in their thinking.

In my early 20s, after undergraduate school, I finally moved to New York City. There I encountered the New York Intellectual. Much to my surprise, I discovered this individual to be, in his or her own way, just as narrow, just as much a product of his or her culture, as the people with whom I had grown up in Lancaster County.

This personal experience has had a profound impact on my work in education. The construct of culture, in fact, has been central to my professional activities in the field. I confronted the construct of culture head on when, after two years of living in New York City, I decided I wanted to be a teacher and got my first teaching job in a Harlem elementary school.

Later, in my Ph.D. program at Stanford University as well as in my subsequent scholarly work, the construct of culture continued to be influential, although in these arenas its influence has been more metaphorical than literal. I have become especially interested in the "cultural" blinders that academic fields of study impose (for example, Piagetians and behaviorists think of learning in fundamentally different ways) and in the gap that exists between those who work in an academic "culture" and those who work in the "culture" of schools. My work over the years, in fact, has focused on (1) bridging the cultural gaps between researchers and practitioners, and (2) rethinking the role that research (which is inevitably biased by a priori "cultural" assumptions) ought to play in applied fields such as education.

THINKING ABOUT CURRICULUM, COMMUNITY, AND CULTURE

Curriculum in Tribal Communities

In Western Australia, when an Aborigine male reaches adolescence, he enters a symbolic death. He is removed from his everyday world. He is isolated from the family and friends he has known since birth, from those who have loved him and those who have cared for him; indeed, he is isolated from *all* families and *all* uninitiated males in the tribe.

During his symbolic death, the adolescent cannot speak. He can only watch as the tribal dances are danced and listen as the tribe's elders recount the sacred myths and traditional beliefs of his people. After six weeks of seclusion and silence, the adolescent undergoes the painful ritual of circumcision, and then he is isolated once more. Finally, when his penis has healed, the young male is reborn and returns once more to the everyday life of the tribe (Howard, 1983).

The process described above is just one in a series of formal educational experiences an Aborigine male must undergo in the elongated process of becoming a fully initiated member of his community. The content of these formal educational experiences varies somewhat, but the experiences always involve the tribe's male elders instructing the initiates in the community's sacred ways and beliefs.

The initiates learn from this process, not just from what is said by the elders, but also from the process itself. Sitting in silence listening to the tribe's elders reinforces what is said about respect for tradition and the elders who keep that tradition. Isolation from females reinforces sacred beliefs about gender differences. The elaborate rites for males, particularly when contrasted with the relatively modest initiation rites for the tribe's females, reinforce traditional tribal notions of male superiority.

Hart's (1974) cross-cultural analysis of tribal initiation rites suggests that the ways of the Aborigines are not unique among tribal communities. The secular aspects of living are taught informally and often subconsciously through the modeling and ad hoc mentoring that occur as part of everyday living. For example, the teaching and learning of vocational skills—which are often essential for individual and community survival—are normally haphazard and left to chance. Transmission of a community's sacred beliefs, the beliefs that turn a community into a culture, however, is almost never left to chance. The transmission of fundamental culture beliefs requires community-sanctioned teachers teaching a community-sanctioned curriculum. That curriculum takes the form of cultural myths and stories, and rites and rituals, which transmit to the young, sometimes directly, but often indirectly, the community's fundamental beliefs about the way the world is and the way the world—and those who live in it—ought to be.

Thus, if we want to understand curriculum in a tribal community, we must understand that community's culture. In tribal communities, curriculum is, quite simply, the most sacred and most fundamental cultural beliefs writ small!

Curriculum in Modern Societies

We live in a very different sort of community than the tribal community inhabited by the Aborigines. Ours is a modern—some say a post-modern—society. In our world, the sacred normally takes a back seat to the secular; science and scientific procedures have replaced myth and ritual; and we venerate change and progress more than we respect cultural traditions.

Our schools reflect these differences. Many of our schools are quite consciously vocational. Furthermore, even schools that do not explicitly focus on the training of vocational skills still are concerned with preparing students for the "world of work," at least in an indirect way. Similarly, science is a centerpiece of modern school curricula, and reforming culture, rather than reproducing it, is what schools claim to be about.

Although there are dramatic differences between our world and the tribal world of the Aborigines, there are also similarities. Certainly, modern societies and their schools emphasize the secular over the sacred, but one could also argue that, in modern societies, the secular has become sacred (Henry, 1963). Similarly, science has increasingly been portrayed as a mythology (Habermas, 1978), scientific procedures have been compared to tribal rituals (Campbell, 1979), and modern society's skepticism about tradition and its veneration of innovation and change have themselves, in recent years, been portrayed as a cultural tradition (Henry, 1963; Meyer, 1977).

Science, for example, has been accused of promoting an orientation toward control which is not a natural and inevitable human instinct but rather a creation of culture. The cultural basis of our control orientation becomes clear when we examine other cultures radically different from our own. Many Native American tribes, for instance, do not attempt to control nature but choose to live in harmony with it. This orientation is fostered by a mythology that portrays, in the words of the chief Seattle, the earth as "the

Redman's mother" and "the sparkling water that flows in the streams and the rivers . . . [as] not only water, but our ancestors' blood."

Our quite different view that human beings are the center of the universe and that the physical universe exists for human beings to use for their own purposes is no less mythological, nor is it necessarily a more pragmatically defensible myth. To be sure, a control orientation has led to the eradication of diseases, the exploration of the moon, and mass communication. It has also, however, led to the atomic bomb, the pollution of our environment, and—when played out in the social realm—the exploitation of whole classes of people as well as the promotion and perpetuation of what Buber (1970) calls "I–it" as opposed to "I–thou" relationships.

It is not surprising that post-colonial governments engaging in the task of nation building consciously use schools to break down tribal loyalties and develop new loyalties to the nation-state (Ramirez & Rubinson, 1979). Nor should one be surprised that school curricula in these developing nations serve to replace the values and world views associated with tribal life (such as a communal ethic and respect for tradition) with the values and beliefs (for example, a belief in individualism and faith in progress) so necessary to make modern economies work (Meyer & Rubinson, 1975). One should also not be surprised that those who have studied the hidden curriculum in our own schools have found a disparity between rhetoric and reality, or that Vallance's (1974) historical analysis has demonstrated that the hidden curriculum, which teaches conformity to community norms, became hidden only after it had worked.

Cultures, whether tribal, modern, or post-modern, inevitably attempt to reproduce themselves. They inevitably try to transmit to a new generation the most fundamental values and beliefs of the old. And they will inevitably attempt to use formal education to accomplish this purpose.

The bottom line of all this is that in any community—whether the tribal society of the Aborigines or the contemporary community in which we live—one can understand the curricula of educational organizations only by understanding the culture in which they are embedded and that they will inevitably try to reproduce.

Although modern societies are no different from tribal societies in this respect, the problem of thinking about curriculum in a cultural context— and, consequently, the problem of teaching curriculum from a cultural perspective—is far more complicated when we move from tribal communities to complex, modern ones. Our culture is a composite culture, or a collection of subcultures, each of which has different values and beliefs, many of which conflict. Furthermore, in our modern, complex society we not only have diverse ethnic groups; we can also use the term culture more metaphorically and talk of such things as the culture of poverty, the culture of professionals, urban culture, and the culture of youth.

The problem is further complicated by the fact that those beliefs, which cut across subcultures and tend to undergird modern society in general, normally embody contradictions and paradoxes: The secular is now sacred, science is now our religion, and a distrust of tradition is now our cultural heritage. Little wonder that sociologists and historians of science demonstrate that scientific communities often violate their own norms of openness and that scientists often behave like religious zealots rather than the self-critical, dispassionate seekers of truth they purport to be (Campbell, 1979). Little wonder that some philosophers and sociologists of science have argued that it is functional—even an organizational necessity—for scientists to do this (Campbell, 1979; Lakatos & Musgrave, 1970). Little wonder, also, that educational sociologists have found that schools—for all their talk of changing the social order—are instrumental in reproducing the status quo (Apple, 1982).

Because of these grand cultural contradictions and because our community is really a collection of many subcommunities, conflict is an inevitable part or modern culture. Therefore, a political perspective, that is, a perspective that focuses on how conflict gets resolved, must be a part of our understanding of and our teaching about curriculum and culture in complex multicultural communities such as our own.

Three Conceptions of Politics

Politics can be conceived of in at least three ways. One conception of politics can be labeled Machiavellian after the author of *The Prince*, the famous sixteenth-century treatise on strategies for gaining and keeping power. This conception of politics assumes that human beings and groups of human beings are self-interested, rational actors who will inevitably try to maximize their particular self-interests in a world of scarce resources. According to this conception, conflict gets resolved through the exercise of power. Sometimes individuals and groups maximize their power by building coalitions with other self-interested actors; coalitions can be built through compromise (giving up something one wants or accepting something one does not want in exchange for another's support of a particular course of action), side payments (giving something, such as a campaign contribution or a position of power, to someone in exchange for support), and the use of ambiguity (keeping a policy proposal vague so that those who disagree with each other will support one policy).

A Machiavellian view of politics is dominant in the field of political science. Not surprisingly, therefore, this view dominates discussions of curriculum politics coming out of the politics of education subfield (see, for example, Wirt & Kirst, 1975; Boyd, 1978).

A second conception of politics can be labeled *Aristotelian* after the ancient Greek philosopher. According to the ancient Greeks, conflict within a community was not resolved through the exercise of power but through the exercise of intellect. Politics, in fact, was conceived of as an academic discipline, albeit a *practical* discipline. A practical discipline does not try to discover what is true, as theoretical disciplines do, but rather what course of action is best. The method used to make such action-oriented decisions is called *deliberation* or *practical reasoning*, a process that considers both means and ends and the interrelationship between them.

Within the curriculum field, an Aristotelian conception of politics is most apparent in Schwab's (1969, 1971, 1973) articles on "the practical." An Aristotelian perspective also undergirds Dewey's (1916) political thought.

A third conception of politics can be labeled the politics of *standard operating procedures* and *standard operating ways of thinking*. This conception is seen most clearly when we examine budgetary practices (see, for example, Sharansky, 1970): The best way to predict a school's budget for any particular year is to get a copy of the budget for the previous year; most organizations are too complex to begin an intricate process like budgeting anew each year and, thus, must be content with making, at most, only minor incremental adjustments.

When this perspective is applied to the area of curriculum, conflicts are seen as being resolved not by the exercise of power or of intellect, but by reliance on tradition and the organization's existing standard operating procedures. Furthermore, when our focus shifts from the sociological to the psychological—that is, when we focus on individuals rather than organizations—this third conception of politics suggests that much potential conflict is muted and unrecognized (see, for example, Lukes, 1974). Steinbruner (1974) employs schema theory to argue that just as organizations require standard operating procedures to manage the complexity of organizational life, individuals require standard operating ways of thinking to deal with the complexity in their environments. According to this perspective, it would be dysfunctional for individuals to focus on the novelty and uniqueness of every new event or individual encountered, or to consider a wide range of alternatives when deciding what action to take at a particular time and place. Cognitive schema screen out uniqueness and make the world seem orderly and predictable. As Pink indicates in Chapter 9, these standard operating ways of thinking also make socially constructed conceptions of reality (which are, by definition, cultural artifacts) appear to be natural and inevitable, and as a result they diminish social conflict.

In the area of curriculum-related research, Dreeben's work, in particular, *What Is Learned in School* (1968), advances this third conception of politics at the organizational level. Clark and Yinger's (1977) description of teacher thinking is an example of the orientation applied to individuals. Curriculum scholars influenced by neo-Marxist and feminist thought (see, for example, Apple, 1982; Giroux, 1981; Lather, 1986; and the other chapters in this part of the book) also tend to conceptualize politics in this way, although they reject the argument that the existing standard operating procedures and standard operating ways of thinking are functional and, by implication, useful. These writers ask, "Functional and useful for whom?" and emphasize the disparity legitimated and perpetuated by a reliance on standard operating procedures and standard operating ways of thinking.

The three conceptions of politics outlined above are more complementary than contradictory. Each has the potential to reveal aspects of culture in complex communities such as our own. Each suggests possibilities for resolving the conflict that will inevitably arise in cultures that are really an amalgam of many subcultures and in which even the general principles that bind the subcultures together embody fundamental paradoxes and contradictions.

Thus, to think about curriculum we must think about culture. To think about curriculum in complex cultures like our own we must also think about politics. Finally, to think about politics in complex societies, we must draw upon different intellectual "cultures" that conceptualize politics in fundamentally different ways.

TEACHING ABOUT CURRICULUM, COMMUNITY, AND CULTURE

A brief description follows of teaching approaches and strategies I have used to teach about curriculum from a community orientation.

Historical Perspective

Understanding curriculum in one's own culture requires that the familiar become strange, that the taken-for-granted assumptions with which we operate in our daily lives are made problematic, and that the standard operating procedures and standard operating ways of thinking that appear natural and inevitable are revealed for what they really are: cultural artifacts. Adding a historical dimension to curriculum courses can help accomplish these purposes.

For example, in 1909 Elwood Cubberly wrote, "Our schools are, in a sense, factories in which the raw products (children) are to be shaped and fashioned into products to meet the various demands of life" (p. 338). The factory metaphor of schooling is still very much with us. This metaphor undergirds Madeline Hunter's (1984) approach to instruction and supervision, mastery learning approaches to teaching, Distar curricula, most versions of competency-based education, the special education teacher's IEPs, and a host of other contemporary educational practices. The metaphorical basis of such practices and procedures, however, has become less obvious over time. As a result, the metaphor becomes all the more powerful because it is no longer thought of as a conception of reality but rather a reflection of the real world.

Thus, in most of my curriculum classes, history plays a central role. I should emphasize—as I emphasize to my classes—that these courses are not history courses. Rather, history is used as a backdrop against which to view contemporary curriculum issues and practices. A historical backdrop adds depth and dimension to contemporary issues and practices and provides a basis for comparison and contrast. By going back in time—for example, by reading about early attempts to conceptualize schools as factories—the metaphorical basis of contemporary standard operating procedures and standard operating ways of thinking can be revealed.

In addition to reading historical texts, I normally try to involve my students in projects that have them doing curriculum history. Normally this work takes the form of oral histories. These have two components: (1) data gleaned from extensive interviews about people's experiences in schools, and (2) an analysis comparing the interview data with ideas discussed in class and in class readings, as well as with the student's own experiences.

I use oral histories for two reasons. First, history texts usually demonstrate one of two biases: They focus either on the history of ideas (see, for example, Cremin, 1961) or on organizational structure and policy (see, for example, Katz, 1975). In both cases, the day-to-day lives of students and teachers in classrooms are underplayed. The student-generated oral histories help compensate for this bias.

Second, like Pink (Chapter 9) and Erdman (Chapter 11), I am concerned about teacher disempowerment. I am a bit more skeptical than those authors about a university course's ability to rectify the situation. I do, however, try not to add to the feelings of disempowerment teachers bring to the university. In my classes I do not want to communicate to teachers the idea that knowledge comes only from books written by officially designated researchers; I want them to know that they, too, can generate knowledge. At the very least, I hope the project—which involves interacting with flesh and blood human beings rather than confronting disembodied theory—communicates this.

A Cross-Cultural Perspective

I frequently focus on curriculum ideas and practices in other cultures for the same reason that I focus on curriculum ideas and practices during other periods of history: Such a focus can demonstrate that what we take to be natural and inevitable could, in fact, be otherwise. My recent work in New Zealand, for example, has provided me with a wealth of cross-cultural examples, which I have used in my teaching. In New Zealand, despite the existence of a national curriculum, a national examination system, and a national inspectorate to ensure comparability between schools and compatibility between each school and the nation's curriculum, I observed more autonomy at both the building and the classroom levels than I have observed in schools in the United States, where no official national curriculum exists and where even state curricula normally reflect a respect for local control.

This paradox occurs because many years ago an enlightened Director General, New Zealand's chief civil servant in the education area, realized what organizational theorists in our own culture are only now beginning to understand: Teachers need a large amount of autonomy both because they need to accommodate the idiosyncrasy in their particular classrooms and because they need to feel a sense of ownership to implement a curriculum with enthusiasm. As a consequence, curriculum, testing, and supervision are conceptualized very differently in New Zealand than in the United States. Curriculum, for example, is viewed as a resource rather than a prescription. There are only a handful of "dos" and "don'ts," and these are normally expressed more as cultural norms general enough to permit teacher discretion than as behaviorally defined teacher-proof procedures. I use differing conceptualizations such as these to reveal the cultural basis of curriculum practices in our country and to suggest alternative ways of thinking and acting.

In addition to comparing curriculum thought and action in our culture with that in other contemporary cultures, I use pre-modern tribal cultures for cross-cultural comparisons. Much as I have asked readers to do in this chapter, I ask my students to look beyond the obvious dissimilarities between the modern and the pre-modern world and find those things that are common. I also use descriptions of education in cultures radically different from our own to reveal what Eisner (1985) has called the null curriculum in our schools, that is, those things that are not taught. For example, I frequently use Eggan's (1974) wonderful description of education in Hopi culture for this purpose.

In addition to reading ethnographies such as the one by Eggan, I frequently ask my students to do their own ethnographic studies. In other words, I ask students to use both the methods and theoretical constructs of anthropology to examine the schools and classrooms in which they currently work or, in the case of those in preservice teacher and administrator education programs, will eventually work.

These ethnographies serve various functions. Sometimes students' findings simply confirm and personalize generalizations encountered in class.

For example, one student, a Chapter One tutor who provided special reading instruction to low-achieving students, was investigating why her tutees, in their classrooms, were consistently given work well below their actual reading levels. Teachers told her, during interviews, that it was because the students did not get their seatwork done and because they needed to practice exercises on standardized tests given by the district. These responses not only confirmed but brought close to home generalizations presented in class about (1) students being punished academically for perceived social inadequacies, and (2) the impact of testing on classroom curriculum.

Sometimes findings have contradicted generalizations presented in class. One white middle class teacher doing an observer-as-participant study in her ethnically integrated classroom, for example, concluded she was actually discriminating against her white middle class students. Her black students' values and behaviors were more consistent with her own ethnic background. Among other insights, her analysis revealed that her black students engaged in far more touching behavior. (Her evidence to support this generalization included candid and posed photographs taken earlier in the year before the study began; in these photos, most of the black students were touching at least one other student, while most white students were not.) The teacher-researcher hypothesized that, since she came from an ethnic background where touching was the norm, she responded far more positively to her black students than her white students.

On occasion, these student ethnographies actually break new ground. In one study, for example, the teacher-researcher discovered that middle school boys labeled learning disabled had group norms that kept them from trying to learn to read in the classroom. Moreover, these same boys, on the playground, had formed a gang in which status was based on reading ability. The leader of the gang, for example, could be challenged by asking him to read a page from a book; if he failed, he would lose status and, possibly, his leadership position.

This past year, I have encouraged students attracted to critical, neo-Marxist theory to engage in what might be called critical ethnographic action research, that is, to build research projects around questions such as: (1) How can classroom complexity be simplified without tracking students? (2) How can administrators sympathetic to a neo-Marxist perspective play the administrative role in a way that is at least partially consistent with that perspective? Elsewhere I have argued that neo-Marxist work to date has been pitched at such an abstract, rhetorical level that critical theorists have generally overlooked the organizational necessities that cut across different ideologies and different economic systems (Donmoyer, 1989). I believe this work, which is still in its infancy, may have the potential to be pedagogically useful not only to the students doing the work but to the field in general.

Regardless of whether any of this work will eventually benefit the field in general, the ethnographic projects certainly have served a useful pedagogical function. I have experienced little of the extreme resistance Pink describes in Chapter 9, and I suspect this has something to do with the fact that much of our class discussions focus on data generated by class members. Such work is not easily written off by fellow students.

Before proceeding, let me make two additional points with respect to the ethnographic projects. First, I do not want to leave the impression that the work done by these amateur ethnographers is always insightful. Some of it is superficial, though I suspect, even at its worst, it is much less superficial than the library research papers I assigned at the beginning of my university teaching career. I suspect that the less-than-satisfactory products have at least something to do with the limitations associated with the structure of university courses—limitations that have led me on occasion to try to "teach" curriculum outside of a classroom context by working in schools on curriculum development, evaluation, and action research projects. One of these attempts is described briefly below.

Second, I want to note, for those considering using this assignment in their own teaching, that it can produce considerable anxiety, particularly in "good" students who have learned to play a more traditional school game successfully. I try to diffuse the anxiety in several ways: (1) by spending considerable time describing data collection and analysis options, (2) by using student papers from earlier classes as models, (3) by assuring students that it is normal to feel that one is drowning in data, and (4) by arguing that most things that are worthwhile have costs attached to them and that focusing on students' own schools and classrooms will likely be far more worthwhile than doing library research (an argument, incidentally, that no one has ever challenged). I also try to minimize grade anxiety by being as clear as possible about my assessment criteria (I place great emphasis on supporting generalizations and inferences with evidence) and by having students do mini-projects that are critiqued but not graded, before undertaking the major ethnographic project.

The Arts and Literature as Modes of Knowing and Methods of Teaching

I have been greatly influenced by the work of aesthetician Susanne Langer (1988) and her "translator" in the field of education, Elliot Eisner (1985). Their influence is apparent in my approach to the use of history and the study of other cultures in my teaching of curriculum. Langer and Eisner suggest that artistic and literary modes of discourse provide knowledge of aspects of experience that cannot be symbolized by either nonliterary language or numbers. In particular, they argue that artistic and literary modes of discourse can better symbolize the affective, or what Mann (1969) has called the "lived in," aspects of experience.

These ideas seem particularly significant for those who attempt to teach curriculum from a cultural perspective because they emphasize the cultural bias inherent in language. Langer (1988), for example, differentiates between two types of symbols, which she labels representational and presentational. Representational symbols—for example, the letters "c-a-t" and the equation $1 + 1 = 2$—have no meaning in and of themselves. They receive their meaning through conventional association based on cultural agreement. We have decided to associate certain sounds with the letters "c-a-t" and to associate these sounds, when combined, with certain real-world objects. The meaning of presentational symbols, on the other hand, is inherent in the symbols themselves. The colors, shapes, textures, and lines of a painting, for example, communicate the meaning of the painting directly to the viewer. A Martian coming to the planet Earth could not understand the word *cat* or the equation $1 + 1 = 2$ without first learning the social rules that give these symbols meaning. Assuming the Martian's sense organs worked as ours do, however, the Martian could "read" a painting by Gauguin. To be sure, there are representational elements in Gauguin's work (a Martian, for example, would not automatically recognize the Christian imagery in it), but most of the meaning of Gauguin's paintings exists in the shapes, colors, textures, lines, which communicate directly to the viewer.

I use the arts and literature to help my students overcome the ethnocentric bias inherent in talk about other cultures and other periods of history. The arts and literature, in other words, permit me to provide a more direct, and a more visceral, experience of other places and times than is possible by simply talking. I will provide two examples of this aspect of my teaching. The first involves using the arts, in particular music; the second demonstrates my use of literature.

Many of my students have difficulty understanding the significance the labor union movement had for the early progressives, because their conception of unions is a product of their experience in contemporary culture, in which unions are large, bureaucratic, and often self-interested organizations. To help overcome this ethnocentric bias, I sing union songs with my students. These songs help students enter an earlier mind-set, when heroes and villains could be easily identified and when union members were clearly a part of the former group.

I also use literature to help students develop a more visceral understanding of the shift from a rural, agricultural society to a modern industrial one, a shift that helped prompt the progressive movement within education and the larger society. For example, in one course, I ask for volunteers to help stage a collection of readings I have put together called *American Montage.* The production is staged simply as readers' theatre. Hence, there are no lines to memorize and no scenery to construct; we use only stools and ladders to stage the work.

The production opens with a choral reading of Frost's "The Land Was Ours Before We Were the Land's." Then various readings and folk songs present aspects of American life before the industrial revolution. Included in this section are an excerpt from *Paul Bunyan,* which reflects Americans' veneration of the rugged individual; an excerpt from *Huckleberry Finn,* the great American novel about a street smart, but unschooled, boy; the rather violent folk song, "The Banks of the Ohio"; a scene from *The Contrast,* the first American comedy, which contrasts down-to-earth, commonsensical Americans with pretentious "academic" Europeans; and an excerpt from *Our Town,* with its portrait of quaint bucolic small town life.

The midway point of the production is signaled by a people machine: One cast member comes forward and begins to make a simple movement and sound, which he or she repeats in machine-like fashion. One by one, each of the remaining cast members joins in with their own movement and sound. When all cast members have joined the machine, it dissolves into a choral reading of Sandburg's *Chicago,* which renders the exhilaration and enthusiasm that often accompanied industrialization and urbanization. Individual readings from Sinclair's *The Jungle* then provide a stark contrast, as do readings from Steinbeck's *The Grapes of Wrath.* Sandburg's poem, "God Is No Gentleman," and a rousing choral rendition of the union song *Union Maid* present a collectivist orientation, which contrasts sharply with Paul Bunyan's rugged individualism. The production concludes with two poems by the black poet Langston Hughes.

With these and other attempts to incorporate the arts and literature in my teaching, I hope to help students transcend the cultural bias inherent in nonliterary language and experience more directly the "lived in" aspects of other cultures and other historical periods.

Sociodramas

Sociodrama is employed to provide students with a sense of the politics that are an inevitable part of curriculum decision making in a multicultural community. Sociodramas normally take the form of meetings or hearings about controversial issues. For instance, we have had school board meetings about whether to implement mastery learning or assertive discipline district wide, and senate hearings about the tuition tax credit bill.

Whatever the focus of the sociodrama, several procedures are followed.

1. Readings on the designated topic are provided so class members have sufficient information to intelligently engage in the role-playing situation.
2. Students choose their roles the week prior to the simulation. To maximize learning, they are encouraged, though not required, to choose roles that would have them defending positions they would not defend in real life. For example, in the tuition tax credit simulations, parochial school teachers are encouraged to be NEA or ACLU lobbyists, while those on the other side of the issue are encouraged to play roles such as the moral majority representative. I emphasize the need to portray the role as correctly and fairly as possible; the purpose is not to satirize or burlesque a particular role or position.
3. Normally I require students to write from the perspective of their roles before the simulation. In the school board simulation about assertive discipline, the activity takes the form of writing to the superintendent either supporting or criticizing the recommendation to the board that assertive discipline be used district-wide. Sometimes students are asked to write more than one letter from more than one perspective.
4. I frequently have like-minded characters meet together, in character, before the official meeting, to coordinate their arguments and avoid duplication and repetition.
5. I not only use a highly structured meeting or hearing setting for the simulation, but, because course members have such limited experience with role playing and simulation, I normally cast myself in a role (the superintendent, board president, staff counsel), which allows me to exercise some control over the action.
6. I also frequently use empty chairs, which allow me to change roles and represent different positions I want represented if they do not come up "naturally" during the simulation. For example, during the simulation on mastery learning, I might, by switching chairs, transform myself into both the school psychologist trained in the tenets of B. F. Skinner and a Carl Rogers-taught school counselor.

Finally, to bring into play a Machiavellian as well as an Aristotelian conception of politics, those participating in the role playing are asked to think aloud about their private, self-interested reasons for supporting or opposing a proposal before coming forward to present their public position on the matter.

"Teaching" Curriculum Outside the Classroom

I will conclude this discussion by briefly considering a more unconventional approach to "teaching" curriculum. This approach moves teaching outside the confines of the university classroom and into the community.

Dewey (1916) provides a rationale for doing this. He suggests that participation in community life is educative. His belief in democracy, in fact, was predicated on the assumption that when people debate and discuss issues with each other, intellectual growth occurs.

> To be a recipient of a communication is to have an enlarged and changed experience. Nor is the one who communicates left unaffected. Try the experiment of communicating, with fullness and accuracy, some experience to another, especially if it be somewhat complicated, and you will find your own attitude toward your experience changing.... The experience has to be formulated in order to be communicated. To formulate requires getting outside of it, seeing it as another would see it.... One has to assimilate, imaginatively, something of another's experience in order to tell him intelligently of one's own experience. (p. 5)

My attempts to move curriculum teaching outside the classroom and into the community have involved approaching curriculum evaluation from the sort of deliberation perspective articulated by Beyer in Chapter 8. For example, I organized an evaluation of an informal open classroom-oriented school around the assumption that curriculum issues and curriculum disputes are, fundamentally, more conceptual than empirical and more value-based than technical in nature. I established panels of individuals who played different roles (teachers, principals, central office personnel, parents) and who viewed education generally and the program in the school being evaluated in particular from differing perspectives. Panel members were guided through a process of deciding what issues to focus the evaluation on; deciding what empirical evidence, if any, would help resolve issues; considering how to gather the evidence; gathering and interpreting it; engaging in extended discourse about nonempirical issues; and making policy and practice recommendations.

This deliberation-oriented approach to evaluation is rooted in a "standard operating ways of thinking" conception of politics; the assumption is that disputes within the field of education result from the fact that people look at education from different perspectives. The study, described above, of the deliberation-oriented evaluation (Donmoyer, 1983) suggests that this assumption is, in large part, correct: Although members of the evaluation panel often used the same language, the meanings they attached to such terms as learning, curriculum, and achievement were often quite different.

A deliberation orientation also assumes that (1) people can expand their standard operating ways of thinking by interacting with others who think differently than they do, and (2) disputes can be resolved by expanding understanding. In the study described above, evidence to support these two assumptions was somewhat equivocal. Indeed, often teachers' standard operating ways of thinking kept them from really hearing what parents were saying. Machiavellian tactics (for example, school staff stonewalling parents' requests to see the school's standardized test scores) were even employed to protect the school staff's standard operating ways of thinking and standard operating ways of doing things (see Donmoyer, 1983).

Thus, the evidence suggests that a deliberation-oriented approach to evaluation does not work perfectly either as a problem-solving method or as a pedagogical device. There was evidence, however, to at least partially support its pedagogical benefit. One teacher, for example, said of the process:

> It was helpful to me personally because I certainly began to understand parents' perceptions. I think better than before ... I learned a lot about just listening to people. Just the kinds of things they were saying, the kinds of concerns, the kinds of perceptions they had. I learned personally how to be a better listener.
>
> Was it a goal of the study to be helpful? Going into it that's not something I thought about ... I tried to be open to what parents were saying ... I thought I would do that for them. I was really trying to be open and listen to them. But I didn't know that I was going to gain so much from it. (Donmoyer, 1983, p. 40)

Similarly, a parent, who in the early stages of the evaluation panel meetings went home and cried, vowing not to return, in the end found work on the evaluation panel empowering:

> It was a maturing thing for me as far as sharing my ideas and having others accept them ... I'd never been confronted by the teaching staff.... To share with others was kind of fun ... I was feeling like I didn't have a lot to contribute, then finding out the opposite was reinforcing. (Donmoyer, 1983, p. 41)

CONCLUSION

By the time an Aborigine male completes the initiation rites and rituals of his tribe, he will have made his tribe's beliefs and values his own. A similar process occurs with schooling in our own culture. In our culture, however, one of our most sacred beliefs is that all beliefs and values should be questioned, and one of our most cherished values is openness. Our culture, in other words, is built on paradox.

A graduate level course in curriculum seems an appropriate place to take our culture's beliefs and values seriously. This chapter has described one curriculum teacher's attempt to do this.

REFERENCES

Apple, M. (1982). *Ideology and curriculum.* London: Routledge & Kegan Paul.

Boyd, W. (1978). The study of educational policy and politics: Much ado about nothing? *Teachers College Record, 80,* 249–271.

Buber, M. (1970). *I and thou.* New York: Scribner.

Campbell, D. (1979). A tribal model of the social system vehicle carrying scientific knowledge. *Knowledge: Creation, Diffusion, Utilization, 1,* 181–201.

Clark, C., & Yinger, R. (1977). Research on teacher thinking. *Curriculum Inquiry, 7,* 279–304.

Cremin, L. (1961). *The transformation of the school.* New York: Vintage Books.

Cubberly, E. (1909). *Changing conceptions of education.* Boston: Houghton-Mifflin.

Dewey, J. (1916). *Democracy and education.* New York: Macmillan.

Donmoyer, R. (1983). Evaluation as deliberation: Theoretical considerations and empirical explorations. Final report to The National Institute of Education, Washington, DC.

Donmoyer, R. (1989). Theory, practice, and the doubled-edged problem of idiosyncracy. *The Journal of Curriculum and Supervision, 4,* 257–270.

Dreeben, R. (1968). *What is learned in school.* Reading, MA: Addison-Wesley.

Eggan, D. (1974). Instruction and affect in Hopi cultural continuity. In G. Spindler (Ed.), *Education and the cultural process* (pp. 311–332). New York: Holt, Rinehart and Winston.

Eisner, E. (1985) *The educational imagination: On the design and evaluation of school programs.* New York: Macmillan.

Giroux, H. (1981). *Ideology, culture, and the process of schooling.* Philadelphia: Temple University Press.

Hart, C. W. M. (1974). Contrasts between prepubertal and postpubertal education. In G. Spindler (Ed.), *Education and the cultural process* (pp. 342–360). New York: Holt, Rinehart and Winston.

Habermas, J. (1978). *Knowledge and human interests.* London: Heinemann.

Henry, J. (1963). *Culture against man.* New York: Vintage Books.

Howard, M. C. (1983). *Contemporary cultural anthropology.* Boston: Little, Brown.

Hunter, M. (1984). Knowing, teaching, and supervising. In P. L. Hosford (Ed.), *Using what we know about teaching* (pp. 169–203). Alexandria, VA: Association for Supervision and Curriculum Development.

Katz, M. (1975). *Class, bureaucracy and schools.* New York: Prager.

Lakatos, I., & Musgrave, A. (1970). *Criticism and the growth of knowledge.* Cambridge: Cambridge University Press.

Langer, S. (1988). *Philosophy in a new key: A study in the symbolism of reason, rite, and art.* (3rd ed.) Cambridge, MA: Harvard University Press.

Lather, P. (1986). Research as praxis. *Harvard Educational Review, 56* (3), 257–277.

Lukes, S. (1974). *Power: The radical view.* London: Macmillan.

Mann, J. (1969). Curriculum criticism. *Teachers College Record, 71* (1), 27–40.

Meyer, J. (1977). The effects of education as an institution. *American Journal of Sociology, 1,* 223–246.

Meyer, J., & Rubinson, R. (1975). Education and political development. *Review of Research in Education.* Washington, DC: American Educational Research Association.

Ramirez, F., & Rubinson, R. (1979). Creating members: The political incorporation and expansion of education. In J. Meyer & M. Hannan (Eds.), *National development and the world system* (pp. 85–116). Chicago: University of Chicago Press.

Schwab, J. (1969). The practical: A language for curriculum. *School Review, 78,* 1–24.

Schwab, J. (1971). The practical: Arts of eclectic. *School Review, 79,* 493–542.

Schwab, J. (1973). The practical 3: Translation to curriculum. *School Review, 81,* 501–522.

Sharansky, I. (1970). *The routines of politics.* New York: VanNostrand Reinhold.

Steinbruner, J. (1974). *The cybernetic theory of decision making.* Princeton: Princeton University Press.

Vallance, E. (1974). Hiding the hidden curriculum. *Curriculum Theory Network, 4,* 5–21.

Wirt, F. & Kirst, M. (1975). *Political and social foundations of education.* Berkeley, CA: McCutchan.

11

Curriculum and Community

A Feminist Perspective

JEAN I. ERDMAN
University of Wisconsin-Oshkosh

I am an associate professor in the Department of Curriculum and Instruction at the University of Wisconsin-Oshkosh. My doctoral degree (1981) is from the University of Wisconsin, where my advisor was Michael Apple, who, in turn, worked with Dwayne Huebner and Jonas Soltis at Teachers College, Columbia University.

I continue to appreciate Michael Apple's ability to understand the organizational constraints under which teachers work and to balance respect for teachers with a critique of schooling within the larger political and social context. I remember being moved by the thoughtfulness and dignity of Bob Tabachnick, and by the sense of community I felt with Ann Becker, with whom I also worked.

In graduate school, I had begun a minor in administration but soon switched to educational policy studies because I felt the administration courses would perpetuate the kind of thinking that I had found most distressful while teaching elementary school, namely, the failure to make connections among organizational decisions, the morale of the faculty, and the curriculum, as the totality of the learning environment.

As a curriculum teacher, my interest in building an inclusive community comes initially from having grown up as the oldest girl in a working-class family of six children during the 1950s. I took for granted that girls were expected to defer to their fathers and brothers and help their mothers. My mother, a homemaker, stressed "getting an education because no one can take that away from you"; when I was in college she began work as a teacher's aide and helped to unionize aides in my hometown.

My father, a machinist and outdoorsman, taught me concern for the "working guy." Perhaps my parents remain such a strong presence in my sense of work in curriculum because I teach at the university in my home-town, and my office overlooks the factory where my father worked.

My appreciation of women's contributions would come later through contact with female professors, including Bonnie Freeman, a visiting professor at the University of Wisconsin, who encouraged me to "at least get a master's degree." I am at home with the call for broadening the range of voices in the conversation about curriculum, and honoring the unknown local educators, many of them women, whose daily routines and formal positions may preclude recognition or publication.

Twenty years of feminist research have documented the systematic suppression of women's ideas (Davis, 1985) and their contributions to community. The new scholarship on women recognizes gender as a fundamental organizing principle of community and identifies male dominance in gender relations in curriculum and in schools (Messer-Davidow, 1985). For example, K–12 and university teachers habitually interact differently with male and female students, overlooking sexist texts and behaviors (Hall & Sandler, 1984; Sadker & Sadker, 1986).

This chapter addresses teaching an elementary curriculum course, including a discussion of the problems of teaching the course within the broader context of a patriarchal culture. Martin's (1985) philosophical analysis of the education of women provides the foundation for some of the things I do in Elementary Curriculum, a required course taken early in the master's degree program. Martin's ideas, applied to curriculum teaching, can be described as follows.

Curriculum must be expanded to include the processes of society with which women's lives have historically been intertwined. The false dichotomy of curriculum for carrying on either the productive processes of community life or the reproductive processes is a consequence of ignorance of alternative ideals of educated women. The reproductive processes of society must stand in relation to productive processes, reflecting a community in which the two sexes live together interdependently. Bringing in the reproductive processes can add caring and connection. However, doing so entails rethinking curriculum.

Martin describes how productive and reproductive processes are gender-related, as are the traits our culture associates with them. Cultural stereotypes attribute analytical and abstract reasoning to males, interpersonal orientation and sensitivity to females. The value hierarchy of our culture places greater status on traits associated with males, and the emphasis on these traits in curriculum reflects this hierarchy. Gender-sensitive curriculum teaching entails striving to develop all capacities in all students, fostering what is already there and working with students to construct what exists to a lesser extent. In calling for the ethic of care that is central to reproductive processes, critical thinking, abstract reasoning, and self-government remain vital.

In a culture in which traits are genderized and sex-role socialization is pervasive, ignoring gender is dishonest. The warped reality, known as patriarchy, narrows women's roles to those of wives and mothers, provides inaccurate historical accounts, perpetuates bias in language use, and removes caring from academic concerns. Ignoring the reproductive processes of society, with their emphasis on care and connection, works to privilege men at the expense of women. When curriculum is defined only in relation to productive processes of the community, trait genderization is seen only as a women's problem. Attention only to the productive processes places a higher value on the masculine than the feminine gender. A first step for curriculum teachers is to raise to consciousness the gender aspects of the hidden curriculum: the denigration and silencing of women and girls, and the tasks, traits, and functions associated with them. This is the main thrust of Martin's work as it informs my teaching of Elementary Curriculum.

As curriculum teachers, we need to broaden the range of voices our students hear; to include works by women and minorities; to teach about the documented history of local women doing community work, often for intrinsic rewards, rather than only about well-known "stars" (although we can honor and learn from them too); and to note the typical pattern of women's volunteer work with young children, with the elderly, and in libraries. We can recognize our communities as outgrowths of vital work by women—the local initiators and volunteers in domestic abuse centers, rape crisis centers, and latch-key programs—and discuss the contradictions inherent in situations wherein those who do the work do not also set policy and receive adequate compensation.

There is always the danger of reverting to androcentric assumptions about what is worth knowing. Many curriculum teachers address the oppressive quality of class bias yet provide only fragmentary glimpses of female and minority struggles to work, go to school, and have decent lives. Intellectually, we need a "wide-awakeness" that requires more than a single definition of human nature. A multifocal, relational perspective on the human experience identifies where issues of gender are relevant. Ideally, gender sensitivity is interwoven with concerns about race, class, linguistic experience, and sexual orientation (Grant & Sleeter, 1986; Greene, 1985;

Tetreault, 1987). It is vital to attend to the salience of economic and organizational constraints on curriculum, and to understand and appreciate that a gender-sensitive—a feminist—perspective can help us envision and build more inclusive communities. Community, from a feminist perspective, emphasizes sensitivity to and inclusiveness of women, minorities, poor people—all groups, particularly those with lesser status and power.

BACKGROUND FOR MY STUDENTS AND MYSELF

As I think about how all members of a community should be heard, I am moved by the following excerpt from a university student's journal written as a requirement for a women's studies class:

> *Nancy:* I couldn't help thinking of the idea of a mute culture within a dominant culture. A "nobody" knowing she's different from the dominant culture keeps silent and is surprised to find out there are others who share this feeling. But they speak only to each other and hide otherwise. But don't tell! At least if you are silent and no one knows, you can continue at least to still belong to you. If "they," the somebodies, find out, they'll advertise and you'll have to become one of them. (Tetreault & Maher, 1987, pp. 20–21)

Most of my curriculum students are female elementary teachers. They feel muted as decisions are made in their districts without their involvement, and they remain silent. When they are asked to react to school-wide policies, as opposed to creating them, they feel the temptation to "close the classroom door" and address only the professional world within their classrooms rather than relating their teaching to school and district policies. When they take Elementary Curriculum, they need to connect the course with their own teaching situations, so that they can view it as more than an academic exercise, a hoop to leap through to garner salary increases.

The thoroughness of preparation and degree of concentration that these teachers and I bring to class are affected by our daily responsibilities and routines. My current responsibilities, which allow more time for reflection than public school teaching does, include co-directing a local affiliate of the National Writing Project, teaching Elementary Curriculum, teaching language arts methods, and supervising student teachers. The latter provides current exposure to schools, which helps with teaching curriculum, but visiting schools takes time away from scholarship—an unresolved dilemma confounded by a 12-hour teaching load each semester. The teachers—my curriculum students—are tired and have a lot on their minds when they come to class after a full day of teaching and a rushed meal with their families. Twenty years ago, before increased departmentalization and specialization among elementary school faculty, there were fewer interruptions during the elementary school day. The elementary grade level teacher's daily routine has become more interrupted and hectic in character (Erdman, 1981). This routine is intensified further by time given to testing students. In summary, my curriculum students and I have diverse responsibilities that make deliberative, intense reflection on course topics crucial. In light of the rushed pace of our professional routines, covering course topics quickly and superficially must be avoided.

These students display a strong sense of collegiality among themselves in class, enhanced by their common interest in nurturing and supporting children—their students. A sense of community is crucial to the process of professionalization whereby a group distinguishes itself from the larger society. I have heard about the strong community among curriculum teachers (evidenced by the array of curriculum literature, organization, and conferences), but perhaps my strongest sense of affiliation is with K–12 teachers, particularly those working in elementary schools, where I spent the first five years of my educational career. I think this sentiment is based on an ethos of caring for children as individuals and an organizational framework of self-contained classrooms that allowed me to know my students well.

In addition, I may affiliate with elementary (and other K–12) teachers because of my perception of the distance between many college and university teachers and public school teachers. The former may be unaware of K–12 working conditions or may minimize their effects on curriculum. My students—teachers—deserve to be listened to as they speak of the constraints of their work; we discuss course readings in order to make connections between what is and what might be. The tension I feel as a curriculum teacher lies in reducing the distance between myself and my students, while at the same time taking an analytical stance toward the perceptions they may hold that their working conditions and school situations are unchangeable.

My students are weary of top-down initiatives from the state and of district administrators brought in from outside, whose goals are to change teachers. As Apple (1986) notes, teachers need our support in the struggle for working conditions that provide autonomy to conceptualize, not merely execute, the tasks of teaching. Despite collegiality within the teaching ranks, the status quo oppression of not being listened to within their districts wears teachers down—words of "empowerment" in university presentations are met with cynicism.

AN ELABORATION AND CAUTIONARY NOTE
ABOUT THE ETHOS OF CARE

In a community, unlike a hierarchy, people get to know each other. They do not act as representatives of positions or as occupants of roles but as individuals with particular styles of thinking. (Belenky, Clinchy, Goldberger, & Tarule, 1986, p. 221)

Belenky et al. (1986), in their groundbreaking work, address the cognitive aspects of caring and describe the transformation of curriculum possible through connected teaching that attends to both the reproductive and productive cultural processes. Their ideas inform my teaching of Elementary Curriculum. They describe powerful learning experiences that come not from words but from action and observation, much of which has never been translated into words. The role of the curriculum teacher is to help students find their own words to make meaning of their experiences, thereby integrating their actions with analysis. Belenky et al. note that standards intended to propel students into independent, contextual thinking can distract women and girls from focusing on intellectual concerns and produce instead efforts to please the teacher, which impede their development. Teachers can support students by thinking out loud with them, thereby modeling thinking as a fallible, attainable activity, and by not "inflicting" views. In connected teaching, no one apologizes for uncertainty because it is assumed that evolving thought will be tentative. The teacher strives to preserve students' newborn thoughts, to avoid turning them into "acceptable lies," to encourage students to "think more." Connected teaching does carry authority, but it is based on cooperation, trust, and encouragement. Belenky et al. (1986) note that females in particular find this energizing.

The emotional labor of teaching is interwoven with cognitive concerns. It includes, but is not limited to, the direct care of and for students. Care has been belittled as custodial and controlling rather than educative (Freedman, 1988). Impersonality is part of a general discounting of the idiosyncratic and contextual nature of teaching, which Beyer, in Chapter 8, describes as the demanding and unpredictable "on the spot" character of teaching.

It is with caution that I stress caring within our culture—advocating nurturing has its dangers. An ethic of care should apply equally to men and women. Women have traditionally been associated with caring, and encouraging this trait can easily reinforce stereotyping, denigration, and exploitation of those who infuse caring behavior into teaching. When care is associated with femininity, it may reinforce institutional tendencies to exploit those who provide the care. Because care has often been provided in private homes, public scrutiny of the political use of an ethic of care has been limited. For example, political organizing for federal day care funding has been very difficult.

TEACHING THE ELEMENTARY CURRICULUM COURSE

I assume that Dewey was correct in his assertion that teachers should help students use their powers for social ends. Toward this goal, I strive to create in my courses "a community where teachers . . . come to value their own experience more, become more reflective about their practice, and receive intellectual stimulation" (Tetreault, 1987, p. 79). I work to facilitate what Belenky et al. (1986) term "really talking," which requires careful listening and implies a mutually shared agreement that together participants are creating the optimum setting so that emergent ideas can grow. Real talk reaches deep into the experience of participants and draws on their analytical abilities. It takes seriously what Bill Pink (see Chapter 9) highlighted as the socially constructed nature of the reality of teaching. Taking class time for real talk assumes that students already possess the capacities to construct powerful truths. An interest in providing real talk underlies the treatment of course readings and assignments in Elementary Curriculum.

Students read an article by Sadker and Sadker (1986) documenting how boys, compared with girls, receive more "airtime" in classroom verbal interchanges and more information from the teacher about both their schoolwork and their social behavior. One student last semester, a male in his 40s, was a first-year sixth grade teacher after 20 years of high school teaching. The move was due to declining enrollments in his high school. He commented about the Sadkers' piece: "I was a little skeptical so I went home last week and I asked the kids and they said, 'Yeah, you do that all the time.' So now I'm going to watch it a little. I was surprised." My students commented that they had never thought about sex bias in elementary school interactions. The power of studying classroom interactions and gender lies in making conscious patterns that were previously unrecognized and encouraging my students to value gender-sensitive, responsive interactions.

I recently readopted Sarason's (1982) *The Culture of the School and the Problem of Change.* Part of my rationale is that my students tend to underestimate their achievements. I will try to provide a reading of Sarason that encourages them to credit themselves for their accomplishments and knowledge, even if principals, curriculum directors, parents, or professors underestimate them. Sarason recognizes the richness and embeddedness of school culture, as well as the difficulties of working in elementary schools.

In the course, we discuss district and state policy initiatives as they affect teaching. Students mention pressure to cover textbooks and skill sheets in preparation for testing. We discuss our experiences, and I share an incident from student teacher supervision when I chanced to observe in a particular kindergarten classroom. Shortly after I entered the room, the children began 30 minutes of rotating to phonics charts and number charts around the room, while the teacher, her aide, and the student teacher "checked off" children for recognition of isolated skills, mostly phonics sounds and numerals. The pace was hurried, and the aide talked loudly to children throughout the period, making for a hectic lesson.

I tell students that I was struck by the aptness of the factory metaphor for curriculum in this room. As the children moved to their desks to begin drawing lines from pictures to letters on worksheets, a child burst into tears and put her head down on her desk. I was not surprised by the child's reaction, but was taken aback by the cooperating teacher's comments—the tears were secondary to "getting ready to read," which was what "the parents expected." I tell students that the disregard of children's feelings has the same source as the disregard for the pressures teachers feel concerning their working conditions—the perception, perhaps more oppressive for children, of having no choice.

The emotional labor of teaching is distorted and circumscribed by narrow conceptions of excellence. Emotional labor is tacit, ineffable, and non-discursive. Its ambiguity creates space that is being filled by technological "neutrality," which favors easily measurable and prepackaged knowledge. In this kindergarten, the emotional labor of teaching was being subsumed under the drive for narrow skills achievement. Caring had been forgotten, even though it is prerequisite to not doing harm. I share with students the observations of Freedman et al. (1982), who report the effects of the institution on elementary teachers. The public school arena has a value system that stresses caring and the integrity of classroom events. However, these values often contradict a school or district-wide emphasis on outcomes and administrative concerns (Erdman, 1987). I note that the kindergarten story illustrates that an interest in outcomes as skills can destroy the trust that is vital to building community.

We discuss reforms of the 1980s that ought to concern us, such as teacher career ladders. The students concur with Freedman et al. (1982) that they are unlikely to share ideas and experiences (as a community of professionals) when the success of one implies the failure of another. The point is that many caring and gifted teachers are unsuited to the managerial roles of master teachers, roles espoused by career ladders that threaten to remove talented teachers from direct contact with young people. Reforms that force teachers to compete with one another for status, and career structures that assume that the best teachers should spend their time managing other teachers, neglect the need for trust as a prerequisite to community among teachers, and give high status to managing and low status to caring for and working directly with students.

For a major paper, students spend a significant amount of time exploring topics (such as the hidden curriculum and the history of childhood) of related interest from a lengthy bibliography that I provide and orally annotate during the first week of class. A few choose topics not included on the bibliography. For example, one student, whom I will call "Julie," chose "classroom management." Initially I assumed that this reflected her interest in "control"—an interest more respectably resolved during one's first years of teaching and surely beneath the capabilities of this experienced teacher. Or had I overestimated her? Further conversation revealed that she wanted to restudy William Glasser's work (1968, 1986) and use her paper to persuade her principal to back off in his espousal of "assertive discipline." This instance exemplifies that students should be honored as intuitive knowers who may use course assignments to garner evidence to negotiate progressive conditions into their schools.

During this early period of topic selection, I discuss with students their judgments about what they need to know before they go forward with their topics. As a curriculum teacher, I strive to abandon hierarchical notions of who knows, decides, and is heard and to emphasize mutual problem-solving explorations. Most appreciate the opportunity to choose. For some—Bill Pink's "reluctant fliers" (see Chapter 9)—choosing a "practical topic" seems to create space, helping them become more open to theoretical concerns. For example, Julie's paper reflected depth and subtlety of understanding and reminded me that the meaning lies not in the topic per se but in learned experience constituted by grappling with ideas in print and discussing them with others in class.

Discussion is a community endeavor as well. Students bring three first-draft copies of their papers to class and share them with their peer editing groups, groups of three that stay together all semester so students get to know one another. The writing audience is broadened beyond the teacher to include other students who become sources of knowledge, affirmation, and critique. Class time is taken for working on assignments. While students are peer editing, I meet with those seeking individual assistance with their writing or with finding resources. This peer editing process honors the non-hierarchical vision of knowing inherent in feminist pedagogy.

TEACHING CURRICULUM WITHIN PATRIARCHY

As curriculum teachers, we can benefit from knowledge of socioeconomic, linguistic, and cultural conditions that are aspects of the problem of teaching curriculum within patriarchal communities. Such knowledge can increase our credibility and affiliation with students and move us toward gender-sensitive curriculum teaching. I will describe three aspects of the problem: socioeconomic and demographic dynamics of local communities, including public school funding; women's socialization to language and how language treats women; and the mass media, including the popular press as a critic of teachers and television as a major out-of-school curriculum.

Demographic and Socioeconomic Dynamics

We need to be aware of demographics and local socioeconomic dynamics because they affect the situations of our students who teach K–12 youngsters from low income families. Local communities have changed dramatically with regard to family makeup and economic opportunities. Two parent, two children households constitute a mere seven percent of U.S. households, and the poverty level has risen during the 1980s, a fact that should not be obscured by a drop in the unemployment rate. My students teach more children living in poverty than ever before—children who come and go from one attendance area to another every few months. Our teaching must recognize the additional demands for sensitivity and caring that this situation places on teachers.

The 1980s have reflected a loss of financial support for schools and a reduction in parental support, the latter exacerbated by the economic plight of families. Aware of financial constraints, the general public, which often feels little control over federal spending, has limited local spending. School bond approval rates, as measured by the number of elections and the value of bonds, have shown a consistent downward trend since the mid-1960s (Piele, 1983). The loss in financial resources has various negative results, including reduced options for small classes and less likelihood for public school administrators to respond to teacher initiatives and suggestions. I will clarify how this relates to teaching in a patriarchy.

Androcentrism has worked to justify diminished resources. The culture sees teaching as women's work, even though in terms of power the profession is male dominated and permeated by masculine values that downplay the centrality of caring about students (Acker, 1983). Diminished resources are culturally embedded in the history of women in teaching. In 1863 Susan B. Anthony noted that teachers were seen as having "no more brains than a woman" because teaching was seen as women's work: Teachers should expect low salaries because they compete with "the cheap labor of women" (Lerner, 1977, pp. 235–236). Anthony identified the connection between the low status of teachers in the community and the presence of women. Teaching has paid a heavy price for its inexpensive female recruits: Teachers continue to battle bias against women as well as against their profession

(Warren, 1985). For example, in 1987, at a school in a nearby farming town, a cooperating teacher described school board meeting comments from townspeople about "high" teacher salaries, salaries "especially too high because the husbands of the women teachers have good incomes, too." Bias against women heightens the need for teachers to garner and preserve resources for themselves and their schools.

Strober and Tyack (1980) elaborate on the connections among the history of teaching, gender, and control of the curriculum by those outside the classroom:

> Women's supposed comparative advantage in nurturance, patience, and understanding of children led the architects of the urban school system to slot women in primary school teaching.... By structuring jobs to take advantage of sex-role stereotypes about women's responsiveness to rule and male authority, and men's presumed ability to manage women, urban school boards were able to enhance their ability to control the curriculum, students, and personnel.... Given this purpose of tight control, women were ideal employees. With few alternative occupations and accustomed to patriarchal authority, they mostly did what their male superiors ordered. Differences of gender provided an important form of social control (p. 98).

The genderization of traits (Martin, 1985) has been applied historically to control teachers and curriculum.

Language

The next problem warranting discussion is that of "language and women's place," the apt title of a book by Robin Lakoff (1975). Donmoyer spoke, in Chapter 10, of the value of noting ethnocentric bias in language. Our efforts toward gender-sensitive curriculum teaching must be grounded in an analytical stance toward language, including how women are socialized to use it, how the language treats women, and how cultural myths about language stereotype women. Distinctions between men's and women's language reflect the cultural expectation that men and women have different interests and roles, hold different types of conversation, and react differently to other people. Lakoff has documented how women and girls are perceived to be uncertain and less credible in coed groups when they speak "the language of women," characterized by qualifiers ("a little bit"), intensifiers ("really," "very"), and the use of a questioning intonation with statements. Besides such patterns, women and girls are assumed to adhere to a level of politeness ("Oh, heck!" rather than "Aw shit!"), which reduces their forcefulness of expression. Men and boys are typically socialized to dominant forms of discourse that emphasize argument and making assertions. Such discourse runs roughshod over the politeness and tentativeness of "women's language."

When women interact with men and use the "ladylike" vocabulary and tentative stance to which they have been socialized, they may be viewed as "nice ladies but not effective." In formal interchanges, language conforms to a patriarchal paradigm wherein "knowledge is a cold, hard, straight and clear thing uttered through but not by subjects. 'One thinks.' 'It is generally believed that . . .' This is knowledge used to intimidate, to overwhelm" (Pagano, n.d., p. 11). Rethinking what it means to be a speaking subject can make us more successful in building equitable, gender-sensitive language communities in which diverse voices are heard and legitimated in our classrooms.

The myth of women as chatty liars needs revision. Women are reliable witnesses of their own experience (Stimpson, 1980). Female "chattiness" is not borne out by studies of verbal interaction in college classrooms: Men talk more than women, talk for longer periods, take more turns, exert more control over the topic, interrupt women more frequently than women interrupt them, and in their interruptions of women more often introduce trivial personal comments that change the focus of the discussion (Hall & Sandler, 1984). In summary, language provides a cultural forum that reinforces the silencing of women's perspective, experience, and wisdom.

Mass Media

The last problem is broader than the situation of patriarchy, although it is infused by that situation. The popular press and television have exacerbated teachers' need for a professional community that provides a high sense of support and purpose. The popular press increasingly reinforces negative images of teachers. Two of the common stereotypes of veteran teachers, as described in the press, are the lazy, superficial, tenured teacher, uninvolved in her work, doing as little as possible; and the "embittered, rigidly inflexible battle-ax whose class resembles an army bootcamp in atmosphere" (Freedman et al., 1982).

Teachers—our students—have been badgered by a near decade of harsh media coverage, and they work during a time characterized by reduced public respect for professionals. Young people—their students—watch television an average of 27 hours a week, making television a pervasive out-of-school curriculum. Television's portrayal of daily life, including professions, is trivialized and distorted by a lack of depth and a search for rating points upon which advertising dollars depend (Fiske, 1987). Television's coverage of women has been equally misleading. For example, television news continues to overplay the image of women as wives and mothers and to underplay their contributions in the paid labor force and as community volunteers (Kuhn, 1978). Prime time persists in depicting women as sex objects: Prostitution is much more prevalent during prime time than in society at large.

WOMEN TEACHERS: CONCLUDING REMARKS

"Juggler" is an apt metaphor for full-time teachers/part-time curriculum students, particularly the women with children. These teachers live in a public and professional culture permeated by "an androcentric denial of teaching as personalized, nurturing work that bridges home and work places [with] the need to produce [inexpensive] ... teachers who don't contest their own lack of power" (Lather, 1983, p. 19). The selective tradition of teaching includes a disrespect for women as teachers, a pejorative rather than creative connotation to their "recipe knowledge," and a disregard for their syntheses of home and school lives. Professional conceptions of "career" discount the "double day" for mothers who teach, cook, care for children, do housework, and grade papers. Occasionally, fathers assume substantial child care responsibilities, but rarely to the degree of mothers. We are silent on the lack of opportunities for job sharing or for the provision of a slower approach to tenure for parents who stay up nights feeding babies or comforting children after nightmares. Single-parent female teachers are often strapped financially, having more in common with working class people than with other middle class teachers.

Both single and married professional women with children may experience comments from colleagues, often made under the guise of "just kidding," that they should be home caring for their children. The "kidding" quickly becomes irritating when one is juggling teaching and motherhood. My students have complained about these remarks, and I have experienced them personally. Unfortunately, when I have most needed my sense of humor, it has deserted me. Women who have had full-time mothers are particularly vulnerable to accepting "guilt" in response to today's misogynist culture. If women were treated as cultural heroes, like World War II's "Rosie the Riveter," our lives would be easier and less conflicted.

We should be aware of cultural and professional bias against teachers and former teachers who are also mothers, so that we do not accept such bias uncritically ourselves and thereby undervalue some of our students. A few of my curriculum students are former teachers and currently full-time mothers who strive to stay in touch with education via graduate work. They plan to return to the classroom if the job market provides openings. The

1980s have subjected women teachers (both mothers who leave teaching and those who stay) to a frightening lack of job security, yet they do not publicly complain. They live in a culture that sees them as uncommitted to education if they stay home with children, and neglectful of their own children if they teach. Complaining publicly may be a losing proposition.

What the curriculum field has considered to be women's issues have tended to be set aside whenever there are competing theoretical claims (for example, correspondence theories and post-modernism) and policy claims (such as shifting federal and state roles), thereby overlooking their transformative potential. This tendency needs to be avoided in order that we may progress in building more inclusive communities, transforming curriculum by infusing the reproductive and productive processes of society in what and how we teach.

REFERENCES

Acker, S. (1983). Women and teaching: A semi-detached sociology of a semi-profession. In S. Walker & L. Barker (Eds.), *Gender, class, and education* (pp. 123–140). Sussex, England: Falmer Press.

Apple, M. (1986). Are teachers losing control of their skills and curriculum? *Journal of Curriculum Studies, 18* (2), 177–184.

Belenky, M. F., Clinchy, B. M., Goldberger, N. R., & Tarule, J. M. (1986). *Women's ways of knowing. The development of self, voice, and mind.* NY: Basic Books.

Davis, B. (1985). Preface. In B. H. Davis (Ed.), Feminist Education [special issue], *Journal of Thought, 20*(3), 8–24.

Erdman, J. (1981). *The structure of principal/teacher expectations: A field study of an elementary school.* Ph. D. dissertation, Madison, WI: University of Wisconsin.

Erdman, J. (1987). [Review of L. M. McNeil, *Contradictions of control: School structure and school knowledge.*] *Educational Studies, 18*(2), 297–304.

Fiske, E. (1987, April). What the media have done to the American curriculum. Paper presented at the Annual Meeting of the American Educational Research Association, Washington, DC.

Freedman, S. (1988, March). A critical look at professionalizing teachers. Paper presented at the Annual Meeting of Professors of Curriculum held in conjunction with the Annual Meeting of the Association for Supervision and Curriculum Development, Boston.

Freedman, S., Jackson, J., & Boles, K. (1982). *The effects of the institutional structure of schools on teachers.* (Contract No. NIE–G–81–0031). Washington, DC: National Institute of Education.

Glasser, W. (1968). *Schools without failure.* New York: Harper & Row.

Glasser, W. (1986). *Control theory in the classroom.* New York: Perennial Library.

Grant, C., & Sleeter, C. (1986). Race, class, and gender in educational research: An argument for integrative analysis. *Review of Educational Research, 56* (2), 195–211.

Greene, M. (1985). Sex equity as a philosophical problem. In S. Klein (Ed.), *Handbook for achieving sex equity through education* (pp. 29–43). Baltimore: Johns Hopkins University Press.

Hall, R., & Sandler, B. (1984). *Out of the classroom: A chilly campus climate for women?* Washington, DC: Project on the Status and Education of Women, Association of American Colleges, 1818 R St., NW.

Kuhn, A. (1978). Education and the sexual division of labor. In A. Kuhn & A. Wolpe (Eds.), *Feminism and materialism. Women and modes of production* (pp. 290–328). Boston: Routledge & Kegan Paul.

Lakoff, R. (1975). *Language and women's place.* New York: Harper & Row.

Lather, P. (1983). Feminism, teacher education and curricular change: Struggling mightily. Unpublished manuscript, Indiana University, Bloomington.

Lerner, G. (1977). *The female experience.* Indianapolis, IN: Bobbs-Merrill.

Martin, J. R. (1985). *Reclaiming a conversation: The ideal of the educated woman.* New Haven, CT: Yale University Press.

Messer-Davidow, E. (1985). Knowers, knowing, knowledge: Feminist theory and education. In Feminist Education [special issue], *Journal of Thought, 20*(3), 8–24.

Pagano, J. A. (n. d.). Teaching toward empowerment integrating feminist pedagogy into general education. Unpublished manuscript, Colgate University, Hamilton, NY.

Piele, P. K. (1983). Public support for public schools: The past, the future, and the federal role. *Teachers College Record, 84*(3), 690–707.

Sadker, M., & Sadker, D. (1986). Sexism in the classroom: From grade school to graduate school. *Phi Delta Kappan,* pp. 512–515.

Sarason, S. B. (1982). *The culture of the school and the problem of change* (2nd ed.). Boston: Allyn & Bacon.

Stimpson, C. (1980). The new scholarship about women: The state of the art. *Annals of Scholarship,* No. 2, 2–14.

Strober, M. H., & Tyack, D. (1980). Why do women teach and men manage? *Signs: Journal of Women in Culture and Society, 5*(3), 494–503.

Tetreault, M. K. (1987). The scholarship on women and teacher education: A case study of Lewis and Clark College. *Teacher Education Quarterly, 14*(2), 77–83.

Tetreault, M. K., & Maher, F. (1987, April). Breaking through illusion: Explorations of pedagogy in feminist classrooms. Paper presented at the Annual Meeting of the American Educational Research Association, Washington, DC.

Warren, D. (1985). Learning from experience: History and teacher education. *Educational Researcher 14*(10), 5–12.

Contestaire

MICHAEL W. APPLE
University of Wisconsin-Madison

Teaching the Politics of Curriculum

From my earlier work in *Ideology and Curriculum* (Apple, 1979) to the later arguments found in *Education and Power* (Apple, 1982) and *Teachers and Texts* (Apple, 1986), one realization—so simple yet so powerful when it is taken seriously—has guided my efforts. This is the reality of inequality and the utter importance of understanding and acting against it. For two decades, I—and many others before me (see, for example, Apple, 1985)—have urged that we not divorce our work as educators from the unequal political, economic, and cultural relations that organize our society and that have such devastating effects on the lives of children, the poor and disenfranchised, workers, women, people of color (these categories are obviously not mutually exclusive), and others.

Yet in our society, especially during the current conservative restoration (Shor, 1986), so many elements conspire to prevent us from recognizing both this reality and our own ethical responsibility to challenge it as educators who care so deeply about the lives of students and teachers. All too often, we are told to treat education as a technical enterprise, and to value teaching and curricula only for their contributions to meeting the needs of business and industry, to a "productive labor force," and to instilling a "common" set of knowledge and values defined by the conservative agenda. As the chapters by Beyer, Pink, Donmoyer, and Erdman make so very clear and as my own conversations and work with many teachers and administrators continually document, technical and conservative approaches are neither the only nor the best ways to do curriculum.

The fact that this is the case should give us reasons for optimism in the future. Not only the authors represented here, or the teachers and other educators with whom they and I work, but many others throughout the country have rejected the impersonal and the merely technical, the ideological agenda of the right, and the overly bureaucratic methods of efficiency experts pretending to be educators. How to turn this rejection against them and into a more mature understanding of where these approaches have come from, who benefits from them, and what we must do to defend and build education worthy of its name is a major question. The stories these authors tell attest that building this understanding is not easy, but is still doable. I am certain we could all add more. The stories of "resisters" are counterbalanced by those in which the teaching has been markedly successful in creating conditions in which our students become more socially and ethically reflective. This is, of course, a large part of our task. And, as with all teaching, there are no guarantees of success. However, to the extent that we create a critically reflective "community" with our students and colleagues and then extend that community to those who are bearing the brunt of the inequalities that dominate our society, we will be acting in a way that is of no little importance not just educationally but socially as well.

What we must do is connect these criticisms of existing educational theories, policies, and practices to the lived experiences of teachers, administrators, and other educators. This needs to be done in a way that is not condescending, that is not so esoteric as to prevent understanding and application, and that is linked to concrete alternatives (see Bastian et al., 1985). Otherwise, what we do is to leave a legacy of mistrust or to simply recreate what we wish to replace—an elitism in which critical theories have no place or time for the day-to-day realities teachers face.

Because of this, we should not dismiss the mistrust of theory—critical or otherwise—by some teachers and administrators in our classes. This mistrust has its progressive side. After all, too many of the curriculum theories and proposals we wish to question and replace have been unconnected to the lives, hopes, and fears of schoolpeople. Just as important, in gender terms, such theorizing often has been done by a group of academics who are usually male and who have applied their theories to the work of teachers, most of whom are women (Apple, 1986). The gender politics in curriculum theory and practice—and the teaching about them—need to be taken much more seriously, something Jean Erdman so nicely points to. This again means that we need to take honest criticism of our position seriously and work even harder to make it understandable and applicable.

In our critical work and in our teaching about curriculum, part of our task is *naming*. We must give words to the suffering, to the struggles of parents, teachers, and others inside and outside schools to build a more democratic and responsive educational system. And we must name—concretely and specifically—who the winners and losers are in our current social arrangements.

Such naming requires that we actively overcome the selective tradition in curriculum studies. When, in our own discourse, education is reduced to the language of behavioral psychology, to standardized techniques, and to economic functions as defined by the powerful, then the intensely ethical and political nature of curriculum and teaching is marginalized. We and our students are kept from seeing such things as the relationship between poverty and achievement, the connections between the growth of industrialized and bureaucratic models of controlling education and the fact that teaching has historically been defined as women's paid work, and the fact that the knowledge of dominant groups tends to be taught in the school curriculum (Apple, 1986). This means that part of our efforts as curriculum teachers must be in providing our students with critical tools (and examples of their use) that have their bases in feminist, antiracist, and critical political traditions. Yet, to do this, it is essential that our students see these more democratic traditions not as new, as "oddities" that somehow have just been discovered, but as having played such a crucial role *continually* in the history of curriculum debate itself (Kliebard, 1986; Teitelbaum, 1988). History plays a part here in making legitimate our continuation of the long tradition of democratic political understanding of and action on curriculum and teaching.

None of this will be easy. Retrogressive tendencies in education are connected in identifiable ways to similar tendencies in the larger society. To act in the educational arena and to have such action have long lasting effects requires joining with others to act in that larger society as well. From such shared political understanding and action, a discourse and practice of democratic education can evolve. And we and our students together, with others, can build for the common good (Raskin, 1986) and show the technocrats why education isn't simply training.

REFERENCES

Apple, M. W. (1979). *Ideology and Curriculum*. Boston: Routledge & Kegan Paul.

Apple, M. W. (1982). *Education and Power*. Boston: Routledge & Kegan Paul.

Apple, M. W. (1985). There Is a River: James B. Macdonald and Curriculum Theorizing. *Journal of Curriculum Theorizing, 6*(5), 9–18.

Apple, M. W. (1986). *Teachers and Texts: A Political Economy of Class and Gender Relations in Education.* New York: Routledge & Kegan Paul.

Bastian, A., et al. (1985). *Choosing Equality: The Case for Democratic Schooling.* Philadelphia: Temple University Press.

Kliebard, H. M. (1986). *The Struggle for the American Curriculum 1893–1958.* Boston: Routledge & Kegan Paul.

Raskin, M. (1986). *The Common Good.* New York: Routledge & Kegan Paul.

Shor, Ira (1986). *Culture Wars.* New York: Routledge & Kegan Paul.

Teitelbaum, K. (1988). Contestation and Curriculum: The Efforts of American Socialists, 1900–1920. In L. E. Beyer & M. W. Apple (Eds.), *The Curriculum: Problems, Politics and Possibilities.* Albany: State University of New York Press.

Conversation parmi animateurs

O. L. DAVIS, JR.
University of Texas at Austin

PAUL KLOHR
Ohio State University

NORM OVERLY
Indiana University

DAVIS: I liked the use of community as a starting point. Most of the examples given by these authors struck me as examples of community built within a particular course. For example, dealing deliberately in a curriculum course with gender, economic, cultural, and other concerns is absolutely important for self-realization.

OVERLY: Agreed. But, these authors tend to see community in a more restrictive political manner than I do. Not that I dismiss the political perspective, but I think my religious background has influenced me. I can't separate my religious teaching from my totality, which includes my professional concerns in education. The sociopolitical view is not the only view of community; there is also the human, personal community. Community isn't just institutional relationships. We need to broaden this concept.

KLOHR: At the national level there were some projects to personalize institutional efforts. ASCD, in an earlier time, was interested in decentralization. In the late 1950s, the Cooperative Action Program for Curriculum Improvement (CAPCI) was an early effort at networking within its professional community. We were trying to focus on some big issues, like involvement of teachers in their own supervision of instruction. We wanted groups of schools within a state or among states to work collaboratively on these issues, sharing their experiences and ultimately providing feedback to the national organization. This is, of course, quite different from the top-down model used by some organizations today. CAPCI was an attempt to develop cooperation at a variety of levels, beginning with teachers within one school building.

DAVIS: This notion of building a community at one site is terribly important. I wish more people appreciated the importance of this—the idea that community is built in one place and seen as an analogue to be constructed in another setting. Today's reality, though, does not reflect such an appreciation. Teachers in every setting are alone; teaching is a lonely profession. Community is indeed more than institutional relationships, but most institutional settings simply offer few opportunities for individuals to *build* a community within that institution.

OVERLY: Or to maintain the community that we are in. When I started teaching, my very first year, I felt that the building I was in really had a sense of community that was separate from, and, in a sense, politically active against, the superintendent. We didn't rebel against the superintendent, but we didn't see things the same way. For example, he had a requirement that we have a schedule posted about the subjects we were teaching and the number of minutes in each subject. As a school, and as individual teachers, we didn't believe in that. Now, whenever the superintendent came around to visit, he parked in a lot that was visible to the kindergarten teacher. As soon as she spotted his car, she sent a student with a blank note to all the teachers in the building to alert us so we could switch from whatever we were doing to the posted curriculum. I realize that this is a kind of political action, but there was also a feeling within the classroom of the human, personal element. I don't see that as being intentionally political, even though it was an effective (political) behavior.

KLOHR: Well, it seems to me that these authors talk about a larger community that differs from the concept of community that characterized the 1960s. The gurus in education then, such as Edgar Friedenberg and Paul Goodman, influenced my work quite a bit. But, they were addressing the problems of community often in a way that seemed very difficult to take hold of from the point of view of curriculum. Their criticisms of the schools and the lack of community within them, other than making one more conscious of the problem, were such that solutions were difficult to project. When Landon Beyer and Bill Pink, on the other hand, talk about the politicization of the teacher and the students, they give me a sense of how one might effect that in one way or another.

OVERLY: But, that's precisely what unsettles me about the pieces in this section, Paul. These authors portray the community writ large: as the government, as the other, as something out there. They want teachers to become participants or directors of the wider-than-school community. Certainly teachers have the right to be energized by and to be a part of the wider traditions in the political community, but the development of a sense of communities of shared interests and commitments on a smaller, more personal level is also needed. Moreover, there needs to be a sense of shared intentionality in relationships, something often missing from existing political relationships.

DAVIS: To my way of thinking, the way that the writers of these essays conceive of their job is to invade the world of another person with the intention of transforming or of the world being transformed. These are not neutral people. These writers indicate that there are political dimensions to their work, whether it be with their children at home or with their students in the classroom. We are invading their lives, however benignly. In recognizing this, rather than being arrogant about it, I think we must approach our role as a sensitive invader and ask their forgiveness. This is a theological statement. We're asking forgiveness for messing up their lives. We have agendas. We would like for others to be enriched or empowered—even when they are satisfied with who they are.

OVERLY: Perhaps that's why I was struck by Pink's metaphor of the different types of fliers. You are making a judgment about those who are resisting, saying "They don't understand." Maybe they simply like the world as they see it. I found the frequent flier metaphor a useful way of categorizing the kind of responses I get in my own classes. It gets to a problem that I have; am I pushing students hard enough? At what point is it okay to allow them to exist in ignorance—if I want to make the judgment? Am I pushing them hard enough to overcome their fear of flying? As a curriculum teacher, I am concerned about those with whom I am unsuccessful. We always hold out the possibility that somewhere down the line they will reflect on the set of experiences we shared and find that it was good. But, there is also the possibility that they may never reflect on it.

DAVIS: You've hit on what's probably a universal concern of all teachers, Norm. Over the years, I've come to see a distinction between the intentional and consequential understandings of teaching. When I work with practicing teachers who've taught all day and come into class in late afternoon, I accept the fact that they want to know little about curriculum or their craft. They're stressed out; they want or need to get a certificate or pay raise. If they learn something, well that's super. But, don't push it. Under these circumstances, it seems to me that the most important element in my teaching is to have them catch fire. I remember Bob Gilchrist telling how, as a curriculum director, he wanted to see his district's teachers setting fires all around. His role was not to fight these brush fires but to fan them! I guess what I'm suggesting is that our efforts need to be understood as modest. We may only be able to build a rich memory. For most of the students, my course is not a Damascus Road sort of experience.

OVERLY: That's true. Beyer's story of Poduska is an encouraging example of the power of such an experience. I doubt that her's was a modal type of response, however. She had much more experience and maturity than most preservice teachers. So, while I do think that teaching from a community perspective is very helpful, I see that act as starting with the student's personal history. I have a considerable problem with the neo-Marxist position. It is a strength, however, to use this perspective in teaching curriculum because it provides another way of looking at what's going on. People just don't naturally look critically at the society around them.

KLOHR: And, that's exactly what pleased me about the essays in this section, Norm; the authors address normative, value-based questions. Regardless of whether we label it neo-Marxist or something else, this focus has been largely lost on the national level for many of us. To have it so clearly reflected in these essays is important. Otherwise, the whole business of community becomes just a set of critical essays that are important and necessary, but not sufficient.

OVERLY: Well, as you might've guessed, I felt most comfortable with the Donmoyer chapter. I found his three conceptions of politics and the exercise of power very useful. This kind of generic approach, if that's the word, is more amenable to my own approach. It may be a way of avoiding the forcing of persons to confront their interpretation of community. That's something that I am struggling with personally. As a curriculum teacher, the battle for me is how teachers can use abstract ideas in their day-to-day working place. How to remain genuinely open when part of the process is trying to get people to change and take a stand. How do you transfer your desires? Aren't we, as curriculum teachers, really wanting to teach students something other than just letting them confirm what they already know?

DAVIS: Before we finish here, let me just say that there is another dimension to community that I would like to have seen: the community of generations. One of the things that struck me when I read these chapters was that there are people who are contributors here who were classmates or students, at different times, of the same teacher. There is an obvious community of interest, a community of experience, a community of scholarship, a community of language, and a community of intention, which is easy to spot. That didn't develop casually. It didn't just happen. It came about through the intent of thoughtful measuring and working as protégés over some extended period of time. This is another sort of community about which the curriculum field has not been self-consciously aware until the last 10 or 15 years.

PART IV

TEACHING FROM THE PERSPECTIVE OF THE FIELD

We are within one era of the centennial anniversary of the birth of curriculum as a field of study. The present and preceding three eras have generated landmark publications such as Parker's *Talks on Pedagogics: Theory of Concentration* and the *Cardinal Principles of Education,* the *27th Yearbook of the NSSE* and Dewey's *Democracy and Education,* Tyler's *Basic Principles of Curriculum and Instruction* and Phenix's *Realms of Meaning,* Pinar's *Curriculum Theorizing: The Reconceptualists* and Eisner's *The Educational Imagination.* The field also has endured battles over curriculum form and substance such as those between Snedden and Dewey on the vocational versus liberal curriculum; the Bode and Childs' imposition controversy, Johnson's and Macdonald's differing conceptions of the role of theory in educational practice, and the Pinar–Apple conflict between poetics and critical theory. Curriculum workers have advanced our understanding of the field through landmark research endeavors, including Hall's Child Study Movement, the Eight Year Study, *Man a Course of Study,* and Goodlad's *A Place Called School.* And, we have witnessed watershed events—James' Harvard Lectures, *Talks to Teachers;* the 1932 Progressive Education Association Meeting, and the curriculum theory conferences in 1947 at the University of Chicago and in 1973 at Rochester. These ideas, struggles, contributions, and events contour curriculum as a field of study. For some, these also represent the starting point for teaching and thinking about curriculum.

The importance of teaching curriculum from the perspective of the field of study is well stated by the authors of these four chapters. Edmund Short begins in Chapter 12 by lamenting the trend toward trivialization in the curriculum field. Short argues that in order to empower persons through curriculum studies, teachers of curriculum must challenge this trend. Stressing the importance of a research base, Short outlines a teaching approach focusing on "the nature of the research logic, theory, and procedure associated with formal critical inquiry" as he moves his students to alternative ways of thinking and coping with practical curriculum concerns.

William Schubert's concern, in Chapter 13, is directed toward the lack of serious consideration given to the question of worth in the curriculum development process. Empowerment, Schubert contends, can occur only when this fundamental question is addressed by curriculum developers. Following a brief description of the historical antecedents to this question, Schubert asserts that the experientialist position is the most appropriate platform from which to explore this issue. Schubert concludes by detailing a variety of pedagogical strategies for engaging students in dialogue on this fundamental debate.

In Chapter 14 Paul Shaker details his 15-year odyssey in the teaching of curriculum with preservice teachers. Committed to a new understanding of curriculum studies, and determined to expose these students to an integrative learning model, Shaker couples an interactive classroom format with nontraditional media such as films and attitudinal instruments and unconventional content such as depth psychology, metaphysics, and phenomenology. The result, Shaker claims, is that "preservice teachers . . . become aware of a feeling of inspiration in their own preparation [and] are given the capacity to elicit the same in their students." At the end of the chapter, he provides a set of curriculum principles for the teaching of preservice teachers.

Concerned about the simplemindedness of pedagogy and content of most curriculum development courses, Craig Kridel outlines, in Chapter 15, an approach that satisfies both his students' routine desire for recipes, lists, and models and his determination to expose them to the "heart of the field." Using photographs, recordings, films, and primary historical material, Kridel resurrects curriculum workers of the past, such as Bode, Counts, and Alberty. In the process Kridel details how fundamental curricular issues, such as indoctrination and control, are discussed from both a historical and contemporary perspective. The experiences in assembling these teaching materials and suggestions for others interested in teaching curriculum from a historical-biographical approach are also described.

12

Challenging The Trivialization of Curriculum Through Research

EDMUND C. SHORT
Pennsylvania State University

My doctoral studies were at Teachers College, Columbia University (1965), working with Florence B. Stratemeyer in the Department of Curriculum and Teaching, chairperson of my committee, and with Arno A. Bellack, Dwayne E. Huebner, and Philip H. Phenix. From my early days in under-graduate preparation for secondary English teaching, I found myself committed to checking assertions made by others through personal investigation and experience before I would accept them. This has become the foundation of my way of working with college students and others in my teaching and research. This approach became grounded for me in Dewey's pragmatism and approach to inquiry. It has led to a high regard for the knowledge base for professional practice, to either question or confirm it, and to a strong conviction that such knowledge can be found by each professional person after undertaking the relevant inquiry. Thus, even in a highly problematic field of study and practice such as curriculum, I believe the road to sound practice is through research and inquiry, and I strive always to initiate my students into the habit and mysteries of reflective inquiry.

In teaching curriculum, I have tried a lot of approaches in both graduate and undergraduate courses: the typical survey course built around a synoptic text, a practical how to do curriculum development course, a sophisticated theory and research course, a standard works course focused on classics in the field and their authors (something like Craig Kridel describes in Chapter 15), and a venture into students' philosophical bases for their curricular platforms and proposals (something like William

Schubert focuses on in Chapter 13). The approach I want to highlight here is a fairly new one for me—addressing a single issue in curriculum for an entire semester. The issue around which I have organized a course is the trivialization of curriculum.

Have you noticed how frequently some assertion regarding the trivialization of curriculum has been made in recent books and articles? Apparently, evidence is mounting for describing what is happening in curriculum in a number of settings as trivialization. If this is a major, widespread trend, it deserves serious attention in our thinking about and teaching curriculum issues. It is a subject worthy of increased attention by curriculum researchers and practitioners. In my judgment, it is a trend that needs to be challenged, and I believe there are some research techniques and some research knowledge that can help in this effort. In any teaching that relates to curriculum studies, it is important to address the topic of trivialization and to introduce students to the knowledge and relevant research approaches that can assist them in counteracting this trend.

Trivialization, in the context of the curriculum, refers to instances in which the curriculum is conceived or enacted in a way that oversimplifies, renders it less stimulating or demanding, requires little judgment and expertise by the teacher, or obscures the real ideologies that are embedded in it. This chapter will first cite a number of persons who assert or present evidence that trivialization is occurring; then it will offer some means by which the tendency toward trivialization can be challenged. The thrust of this approach will be to argue that research has been done (or that could be done) in curriculum studies is essential if trivialization in curriculum policies and practices is to be seen for what it really is—an uncritical stance and an unacceptable tendency for educators to pursue. Some of the available research that assists in revealing the shallowness of the norms inherent in trivialization will be cited. Finally, the chapter will argue the necessity of teaching the understandings made available through critical research in any course offered in curriculum studies in order to empower persons to discover and overcome the effects of trivialization.

RECENT REFERENCES TO TRIVIALIZATION

A number of writers have recently commented on practices that contribute to the trivialization of curriculum. Frymier (1986, p. 648) argues that the process of centrally legislating curriculum leads to freezing the curriculum and hampers curriculum improvement. He also refers (1987, p. 14) to the "neutering of teachers" as a result of increased centralization and bureaucratization—processes that take away teacher's right to make curricular and instructional decisions. White (1987, p. 24) discussed the narrowing of the conceptualization of teaching that is often embedded in the curriculum of teacher education, and concluded that this results in the trivialization of teaching. Ornstein and Hunkins (1988, pp. 307–308) summarize in their textbook review of the current curriculum situation the tendency toward trivial curriculum. Urban (1987, p. 33) points out the routinized and trivialized classroom learnings that result from mandated teacher evaluation systems in Georgia, which are based on set repertoires of performances. Welsh (1986, pp. 122–132) reports as a teacher in *Tales Out of School* that content coverage and testing are driving the curriculum, while the students dismiss the content as unimportant for living their lives or perhaps engage it only enough to avoid hassles.

Character education is being trivialized through the political biases of Department of Education officials in Washington, reports Lewis (1987). Darling-Hammond (1987, pp. 28–29) observes that teachers are often asked to substitute "procedure-following for the enhancement of learning" through what is prescribed by a heavily regulated curriculum. Zumwalt (1988, p. 158) fears good teachers are dropping out of teaching because they refuse to see teaching simply as workbook supervision, covering the text, or preparing students for standardized tests. Tanner (1988, p. 133) and Sewall (1988) take note of the phenomenon of "dumbing down" textbooks to avoid controversial material. Wise (1988) sounds an alarm over an array of curricular mandates, predetermined through legislation, that leave teachers and their clients unable to control their own learning situations and thus unable to attain the quality of educational outcomes desired by the public. Shulman (1988), in discussing the development of professional assessments of teaching, cautions against the trivializing of teaching by testing whether the teacher has been teaching to the test. People who advocate a rigorous, less flexible core curriculum for all students are doing so on the grounds that many "junk courses" now exist and that these should not be offered (Kearns, 1988, p. 569).

The research literature also provides evidence of the existence of trivialization of curriculum and teaching. Apple (1986, p. 32) has identified the loss of control over decision making by teachers and other local educators when the conception and execution of curricular and instructional plans are separated from each other. The former is done higher in the hierarchy, and the latter is left to the teachers—thereby deskilling teachers, that is, reducing their tasks to ones that can be carried out with a minimum of professional knowledge and judgment. Curriculum packages containing preset content, teaching procedures, and student responses contributed greatly to trivialization of learning and teaching. Shor and Freire (1987, pp.

75–76) summarize this effect of "teacher-proof" curriculums that tell teachers how to assign and test regardless of student differences, as if learning were easily designed, monitored, and measured by managerial models of teaching rather than professional ones. Case studies by McNeil (1986, pp. 209–210) forcefully demonstrate teachers' loss of power to make critical professional decisions in planning as well as in enacting curriculum. Controlling students rather than educating them becomes the primary goal, and role enforcement supported by a bureaucratic ethic, rather than creative educational planning and teaching, dominates teachers' thoughts and actions.

Standardization of the curriculum is another factor contributing to its trivialization. Apple (1986, pp. 187–188) has summarized studies that document the use of highly systematized and rationalized curriculums that employ standardized textbooks, learning competencies, teaching processes, and testing procedures. Goodlad (1984, pp. 197–270) also found evidence of similar practices and the consequent stifling of active, unfettered learning. McNeil (1988c) cites evidence of what she calls proficiency-based curriculums—ones in which content is reduced to elements that can be sequenced, numbered, monitored, tested, and reported on, with the student obligated to accept, master, and test-out on them as if there were no problems or alternative ideas inherent in the content. Ease of testing becomes a leading criterion for curriculum content. Madaus (1988) documents the effects of these testing practices on curriculum over the last several decades and concludes that measurement-driven instruction is, and always has been, devastating to both the curriculum breadth and teaching flexibility needed to ensure high quality education. The curriculum is narrowed to preparing for exams. Madaus asserts that test results should be only one element to be considered in deciding on curriculum goals and enactment policies, and the tendency to standardize the curriculum through the use of easy-to-administer tests should be resisted, even by measurement experts.

Shor and Freire (1987, pp. 5, 9–10, 18, 122) report that students are withdrawing into a "culture of silence" because the content of the curriculum is so trivial or dull that it can no longer engage them meaningfully in significant learning. Massive transfer of knowledge by teacher lectures and/or demands to master or memorize the official content brings on what may be called a "performance strike" by students. Or they invent phony, defensive language to disguise their disengagement with the material presented. Frequent testing has not always had the positive motivational effects on students that advocates assert, according to Madaus (1988, pp. 98–105). Teachers' efforts to control and thereby enhance learning frequently backfire into a situation where classroom order, control, and compliance with rules and instructional procedures become dominant and teachers begin to teach defensively (McNeil, 1986, pp. 157–190). They accommodate to the pressures they themselves are under from external mandates by choosing instructional processes they think will lighten their workload or will minimize student resistance as much as possible. They also may choose to simplify content and reduce demands made on students in order to ensure their success on tests (Sedlak, et al., 1986, p. 101).

McNeil (1988b) designates four strategies used by teachers to trivialize curriculum content: (1) the *fragmenting* of knowledge into lists of facts, outlines of key points, fill-in-the-blank exercises, and the like, with no opportunity for student discussion of this fragmentary knowledge in relation to "richer" information they may have gained from other sources; (2) the *mystification* of knowledge by suggesting that its complexities are too great for students to understand and that they need only be aware of the topic (this despite evidence that the teachers themselves know and understand such topics); (3) the *omission* of controversial, anomalous, or contemporaneous material, presumably in order to avoid long discussions that get in the way of covering required content and preparing students efficiently for their tests; and (4) *defensive simplification*, meaning the ritual of seeming to deal with topics while actually not teaching them or requiring them to be learned. Here the intent is to avoid active resistance by students to what is perceived by them as difficult content to master. This procedure parallels what has been observed by other researchers (such as Powell, et al., 1985, and Sedlak, et al., 1986) and is often defined as a compact agreed to by both teachers and students and perceived to be mutually advantageous given the institutional constraints under which they both live in schools.

The existence of the trivial curriculum in some schools is, therefore, well documented, and some of its causes are being identified. Irrelevant content, watered down texts, oversimplified treatment of subject matter, routinized teaching procedures, readily consumable and measurable course requirements, acceptance of appealing electives in place of basic knowledge—these are characteristic of the trivial curriculum. In summary, the trivial curriculum is a result of a number of factors: (1) teacher deskilling, (2) mandated curriculum and testing practices, (3) credentialing schemes, (4) the operation of schools on bureaucratic rather than professional and educational norms, and (5) the contradictions inherent in teachers being required to follow prescribed practices in both the content and the implementation of the curriculum without having the power necessary to influence the policies governing these prescriptions (Saras & Short, 1988). The question is whether the trend toward the trivialization of the curriculum will continue or be reversed.

CHALLENGING THE TREND

Why should this trend be reversed? What can be done to reverse it? The trend toward trivialization of the curriculum can be seen to be undesirable from a number of different perspectives. From one perspective, that of cost–benefit analysis (Apple, 1986, p. 181), we are not getting our money's worth from our investment in education if what is being learned by a large number of students is limited, trivial, and superficial. This suggests that those factors contributing to the trivialization of curriculum that are a result of current policy choices must be re-examined. While control of school knowledge, regulation of school practices, and hierarchical authority in decision making and planning may have appeared to be appropriate ways for policy makers to ensure excellence in education, the evidence is to the contrary. These policies have contributed in various ways to the trivialization of curriculum, and the support of these policies is consequently fiscally irresponsible. To attain the stated goals for education in the United States, which are largely shared by citizens and professional educators alike, funds need to be diverted to alternative policies that support authentic teaching and learning and that recover some degree of congruence between the enacted curriculum and the stated curriculum. This is not to whitewash the stated curriculum if it too needs to be re-examined. This simply recognizes that incentives and sanctions that support desirable curriculum responses by administrators, teachers, and students must be put into place if the tendency toward curriculum trivialization is to be reversed.

From another perspective, that of consistency between intentions and actions, we must recognize the discrepancies that exist in the curriculum realities we face. On purely prudential grounds, no legitimate evaluation of what is happening to teachers and students in places where trivialization is in evidence can overlook the facts regarding discrepancies between what we say we want and what we are getting as a result of this tendency. Limited or distorted forms of evaluation may find satisfactory results on various measures of achievement or improvement. This, however, can be a function of discrepancies between the measures designed or chosen and the stated curriculum intentions (Madaus, 1988). An honest effort to use appropriate forms of curriculum and instructional evaluation must be inaugurated in order to obtain an accurate picture of the congruence or lack of congruence between intentions and results. And then we must let the evidence obtained in this manner speak for itself, apart from anyone's wishful thinking or unwillingness to look at the facts. Where these carefully gathered facts suggest that something undesirable is occurring as a product of the trivialization of curriculum, something different must be initiated to reverse the trend. We must inquire into what factors are causing or contributing to trivialization in a particular setting and begin to identify what it will take to rectify the situation. Letting things slide is not a good strategy for ensuring that curriculum intentions are as fully realized in practice as possible.

A third perspective is the ethical perspective. We should not allow students or teachers (or administrators, policy makers, or the public) to believe that a good education is obtainable under conditions associated with the trivialization of curriculum. To do so is unethical. We must challenge people's self-deceptions that what they are experiencing is authentic education. While we may sympathize with their attempts to cope with unfortunate circumstances by the various survival strategies they feel compelled to employ, we must ethically admit that what is happening is not good education and that we must not settle for trivialization as the best that can be hoped for. Things can be changed to permit schooling to be truly educative, not simply adaptive to undesirable forces and circumstances. To challenge this tolerance of the trivial, the mediocre, and the influences that contribute to them, some major systematic changes will be necessary as well as some readjusting of particular classroom practices. But even more necessary will be the reassertion of a vision of what constitutes a desirable education, a justifiable, nontrivial curriculum, and good structures and strategies for enacting it, as suggested by Schubert in Chapter 13. No doubt, part of the cause of the rise of the trivialized curriculum is the loss of vision or commitment to a conception of curriculum and what constitutes an educated person by those who influence the policies and practices of schooling. If this has been lost or was never well articulated in the stated curriculum, let alone in the minds of all parties concerned, then the first task is to rethink and reformulate an understanding of what is desired in a good curriculum. Then we must act ethically to realize that ideal in the daily activities of education.

In summary, the trend toward the trivialization of the curriculum needs to be challenged for reasons of public accountability, intellectual integrity and honesty, and those ethical norms that represent the desire for the best education possible for our children and the least damage to students, teachers and other educators, and ultimately the society at large. As curriculum teachers, will we be able to challenge the tendency toward trivialization? Perhaps, but only if we understand the phenomenon and why it needs to be challenged.

ROLE OF TEACHING IN CHALLENGING TRIVIALIZATION

Those of us teaching courses in curriculum studies and related topics have the opportunity and the obligation to help people understand trivialization and how to rectify it. To ignore this problem is to enhance the hiddenness of curriculum trivialization and to prolong its existence. There are several ways of dealing with this topic in teaching curriculum courses. One is to recognize the research that has been done on the problem and to make it accessible to students. I find student responses to reading the work of Apple (1986), McNeil (1986, 1988a, 1988b, 1988c), and others cited in this chapter quite dramatic. They range from almost outright disbelief, to horror, to intelligent concern. Seldom do students come away from such knowledge unaffected. Often they identify similar instances of trivialization in their own school settings, which they had never recognized or labeled as such before. Often they undertake research projects to determine whether trivialization, in its various forms, exists in particular schools and to look into the policies and practices that give rise to it. Often they become motivated to work toward reversing the trend toward trivialization when they have demonstrated its existence and/or its effects. Some challenging reports have been written as a result (Saras & Short, 1988).

My experience in teaching curriculum this way is somewhat like teaching literature. I lay out the various works to be read and let them speak for themselves. Some of them move students more than others and some not at all. Some students barely respond to any of these works themselves, though they may respond to the seminar discussions we hold on them. Whatever happens or does not happen is all right with me. I have no compulsion to demand that things be seen as the authors see them or as I see them. Nevertheless, as I have said, evidence of trivialization tends to convince students that it is a problem to which a response is required. So, from my point of view as a curriculum teacher, the things I do in dealing with this topic are not different, pedagogically, from any other teaching I do. I help clarify what is read, raise questions about its meaning and import, and try to evoke imaginative but realistic courses of action that students might feel compelled to take in light of their new understanding of curriculum trivialization. Most of the time this approach turns out to be quite satisfactory.

More important than anything I engage in as a teacher during actual classes and related activities is my choice of what to lay before students to read and confront. This factor is highlighted by Shaker in Chapter 14. My primary contribution, perhaps my only special contribution, is in deciding the content through which trivialization can be recognized and/or issues about it can be raised. For anyone who teaches curriculum and who chooses to deal with the topic of trivialization, the topics chosen for reading and discussion are the most crucial decisions to be made. Should they be of the kind that assert the existence of a trend toward trivialization, with or without concrete examples? Should they present solid evidence of instances of it? Should they be research findings? One needs always to look for new readings or examples of whatever type one thinks might be appropriate. If some curriculum teachers are not aware of what is available, the choices will necessarily be limited. That is why I gave so much space in this chapter to citing and summarizing the material I have come across and used; it may save others a great deal of searching. Of course, there are bound to be reports that I have overlooked or others that will become available as time goes on.

In my own classes, I stress research-based reports because I want my students to have real evidence, not simply assertions. Inquiry-desired knowledge is what I want them to value and to create themselves. Teaching this research knowledge seems to contribute to empowering persons to discover and to help overcome the undesirable consequences of trivialization in situations they may face. I do not want to be charged with instigating political action through direct instruction, so I always teach the research knowledge on this topic as I do any kind of knowledge, that is, critically. I ask students to explore the reports of scholars both sympathetically, to find out what the scholars found out, but also critically, to ascertain any flaws in their inquiries or biases in their conclusions. This leads inevitably to teaching how this kind of research is done. We examine the theoretical and procedural aspects of work by Apple, McNeil, and others in a dialogical process (Gitlin & Goldstein, 1987). Not only is this critical process helpful to understand the studies being read and their research procedures; it also suggests a model of inquiry for the students' own work. Students come to realize that we tend to accept uncritically the factors that contribute to the trivialization of the curriculum, because we do not recognize the contradictions between stated goals or norms and what is practiced. When inquiry methods for detecting these kinds of contradictions are identified in the studies we examine, students become quite eager to learn for their own purposes the mode of inquiry that will enable them to do the same thing.

Ultimately, then, I am asked to teach this form of inquiry directly to them. We focus on the nature of the research logic, theory, and procedure associated with formal critical inquiry. The best book I have found to assist with this task is one by Carr and Kemmis (1986). Because it focuses on formal critical inquiry within an action-research context, this treatment is readily understood in terms of how it can be used in a particular school setting and how decisions to change the trivial curriculum can arise right out of evidence unearthed in that setting about its existence, causes, and effects. What is at the heart of this process of formal critical inquiry, of course, is uncovering the real norms operating in the situation and demonstrating how they and their associated practices are at odds with the stated or assumed norms that underlie or provide the implicit rationale for the curriculum being enacted. The primary tool of the critical inquirer is to assume a normative stance from which to examine the operative norms and the intended norms and to observe the contradictions between the researcher's stance and these other norms. Not surprisingly, a great many things can be seen in this way that might not otherwise be detected if one observed from a frame of reference that was itself congruent normatively with what was being studied. Students are usually quite impressed with the power of this method of 'looking through other eyes or perspectives or norms.'

A natural follow-up to this direct instruction in how critical inquiry is conducted is to have students do it. I am almost never able to learn how students fare in this endeavor because they do it after they leave my courses and conduct their action inquiries in their own educational settings over an extended period of time. I hear from time to time that they are doing critical action research and that the process has been easy enough to follow. Whether they are actually able to make a dent in the trivialization of the curriculum I must wait and see, but I suspect they will, at least to some degree.

CONCLUSION

What can I say from my experiences with this chain of teaching topics and strategies? Not much, because I haven't done it very often yet. Still, I find I have few problems with this approach and lots of positive things happen— many more than when I deal with conventional curriculum topics in conventional ways. Last semester all but one student got excited about the problem of trivialization. Everyone read a great deal on the topic and related matters without being forced to do so. Discussions were never dull and in every case led us into conventional curriculum issues and topics, so that I did not have to follow a regular textbook outline to be sure we dealt with the basic knowledge of the field of curriculum. Students moved quickly into familiarity with critical inquiry—a goal I do not often attain or even attempt in my traditional classes. In short, it was highly motivating, expansive in terms of the range of study we were able to undertake, and transformative of students' ways of thinking and dealing with practical curriculum issues.

I end with a plea that those of us who teach curriculum studies should try something like I have outlined here with their students. Try to expose them to the reality and the dilemma of curriculum trivialization. Give them access to research studies that inquire into it and the knowledge that such studies provide. And equip them with the appropriate inquiry skills needed to deal with it in their own ways in their own realms of action. See if you have similar results.

REFERENCES

Apple, M. W. (1986). *Teachers and Texts.* New York: Routledge & Kegan Paul.

Carr, W., & Kemmis, S. (1986). *Becoming Critical: Education, Knowledge, and Action Research.* Philadelphia: Falmer Press.

Darling-Hammond, L. (1987). The Over-regulated Curriculum and the Press for Teacher Professionalism. *NASSP Bulletin, 71*(498), 22–29.

Frymier, J. (1986). Legislating Centralization. *Phi Delta Kappan, 67*(9), 646–648.

Frymier, J. (1987). Bureaucracy and the Neutering of Teachers. *Phi Delta Kappan, 69*(1), 9–14.

Gitlin, A., & Goldstein, S. (1987). A Dialogical Approach to Understanding: Horizontal Evaluation. *Educational Theory, 37*(1), 17–27.

Goodlad, J. I. (1984). *A Place Called School: Prospects for the Future.* New York: McGraw-Hill.

Kearns, D. T. (1988). An Education Recovery Plan for America. *Phi Delta Kappan, 69*(8), 565–570.

Lewis, A. C. (1987). A Word About Character. *Phi Delta Kappan, 68*(10), 724–725.

Madaus, G. F. (1988). The Influence of Testing on the Curriculum. In L. N. Tanner, Ed., *Critical Issues in Curriculum.* 87th Yearbook of the National Society for the Study of Education, Part I. Chicago: University of Chicago Press, pp. 83–121.

McNeil, L. M. (1986). *Contradictions of Control: School Structure and School Knowledge.* New York: Routledge & Kegan Paul.

McNeil, L. M. (1988a). Contradictions of Control, Part 1: Administrators and Teachers. *Phi Delta Kappan, 69*(5), 333–339.

McNeil, L. M. (1988b). Contradictions of Control, Part 2: Teachers, Students, and Curriculum. *Phi Delta Kappan, 69*(6), 432–438.

McNeil, L. M. (1988c). Contradictions of Control, Part 3: Contradictions of Reform. *Phi Delta Kappan, 69*(7), 478–485.

Ornstein, A. C., & Hunkins, F. P. (1988). *Curriculum: Foundations, Principles, and Issues.* Englewood Cliffs, NJ: Prentice-Hall.

Powell, A. G., Farrar, E., & Cohen, D. K. (1985). *The Shopping Mall High School: Winners and Losers in the Educational Marketplace.* Boston: Houghton-Mifflin.

Saras, L. J., & Short, E. C. (1988). The Trivial Curriculum in American Education. Unpublished paper, College of Education, The Pennsylvania State University.

Sedlak, M. M., Wheeler, C. W., Pullin, D. C., & Cusik, P. A. (1986). *Selling Students Short: Classroom Bargains and Academic Reform in the American High School.* New York: Teachers College Press.

Sewall, G. T. (1988). American History Textbooks: Where Do We Go From Here? *Phi Delta Kappan, 69*(8), 554–558.

Shor, I., & Freire, P. (1987). *A Pedagogy for Liberation.* South Hadley, MA: Bergin & Garvey.

Shulman, L. S. (1988). The Design of Teaching Assessments. Address given at the

Annual Conference of the Association for Supervision and Curriculum Development, Boston, March 13.

Tanner, D. (1988). The Textbook Controversies. In L. N. Tanner, Ed., *Critical Issues in Curriculum.* 87th Yearbook of the National Society for the Study of Education, Part I. Chicago: University of Chicago Press, pp. 122–147.

Urban, W. J. (1987). The Illusion of Education Reform in Georgia. *Journal of Thought, 22*(2), 31–36.

Welsh, P. (1986). *Tales Out of School.* New York: Viking.

White, J. J. (1987). The Teacher as a Broker of Scholarly Knowledge. *Journal of Teacher Education, 38*(4), 19–24.

Wise, A. E. (1988). Legislated Learning Revisited. *Phi Delta Kappan, 69*(5), 328–333.

Zumwalt, K. K. (1988). Are We Improving or Undermining Teaching? In L. N. Tanner, Ed., *Critical Issues in Curriculum.* 87th Yearbook of the National Society for the Study of Education, Part I. Chicago: University of Chicago Press, pp. 148–174.

13

The Question of Worth
as Central
to Curricular Empowerment

WILLIAM H. SCHUBERT
University of Illinois at Chicago

I have taught curriculum and instruction courses in doctoral, master's, and bachelor's programs at the University of Illinois at Chicago since 1975, when I completed my doctoral work in curriculum studies at the University of Illinois at Urbana-Champaign under the mentorship of J. Harlan Shores. Known for his contributions to curriculum (especially Fundamentals of Curriculum Development, *1950, 1957), Shores was a first-rate mentor whose door was always open to students. He carefully developed an individualized program that facilitated my sense of direction and quest for self-education. Other faculty members also contributed greatly to my image of curriculum inquiry and how to teach it. I also consider certain authors as mentors, though I have not met them—from Plato to Dewey, Whitehead, James, and even Dickens and Twain (among other artists and philosophers). My list would be very long and likely full of omissions if I tried to mention contemporary scholars whose influence has mentored me over the past 15 years. Many of them are represented in the pages of this book, by authorship and citation.*

My teaching is influenced profoundly by my family of educators: Walter Schubert, my father—administrator and coach; my mother, Madeline Schubert—social studies and mathematics teacher; my grandmother and great aunts who taught in rural schools in Indiana; Charles Hampel, teacher and administrator; and professors at Manchester College, where teaching counts more than research. These dedicated teachers taught me to care for students, relate to their lives, and have high but realistic expectations. Much that I learned about teaching came from per-

sonal attempts to imagine, invent, and do curriculum for seven years as a teacher in Downers Grove, Illinois, and more recently from interactions with a wonderfully insightful array of students at UIC. Finally, the essence of curriculum theory and teaching for me derives from sharing ideas with Ann Lopez Schubert, as we reflect on our own growth, that of our family, students, and others.

Serious consideration of the question of worth is both necessary and neglected at all levels of curriculum development. It is necessary because of the widespread trivialization of curriculum, as depicted in Chapter 12 by Edmund Short. While acknowledged as a primary focus of curriculum theory and discourse by curriculum scholars and planners, the question of what is worthwhile is usually neglected at the school site level by leaders, teachers, and students. I argue here that curriculum can be empowering only when all levels of curriculum makers (from scholars and developers to teacher educators, supervisors, teachers, and students) address the fundamental curriculum question: What knowledge and experience are most worthwhile? Addressing this question provides continuous realization of greater meaning and direction. Only when those at each level make this question a part of their consciously developed biography, as Craig Kridel advocates in Chapter 15, can educators and students engage in empowering experience. To become empowered is to become the author of one's own growth, personally and socially. Like Paul Shaker in Chapter 14, I too have found that when pursuit of a question brings meaning and direction for educators, they readily accept its challenge as a source of empowerment.

HISTORICAL PERSPECTIVES

The question of worth is usually traced back to Herbert Spencer's *Education* (1861), the first chapter of which is entitled "What Knowledge Is of Most Worth?" Clearly, however, even a survey of educational history (Boyd & King, 1975; Butts, 1973; Ulich, 1950, 1954) reveals that the question of worth is much older. From Plato in the West and Confucius in the East, to John Dewey and Alfred North Whitehead in this century, one finds the question of worth to be central to the ancient and modern worlds of educational discourse. It is indeed interesting that prior to the advent of curriculum as a field of study early in the twentieth century (Schubert, 1980), the question of worth was central to major social and philosophical treatises that dealt with issues concerning the substance of education. As Shaker points out in Chapter 14, classic statements on education throughout history (such as those by Aristotle, Quintillion, Augustine, Abelard, Descartes, Kant, Rousseau, Tolstoy, Montessori, and many others) always couched arguments about what is worth knowing in a context of social and individual improvement. In the twentieth century, when specialization from industry combined with the thrust to achieve universal schooling, curriculum specialists were born, and with them the curriculum field. Kliebard (1986) designates the 1890s as the crucible of specialized attention to curriculum matters. In my own work (Schubert, 1980, 1982, 1986), I have found it useful to designate three recurring curriculum orientations or tendencies (intellectual traditionalist, social behaviorist, and experientialist). While each of these has been used as a basis of commentary on a range of curriculum topics (Schubert, 1986), each provides a different interpretation of the question of worth in curriculum discourse and practice.

For the intellectual traditionalist (from William Torrey Harris and Charles Eliot in the late nineteenth century to today's popular writings by Mortimer Adler, E. D. Hirsch, Allan Bloom, Diane Ravitch, and Chester Finn), that which is worthwhile becomes tied to classics in the Western cultural heritage. At best, it is implied that this tradition consists of great works that reveal insight and understanding that transcend Western culture itself and cut across barriers of race, ethnicity, place, social class, and the like. This transcendence is possible because it is asserted that great works, more than any other sources, deal with what Robert Ulich called "the great events and mysteries of life: birth, death, love, tradition, society and the crowd, success and failure, salvation, and anxiety" (1955, p. 255). The best and most creative expressions of the human mind and spirit deal with these mysteries and events. Thus, the most worthwhile learning for human beings comes through exposure to the great works. Such exposure and the reflection and contribution it engenders are, for the intellectual traditionalist, the greatest empowerment available to subsequent generations. Thus, it must *be* the curriculum.

The social behaviorist position grew out of the widespread reverence for science and the emergent respect for its technological offspring at the onset of the twentieth century. Franklin Bobbitt, W. W. Charters, and others engaged in "scientific curriculum making," whereby they studied the activities and ideals of successful members of society and used what they found as grist for the mill of curricular purposes. This represents the avoidance of educator responsibility in determining purposes, which is evident in today's tendencies to view curriculum developers as technicians whose job is to further someone else's ends.

Evolving from a long tradition of educational thought from Rousseau, Herbart, Pestalozzi, Froebel, and others is the experientalist tradition, which finds its fullest statement in the work of John Dewey (1900, 1902, 1910,

1916, 1929, 1938). Dewey argued that the question of worth should be pursued along three interrelated dimensions: pedagogical, scientific, and democratic. Pedagogically, Dewey situated genuine learning in a movement from the psychological to the logical. The "psychological" for Dewey is rooted in concerns that grow from everyday experience. Good teaching consists of enabling students to engage in dialogue (origins of democracy), through which they begin to see common human interests (Habermas, 1971). Common human interests, once perceived as shared concerns, are the doorway to appreciation of knowledge from the disciplines (that is, the Deweyan "logical"). When referring to the Deweyan logical, or disciplinary knowledge, as a basis from which insight can be derived for common human interests, it is clear that such knowledge is a source of meaning for under-standing Ulich's "great events and mysteries of life," noted in discussing the intellectual traditionalist position. In other words, the pedagogy of the ex-perientialist turns the intellectual traditionalist on its head. Instead of study-ing extant knowledge to gain insight into the great mysteries and events, the experientialist holds that genuine human concerns and interests derived from everyday experience embody the great mysteries and events of life, and that they are, in fact, the reason for seeking insight from the disciplines of knowledge and from the great books. Science, the second dimension of the experientialist or Deweyan position on worth, is a method of inquiry that is not exercised by credentialed experts alone. It is the everyday, intel-ligent problem solving of all human beings. Moreover, it is an imaginative, inventive, reflective, even poetic way to conceive of meaning and direction, consider precedent, develop hypotheses, and assess probable and actual consequences of decision and action. Democracy, the third dimension of Dewey's position on worth, asserts that everyday science is magnified im-measurably through cooperative human community. For Dewey, democracy is considered to be a great deal more than exercising the vote to enhance policy by majority and protecting the minority. It is conjoint living and de-liberation that continuously reconstructs meaning and direction in human lives.

In recent years, the experientialist position has again surfaced with some strength in curriculum discourse (see Apple, 1986; Giroux, 1988; Pi-nar, 1988; and van Manen, 1986). It can be argued that the experientialist assumptions of progressive educators of the first third of the twentieth cen-tury have been rekindled and augmented by contemporary authors whose inquiry is practical, pragmatic, phenomenological, and/or critical (see Schubert, 1986; Schubert, Willis, & Short, 1984). Zissis (1987), for instance, has identified six value assumptions in the writings of Francis Parker, John Dewey, Boyd Bode, William Kilpatrick, George Counts, Harold Rugg, and L. Thomas Hopkins, as follows: (1) search for the good life, (2) person as creator, (3) knowing as multidimensional, (4) knowledge as intersubjective, (5) education as intrinsic, and (6) democracy as participatory. She goes further to show that such values characterize a significant domain of recent literature as well. This experientialist approach to the question of worth leads to a broad spectrum of empowerment on the part of those engaged in the educative process.

EXPERIENTIALISTS, WORTH, AND EMPOWERMENT

The experientialist position is the only one of the three sketched above that provides for empowerment of all those involved in places where curriculum is developed. The emphasis here is on the experience of developing curriculum. In contrast, the social behaviorist and the intellectual traditionalist cling to a curriculum that was developed by others and is bestowed on those in the curriculum situation, that is, the teaching-learning setting. "Curricular empowerment" means that the experientialist teacher, curriculum developer, scholar, and all engaged in the curriculum situation play proactive roles in curriculum. In other words, the "author" root in authority (the dictionary reference to empowerment) is emphasized. Whoever is involved in the process of curriculum development (whether in a graduate school seminar, a preservice teacher education classroom, a school-based inservice setting, or an elementary school classroom) is acknowledged as having a genuine and deserved right to be an author of the meaning and direction of his or her growth journey, that is, curriculum. Each participant is not merely a receiver of curricula developed by others. Each is an active creator, along with those who have special expertise, of the curriculum that gives increased meaning and direction to an individual's life.

The contrast of this position with that of the social behaviorist and intellectual traditionalist is striking. The social behaviorist finds authority in the preferences expressed by the activities and ideals of successful members of society. This position includes no method for critiquing such dominant practices and ideals. The dominant values are *ipso facto* acknowledged as those to be emulated. This alone presents the serious problem of no checks and balances on educational purposes, for educators are to mere technicians. But the problem runs deeper. By assuming that the collective preference of successful members of society is an expression of democracy, the social behaviorist unwittingly confuses material success with success defined in terms of pursuit of greater meaning and direction. Moreover, curriculum developers are effectually removed from the process of democracy. "Science," in the sense of discoveries by credentialed experts, not everyday problem solving, is granted paramount authority. Assuming that educational leaders, teachers, and even students are mere receivers of curriculum precludes them from playing a significant role in the creation of their lives. The concomitant impact on students is profound. Students are taught to be receivers, not authors, of meaning and direction.

The intellectual traditionalist, like the social behaviorist, betrays democracy by advocating, at best, a democracy limited to the aristocracy (Gutmann, 1988). If only those who have had access to the classics and disciplines of knowledge are deemed capable of setting worthwhile direction for their lives, if only they are able to create meaning and direction adequately, what about those who are less privileged? Even if a grounding in classics were available for all through reconstructed universal schooling, it would still put educators and students alike in the role of receiver. The question persists: How can those who merely receive meaning and direction learn to create it? If creating worthwhile lives (personally and collectively) is the goal of democracy, the ability to do so is not fostered by a bestowed curriculum. In the next section I illustrate how the teaching of curriculum from an experientialist perspective can enable teachers to have greater authorship of their lives and work (how they can become more empowered), by involving them in fundamental questions about what is worthwhile.

TEACHING TEACHERS THE CENTRALITY OF WORTH

To directly focus on worth in curriculum discourse requires the revision of teaching about curriculum to enable students of curriculum to ask in many different ways: What is worthwhile to know and experience? To ask this question individually and collectively leads teachers to realize authorship of curriculum, not just for students but *with* them. Toward the end of enhancing the empowerment of curriculum makers at all levels, I will next describe and interpret pedagogical strategies that I use in the preservice and inservice education of educators. First, I present an organizing center that focuses student attention directly on what it means to be a good teacher. Second, I describe group process activities that I have used to enable teachers to reflect on the meaning and direction of their personal and professional lives. Third, I characterize settings or environments for curriculum study that foster empowerment through consideration of worth.

Organizing Center

The important and neglected work of Virgil Herrick et al. (1956) on "organizing centers" asserts the necessity of having a central point around which all curricular and teaching processes could be coordinated. In commenting on the value of organizing centers, Macdonald, Anderson, and May (1965, p. 107) note that "perhaps the most crucial and central concept related to the teaching operations is the idea of the organizing center." The organizing center for curriculum study should be the fundamental question of worth, noted earlier in this chapter. For the teacher, I have found that the question of worth may be more abstract than the practical details of classroom decision and action; thus, teachers may need a version of the question of worth that fits their concerns more fully. Research I (Schubert, 1988) have conducted on the sources of meaning and direction in the experience of good teachers reveals that they

1. Maintain a holistic perspective on situational problem solving
2. Enjoy being with students
3. Draw insights from student experiences outside of school
4. Hold a sense of mission about the importance of teaching
5. Exhibit love and compassion for students
6. Determine ways to build on student strengths
7. Have a clear sense of meaning and direction and are in the process of revising the same
8. Guide their work with a quest for that which is worthwhile and just
9. Consider the issue of developmental appropriateness as problematic in each new situation
10. Actively engage in self-education

   I have also found that good teachers develop a repertoire of strategies and resources from study and experience. Together, this repertoire and the guiding beliefs outlined above concretize the question of worth in the form of the question: What does it mean to become a good teacher, and how can I be one? I concluded a number of years ago that this question, the implicit and explicit driving force by which good teachers strive to grow, should become the organizing center for preservice and inservice education. I am convinced that it is, in fact, the question of worth that prompts the self-development of teachers.

   Thus, the inservice and preservice education of teachers should enable them to develop the philosophy, strategies, and resources to further their quest to be better teachers. One approach being tried in an alternative program at the University of Illinois at Chicago consists of combining methods courses and student teaching in an ongoing set of seminars with the same cadre of teacher education candidates and faculty members throughout an entire academic year. Students are engaged in school experiences all morning four days a week, a setting from which topics for seminars emerge and to which they can be related (Ayers, 1988). This pedagogical approach begins with the experientialist assumption of starting with the psychological (student experiential interest) and moving to the logical (extant knowledge about teaching and curriculum). Rather than organizing the teacher education methods curriculum around one or another subject area, as is usually done, the organizing center is becoming a good, or worthwhile, teacher. Students are asked to prepare card files and journals that reflect their development in pursuit of this purpose. They collect information—from professional literature, personal contacts, concrete approaches, instructional materials, and so on—that facilitates becoming a good teacher. Especially relevant is the process of refining a belief system or philosophy that guides their teaching.

On a different scale, I ask practicing educators in master's degree courses and inservice staff development programs to keep journals or similar records about conscientious attempts to grow and develop around the organizing center of what it means to be a good teacher. Such records might be largely philosophical, or they might consist of collections of relevant research findings or practical plans and approaches gleaned from reports of others in similar circumstances. At the doctoral level, too, the question of worth is addressed by asking: What dos it mean to make worthwhile contributions as a curriculum scholar, consultant, curriculum leader in schools, or teacher educator? I encourage such questioning in a doctoral course on foundations of curriculum and program design (Schubert, 1987) and in advanced seminars and study groups (Schubert et al., 1987).

Group Process Activities

I have used group process activities at all of the above levels of curriculum studies to encourage students' reflection that connects sources of meaning and direction in their lives with both extant educational knowledge and everyday concerns of their lives in classrooms. These activities are designed to enable educators to assess the concerns that grow out of the teaching-learning situations that they regularly experience, by having them reflect on their own deeper values and principles. Over the past 15 years I have used activities such as those illustrated below to engender reflection and imaginative educational improvement. The activities first emerged in quite different form for me as an elementary school teacher who wanted students to think seriously about reading stories, social studies material, and other subjects. I have come to believe that learners at all levels need experiences that enable them to consider new subject matter in light of their own experience. The activities that follow are, thus, means, not ends. The goal is to enable other educators to seek out and reflect on new perspectives without the activities. I have, however, concluded that most need springboards to begin the process, because schooling at all levels so rarely connects with life experience.

Magical Powers.   I tell students that they are endowed with magical powers (half humorously, of course). I ask them to imagine five characteristics that they would like to bestow on everyone in the world. In small groups they explain and clarify their lists of characteristics. They attempt to find commonalities such that they can agree on at least one characteristic or give a name to a constellation of characteristics. I ask them to imagine how they might build curricula designed to enable students to develop the characteristic. Questions usually arise about the relative, intangible quality of such characteristics as love, creativity, happiness, and empathy, and whether they can be taught at all. I usually argue that if some humans do develop such characteristics, then they must learn them. If they are learned, is it not possible to orchestrate conditions that help the characteristics develop, that is, to teach them? After addressing such questions and issues, students consider how the characteristics might be translated into purposes, learning experiences, and organizational patterns, and how acquisition of the characteristics might be evaluated. Thus, they are led through considerations of the Tyler Rationale (Tyler, 1949). After developing the rudiments of a curriculum, thinking their way through it as it were, the students reflect together on the process in which they engaged. I ask them to consider how it might have been similar or different if they had been developing curriculum for an actual situation. They also consider how they currently incorporate characteristics they deem important to acquire that are not usually among the subjects taught in school. What if such characteristics replaced those subjects? How might they map the characteristics on a program of more traditional subjects?

Like the other group process activities that follow, this activity is empowering because it treats the students as authors of curriculum. In doing so, the activities embody the Deweyan dimensions of pedagogy, science, and democracy. They are pedagogic in that they begin with the psychological interests derived from experience and proceed to fundamental matters at the center of educational literature and discourse (that is, the logical). The method of inquiry or science is everyday problem solving, reflection, intuition, and attention to consequences. Finally, dialogue and deliberation, hallmarks of democracy, refine and bolster the experientialist science and pedagogy.

Although educators are often wedded to curriculum organized around separate subjects, they find this exercise helpful to open the question of worth. Some who become bored with their subject matter seem invigorated with the prospect of actually teaching what they deem most important in life. Others, less missionary in outlook and hope, see aspirations beyond subject matter to be too ideal. Even these differences, however, lead to useful debate and discussion.

Impacts on Outlook.   I ask educators to recall significant situations in their lives that brought about a change in their philosophy of life, perspective, guiding beliefs, or outlook. I request they they delineate the conditions under which the impact occurred, including the setting (formal or informal), personalities involved (friends, authorities, family), and prevailing attitudes (traumatic, hostile, calm, understanding), among others. I remind participants that teaching is a process of attempting to have impacts on the outlooks of others. With this in mind, they look for common threads in the different kinds of impacts on their own outlooks as individuals; likewise, in small groups they discuss their observations with others. Once common threads of conditions, personalities, attitudes, and the like are identified from participant experience, I ask participants to reflect on them within their own classrooms. Do the same threads appear? Why or why not? Might it be useful to try to incorporate some of them more fully?

Participants are often astounded to bring to the forefront of reflection significant learning from their own lives. For some reason educators rarely connect salient impacts on their outlook (which usually occur outside of school) with their work in school. Too often we become so wrapped up in the taken-for-granted procedures of schooling that we fail to ask how schooling might contribute to the improvement of the life of the learner. Asking teachers to focus on what has contributed to the improvement of their own outlook encourages them to look at this central dimension when planning experiences with and for students.

Invention from Nearly Nothing.   Teachers often lament the fact that they do not have enough supplies. If they had more instructional materials, they tell me, they would be more creative. Sometimes, it seems that the opposite is the case; that is, invention derives from limitation more than from plenty. To point this out, I ask participants to find an insignificant object. I sometimes give them the object in a surprise bag, request it to be found in their purse or pocket, or solicit it from the back of their classroom closet where unknown wonders sometimes remain from previous years. Again, in small groups (using all of the objects or one at a time) I ask participants to build curriculum and plans for teaching. I tell them that they have a unique administrator who is at once very liberal and very conservative. He or she is liberal in the sense that anything justifiable may be taught, but conservative in that only seemingly insignificant materials can be used as instructional supplies. Participants discover or are presented with topics that stimulate different kinds of lessons, which might not have been entertained if they had a richer stock of materials. Illustrations include, What is the larger idea or societal function represented by the object? What chain of events brought the object to this classroom? What values and needs created the desire for such objects? What stories could be told by putting together all the objects in a small group of participants? What if the world suddenly had none of these objects? What other uses could there be for any of the objects?

Teachers involved in this activity often see their selection of instructional materials, previously thought limited, as having much greater potential. Sometimes I explicitly tell them that the activity is an analogy. They should not transport the particular "insignificant" objects and the lessons derived from them back to their classroom. Rather, they should develop similar strategies from persons and experiences with whom they are involved. Some report back excitedly on attempts to do this.

Setting or Environment

Group process activities, such as those described above, are useful but insufficient to providing an empowered sense of worth. Educators need to live their professional lives in a democratic setting—a place in which dialogue provides a sense of meaning and direction. Dialogue, in university and inservice settings alike, can be enhanced by study groups, mentoring relationships, and tutorial arrangements. Collegiality is the mainstay of growth in such arrangements. The activities described above are transitions to larger realms of lived experience for educators.

This kind of environment builds on the culture of schooling depicted in its complex diversity by Sarason (1982). Building school improvement efforts on this image of school culture involves developing collaborative relationships between schools and other institutions (such as universities) and within schools. In the spirit of Dewey and field psychologist Kurt Lewin (1948), Corey (1953), Miel (1946, 1952), and others who called for action research to improve educational situations, contemporary writers have written of long-term efforts to engage in school improvement. Lieberman (1986) brings together an array of contributors to the research, craft, and concept of school improvement. Lieberman (1988) also brings together researcher-consultants who have conscientiously attempted to build a professional culture with practitioners in schools. Griffin (1983) provides explications of collaboration and interactive action research within the realm of staff development, while Bolin and Falk (1987) relate collaborative school improvement efforts to personal choices and professional issues in the renewal of teachers. Schwab (1983) argues that continual practical improvement at the building level necessitates ongoing deliberation and assessment of the shifting balance among four curricular commonplaces: teachers, learners, subject matter, and milieu. He calls for a curriculum group made up of teachers, building leaders, other school staff, parents, students, and community members who engage in deliberation that informs and refreshes situational decision and action.

Different forms of democratic environments that have emerged in other cultures have had considerable impact on curriculum thought and action throughout the world. Two of these stem from the work of Lawrence Stenhouse in England and Paulo Freire in Brazil, respectively. Stenhouse (1975, 1980; Rudduck & Hopkins, 1985) presents the "teacher as researcher" approach. This consists of long-term collaborative action-research ventures in which university faculty and teachers strive on equal grounds for insight into educational processes in particular classrooms, tapping the mutual expertise of each group. In England, teachers enlivened the example by developing teacher-researcher collaboration themselves and creating conferences and publications to share their experience in teacher-oriented language. Based on this work and other sources in the literature and practice is the concept of school-based curriculum development (Skilbeck, 1984) that has gained currency in Australia and Great Britain.

Freire's (1970) *Pedagogy of the Oppressed* is based on his experience in educating Brazilian peasants to realize that developing literacy is being able to name their world and negotiate in it with greater expertise. In subsequent work, Freire (1973, 1985) continued to develop pedagogical strategies and political perspectives that enable learners from all social classes (despite their level of oppression) to develop critical consciousness that exposes what is oppressive and dominating, to recognize false consciousness, and to make unjust values and distorted conceptions problematic. The pursuit of what is worthwhile to know and experience, he asserts, must be coupled with emancipatory and active power relationships. Thus, learning about curriculum, or anything else, must take place in dialogue in which problems are posed cooperatively by teachers and students alike. Carr and Kemmis (1986) have joined together action-research traditions and those of critical *praxis* to move in this direction.

The above body of literature serves as an eclectic repertoire of theory and practice from which to build a setting that will enable educators to become more empowered. The beginning is to realize, as Edmund Short admonished in Chapter 12, that there is great danger in the trivialization of curriculum. Curriculum becomes significant when it is experienced as being connected with the growth of meaning and direction in one's life. The methods I have described have been useful to me and to my students in making that connection initially. However, as Shaker points out in Chapter 14, teaching methods must be seen as transition mechanisms; they are not ends in themselves. The group process aspects of the activities illustrate in microcosm what a more holistic environment might be. It is an environment organized around the question of worth; it involves a group of persons who strive to grow together by starting with immediate concerns and moving to greater understanding and empowerment through the consideration of theory, research, and each other's experience.

In Chapter 15, Craig Kridel shows that a historical and biographical approach to teaching curriculum can enable students to see curriculum study as integrated with the history and biography of their own experiences. I, too, have found this kind of environment in study groups of graduate students that spin off from classes (Schubert et al., 1987). I have also found it in master's degree internships and doctoral research projects. Moreover, I have experienced this environment in collaboration with schools in which consultants, school leaders, teachers, and students are all recognized for the special expertise and insight they can contribute.

CONCLUSIONS AND DIRECTIONS

The central point of this chapter is that teaching curriculum must be organized, at all levels, around the central question

- What is worthwhile to know and experience?

This invokes related questions, such as

- What kind of life should I create for myself, and how can I do so?
- What is the impact of my life on the growth of other persons and of society?
- How can I improve such contributions?
- What assumptions guide my asking of these questions?

The seriousness of curriculum inquiry is indisputable when it addresses these questions. Teachers, educational leaders, and others who study curriculum in view of these questions begin to perceive the indelible connection between the pursuit of meaning and direction in their own lives (both personal and professional) and the pursuit of curriculum for schools and other educative settings. They see curriculum development as a holistic process that can overcome the deskilled lives of many educators (Apple, 1986). In other words, such curricularists move beyond the separation of purpose, implementation, and evaluation, which is so prevalent in conceptions of curriculum that designate teachers as mere implementors. Teachers whose purposes are bestowed upon them by larger forces (states and school districts) beyond their control, and whose work is evaluated by testing agencies, have their craft and art broken apart. They are deskilled. However, to address fundamental questions about worth, as illustrated above, is the beginning of empowerment that overcomes deskilling. It rejoins what has been broken apart by the deskilling process and empowers teachers and curriculum leaders to ask questions of worth and follow them through. Clearly, such asking is necessary but insufficient to empowerment. Institutions must be reconceptualized and reconstructed to enable lived experience of those who can actualize the basic tenets of experientialist curriculum. Zissis (1987) holds that such institutions involve all participants in a continual search for the meaning of the good life. Moreover, these individuals are considered creators of knowledge through a variety of epistemological bases as they participate democratically to address intrinsically valued problems.

Although the matter of reconstructing institutions is beyond the scope of this chapter, it is important to raise two concluding points in an effort to clarify meaning and direction. One point focuses on schools and the other on students. Students are the most neglected potential participants in curriculum development. By their interaction in the classroom and by the way they receive and respond to curriculum and teaching, they are curriculum developers. Because they profoundly influence curriculum already, they deserve to be involved in the process. If one consistently extends experientialist tenets to the realm of students, it is obvious that they, too, must address the fundamental curriculum questions. Thus, the organizing center for curriculum at the classroom level, as well as at many different planning levels, should be to ask: What is worthwhile to know and experience? This connects schooling and life concerns, it integrates the artificially separated subject areas, and it points the way to the democratic search for meaning and direction. The institutional point, one too often ignored in colleges of education that are interpreted as colleges of schooling, is to ask if schools as we know them are, indeed, places where fundamental curriculum questions can be asked by teachers and students. If so, why are such questions so seldom addressed in schools? If not, what kinds of institutions or arrangements are needed for individual and social empowerment through serious reflection on what is worthwhile to know and experience?

REFERENCES

Adler, M. J. (1982). *The Paideia proposal.* NY: Macmillan.
Apple, M. W. (1986). *Teachers and texts.* New York: Routledge & Kegan Paul.

Ayers, W. (1988). Giving headaches: On teaching and the reform of teacher education. Presentation at the Midwest Region Holmes Group Conference, Chicago, May 14.

Bloom, A. (1987). *The closing of the American mind.* New York: Simon & Schuster.

Bobbitt, F. (1918). *The curriculum.* Boston: Houghton-Mifflin.

Bobbitt, F. (1924). *How to make a curriculum.* Boston: Houghton-Mifflin.

Bolin, F., & Falk, J. (Eds.). (1987). *Teacher renewal.* New York: Teachers College Press.

Boyd, W., & King, E. J. (1975). *The history of Western education.* New York: Barnes & Noble.

Butts, R. F. (1973). *The education of the West.* New York: McGraw-Hill.

Carr, W., & Kemmis, S. (1986). *Becoming critical: Education, knowledge, and action research.* London and Philadelphia: Falmer Press.

Charters, W. W. (1923). *Curriculum construction.* New York: Macmillan.

Corey, S. M. (1953). *Action research to improve school practices.* New York: Bureau of Publication, Teachers College, Columbia University.

Dewey, J. (1900). *The school and society.* Chicago: University of Chicago Press.

Dewey, J. (1902). *The child and the curriculum.* Chicago: University of Chicago Press.

Dewey, J. (1910). *How we think.* New York: D. C. Heath.

Dewey, J. (1916). *Democracy and education.* New York: Macmillan.

Dewey, J. (1929). *The sources of a science of education.* New York: Liveright.

Dewey, J. (1938). *Experience and education.* New York: Macmillan.

Freire, P. (1970). *Pedagogy of the oppressed.* New York: Seabury.

Freire, P. (1973). *Education for critical consciousness.* New York: Seabury.

Freire, P. (1985). *The politics of education.* South Hadley, MA: Bergin & Garvey.

Giroux, H. A. (1988). *The teacher as intellectual.* South Hadley, MA: Bergin & Garvey.

Griffin, G. A. (1983). *Staff development.* Eighty-second Yearbook of the National Society for the Study of Education, Part II. Chicago: University of Chicago Press.

Gutmann, A. (1988). Democratic education in difficult times. Invited address at the Annual Meeting of the American Educational Research Association, New Orleans, April 6.

Habermas, J. (1971). *Knowledge and human interests.* Boston: Beacon.

Herrick, V., et al. (1956). *The elementary school.* Englewood Cliffs, NJ: Prentice-Hall.

Hirsch, E. D. (1987). *Cultural literacy.* Boston: Houghton-Mifflin.

Kliebard, H. M. (1986). *The struggle for the American curriculum 1893–1958.* New York: Routledge & Kegan Paul.

Lewin, K. (1948). *Resolving social conflicts.* New York: Harper.

Lieberman, A. (Ed.). (1986). *Rethinking school improvement.* New York: Teachers College Press.

Lieberman, A. (Ed.). (1988). *Building a professional culture in schools.* New York: Teachers College Press.

Macdonald, J. B., Anderson, D. W., & May, F. B. (Eds). (1965). *Strategies in curriculum development: The works of Virgil E. Herrick.* Columbus, OH: Merrill.

Mager, R. F. (1962). *Preparing instructional objectives.* Palo Alto, CA: Fearon.

Miel, A. (1946). *Changing the curriculum: A social process.* New York: Appleton-Century.

Miel, A. and associates. (1952). *Cooperative procedures in learning.* Bureau of Publications, Teachers College, Columbia University.

Noddings, N. (1984). *Caring.* Berkeley: University of California Press.

Pinar, W. F. (Ed.). (1988). *Contemporary curriculum discourses.* Scottsdale, AZ: Gorsuch Scarisbrick.

Ravitch, D., & Finn, Jr., C. E. (1987). *What do our 17 year olds know?* New York: Harper & Row.

Rudduck, J., & Hopkins, D. (Eds.). (1985). *Research as a basis for teaching: Readings from the work of Lawrence Stenhouse.* London: Falmer Press.

Sarason, S. (1982). *The culture of the school and the problem of change.* Boston: Allyn & Bacon.

Schubert, W. H. (1980). *Curriculum books: The first eighty years.* Lanham, MD: University Press of America.

Schubert, W. H. (1982). Curriculum research. In H. Mitzel (Ed.), *Encyclopedia of Educational Research.* New York: Macmillan, pp. 420–431.

Schubert, W. H. (1986). *Curriculum: Perspective, paradigm, and possibility.* New York: Macmillan.

Schubert, W. H. (1987). Foundations of curriculum and program design. *Teaching Education, 1* (1), 86–91.

Schubert, W. H. (1988). Teacher lore: A basis for understanding praxis. Paper presented at the Annual Meeting of the American Educational Research Association, New Orleans, April 9.

Schubert, W. H., Thomas, T., Wojcik, J., Zissis, G., Hulsebosch, P., Koerner, M., & Millies, S. (1987). Teaching about progressive education: From course to study group. *Teaching Education, 1* (2), 77–81.

Schubert, W. H., Willis, G. H., & Short, E. C. (1984). Curriculum theorizing: An emergent form of curriculum studies in the United States. *Curriculum Perspectives, 4* (1), 69–74.

Schwab, J. J. (1983). The practical 4. *Curriculum Inquiry, 13* (3), 239–265.

Skilbeck, M. (1984). *School-based curriculum development.* London: Harper & Row.

Spencer, H. (1861). *Education.* New York: D. Appleton.

Stenhouse, L. (1975). *Introduction to curriculum research and development.* London: Heinemann.

Stenhouse, L. (Ed.). (1980). *Curriculum research and development in action.* London: Heinemann.

Tyler, R. W. (1949). *Basic principles of curriculum and instruction.* Chicago: University of Chicago Press.

Ulich, R. (1950). *History of educational thought.* New York: American Book Company.

Ulich, R. (1954). *Three thousand years of educational wisdom.* Cambridge, MA: Harvard University Press.

Ulich, R. (1955). Comments on Ralph Harper's essay. In N. B. Henry (Ed.), *Modern philosophies of education.* Fifty-fourth Yearbook (Part 1) of the National Society for the Study of Education (pp. 254–257), Chicago: University of Chicago Press.

van Manen, M. (1986). *The tone of teaching.* London: Heinemann.

Zissis, G. (1987). *Value assumptions underlying the experientialist critique of curriculum literature, 1883–1929.* Unpublished Ph.D. dissertation, University of Illinois at Chicago.

14

Foundations of Education as a Curriculum Laboratory

PAUL SHAKER
Slippery Rock University
of Pennsylvania

My B.A. (history), M.A. and Ph.D. (curriculum and foundations) are from the Ohio State University. I have also studied at the University of Chicago and the University of Akron. My mentor at Ohio State was Paul R. Klohr and his mentor was Harold Alberty. John Champlin, Charles Galloway, and Elsie Alberty also served as advisors. Many of the contributors to this volume are supportive colleagues and peers whose work has continued my education. In addition to 10 years on the faculty of Mount Union College, I have lived and worked in Saudi Arabia and Japan and am currently planning extended work in Kuwait.

My teaching has been shaped by the exemplary teachers and professors I have encountered as a student. Several of my graduate school professors, like Ross Mooney, were deeply committed to eliciting growth in learners, and others, like Edgar Dale, embodied many timeless traditions of education in their life and work. In the world of theory, my ideas have been influenced by Socrates, Plato, Rousseau, Dewey, and Jung. During my career I have continued to study depth psychology, particularly the interface between instinct and psychology.

My intellectual life is influenced by my second-generation Lebanese-American roots. Raised close to old world traditions, I have throughout my education and career felt that my perspective is a non-Western, Near Eastern one, influenced by certain Oriental attitudes. This has been confirmed by study and my experience of living in Arabia.

The teaching of curriculum is frequently oriented toward the examination and discussion of theory and curriculum textbooks. Alternately, it can employ as methodologies the development of a curriculum or the

228

study of existing curricula. With this last purpose in mind, I offer an auto-biographical synopsis of one teacher's 15-year odyssey in applying curriculum theory to curriculum development at three institutions in their programs of teacher education. The curricula themselves are described with attention to the theoretical foundations from which they were derived and with reflection on their impact on preservice teachers. A central purpose in what follows is to trace the work of a curricularist as college teacher from theory to design and implementation, and, finally, to evaluation of outcomes. Those concerned about the teaching of curriculum may be interested in the process of translating reconceptualist curriculum theory to curriculum and of the specific consequences of the unorthodox foundational sources.

ORIGINS:
THE HISTORY OF WESTERN EDUCATION

As a secondary history teacher, I came to graduate school in curriculum studies to search for unifying concepts that could aid the teaching of social studies. It was also a personal goal to bring my formal education to a kind of closure. As an undergraduate my education had been characterized by a comprehensive interest in world history, which had, appropriately, focused on people, places, and events, rather than themes, theories, or hypotheses. Now, as a graduate student at Ohio State University, I was moving from traditional work in the literature of education to less traveled ground in philosophy, psychology, and other disciplines. At the same time, I began teaching the History of Western Education. Given the opportunity to design a curriculum for this required foundations of education course, I employed several basic assumptions: (1) that primary source material should be given priority over survey textbooks; (2) that certain unconventional sources would be valuable in pedagogy courses; and (3) that nonprint media were an important component of the curriculum. The course employed a "history of ideas" approach, tracing Western education's evolution by the study of some paradigmatic texts of the field.

These assumptions derive from what was beginning in 1973–1974 to be called "reconceptualist curriculum theory" (Klohr, 1974; Pinar, 1974, 1975, 1988). Specifically, the curriculum was quite personal in its inception: (1) It employed phenomenological interpretations of events; and (2) it attempted to engage students in developing their own analyses of the material. Underlying these themes was a commitment to addressing students holistically and through recognition of unconscious as well as conscious motivations. For these reasons the curriculum had to arouse a strong level of interest in all class participants. It had to address affective issues as well as those of self-realization. According to this analysis, the course had to be related to the developmental needs of the students as well as their cognitive, professional preparation. The psychology of C. G. Jung gives a clear foundation for this curricular approach. The central motivation of individuals, according to Jung, is the quest for psychological development, that is, self-realization. The new curriculum continually pointed in this direction.

Teacher education courses are more than group work in self-realization. But to promote attention and learning, the curriculum must attend carefully to the reality of students' motivation. Conventional content goals can be met in a curriculum that also advances psychological development. There are elements of Dewey as well as Jung in this point of view: It points to the former's emphasis on interest and growth, and the latter's definition of the drive for individual fulfillment (individuation). All curriculum design involves selectivity, and in this approach professional and institutional topics were sacrificed. Foundations of education course work can derive from several rationales (Beyer & Zeichner, 1982), however, and my analysis was that this course targeted the most pressing need of my students. These preservice teachers were proceeding through their preparation without the benefit of an integrative rationale for learning. Thrown into college without such a framework, they lacked motivation and an understanding of the purposes of their professors. Courses, in this situation, were mere milestones to be tallied and passed without attaching further meaning. Neither general education nor teacher education provided such a context for their many specific requirements. The foundations curriculum assumed this purpose.

The methods of instruction reinforced the course's aims by, for example, making primary source material more accessible through the use of guiding study questions and abridged selections from demanding texts. These techniques helped to ameliorate differences in reading speed and comprehension. I employed an interactive classroom format with emphasis on higher order questioning. A variety of films were brought to bear on the content themes, often by using only a few minutes of footage to underscore a key point. One illustration is the use of the opening scenes of *The Blue Angel* to bring to life the nineteenth-century classroom Kant (1966) alludes to and, on another plane, the psychological mechanism of repression. *The Blue Angel* is set in a nineteenth-century Gymnasium, which is given its ambience by the discipline of the teacher, and in a decadent nightclub where Lola-Lola fires men's desires. The stage was set for the description of Kant's ideal education and the transformation that the psychology of the unconscious introduces to it. The place of passion and feeling is restored in the curriculum. Excerpts from *Drive, He Said* and *Five Easy Pieces* (provided by the *Searching for Values* film series) dramatized the frustrations

and contradictions that are part of experiencing psychological development. These latter themes—respectively, that one must decide in life between personal autonomy and identification with popular culture; and that
the objective, logical character of the ego must be balanced with the call of
feeling, the affective—were elaborated by the study of *Emile* (Rousseau,
1762/1964). Other texts included Montessori's *The Child in the Family*
(1971), Jaspers' *Socrates, Buddha, Confucius, Jesus* (1962), and *Meno* by
Plato (1956).

I taught four sections of this course on three campuses during the fall
and winter quarters of 1974–1975. The curriculum received strong positive
evaluations and appeared to succeed at awakening the students to the larger
meaning of the education they could receive and, in turn, provide for others.
A decade later, when viewing the film *Educating Rita*, I saw in the reactions
of the nontraditional working class student Rita a dramatization of this consequence of learning. The personal growth we as teachers are privileged at
times to experience in our students is not revealed by statistical data. It is,
however, apparent and moving experientially. Preservice teachers who become aware of a feeling of inspiration in their own preparation are given the
capacity to elicit the same in their students. With encouragement from students and supervising faculty, Professors Elsie Alberty, Paul Klohr, and Robert Sutton, I took a next step.

EVOLUTION: EDUCATION AND
THE EVOLUTION OF CONSCIOUSNESS

I next began to develop a course that took the ideas outlined above
further. This would become the center of my dissertation work. An experimental number was assigned, scheduling on two campuses arranged, and
permission for undergraduates to apply the course toward a requirement in
the preservice program secured. Freed from the constraints and expectations of a "history" or "philosophy" designation, my course was entitled
"Education and the Evolution of Consciousness" and was directed at examining the nature of consciousness and the role of education in its development. Text material included pedagogical writings, philosophy, phenomenology, and "esoteric" psychology. I employed another series of film
excerpts in support of the print resources. These included: *Civilisation XII.
"The Fallacies of Hope," Art of the '60s, Fishing at the Stone Weir* from Man:
A Course of Study, *Huckleberry Finn and the American Experience*, and
Life in the Thirties. The course was heavily subscribed, with an enrollment
of 63 upperclassmen and 21 graduate students (including Janet Miller

[Chapter 6] and Craig Kridel [Chapter 15]), whose work was evaluated by the supervising professor.

The curriculum of the course blended familiar sources (for example, John Dewey, Maxine Greene, and Philip Phenix) with ones on the fringe of higher education (such as C. G. Jung, phenomenologists) and clear pariahs (Georges Gurdjieff, P. D. Ouspensky, R. M. Bucke). This design was within a reconceptualist framework, as illustrated by an emphasis on the individual, the exploration of new sources of knowledge, and constant attention to a holistic view of persons. Sections of the following texts were required reading: *Cosmic Consciousness* by R. M. Bucke (1969), *Experience and Education* by John Dewey (1973), *In Search of the Miraculous* by P. D. Ouspensky (1949), and *Towards Deep Subjectivity* by Roger Poole (1972).

My methodology was similar to that used in the History of Western Education, with study questions, primary sources, class discussion, essay examinations, and use of media. To this I added a set of lectures, written and distributed, which unified material that otherwise might have been perceived as digressive. The course had to maintain an academic form and not dissolve into an esoteric study group.

Education and the Evolution of Consciousness demonstrated the significance of certain neglected psychological material in teacher education as well as the direct benefit the curriculum had on the students. The course helped to validate some reconceptualist claims about the scope and power of phenomenological and depth psychological curriculum. Furthermore, it directly confronted the assumption that the study of consciousness fostered a self-centered, asocial value orientation and argued for compatibility between one's conceptualization of self-realization and the demands of the social order. (This theme is addressed by George Wood in Chapter 7.) Education and the Evolution of Consciousness aimed to reclaim for higher education a vital and personal learning experience, which has increasingly become associated with New Age entrepreneurs and cult figures. The lapse of relevance that permits neglect of psychological self-development on the part of formal education is unnecessary. In light of our discipline's sources in the philosophy of Socrates and others who emphasized self-understanding and an unrestricted search for knowledge in both familiar and unfamiliar sources, the neglect is as tragic as it is ironic.

A number of evaluations of my course became part of my dissertation (1975), and they suggest one conclusion in particular: The course allowed class members to recognize and respect each individual's journey through the stages of psychological development. It also challenged the common tendency to accept the status quo in one's personality. Education and the Evolution of Consciousness provided concepts for creating higher order goals for teachers as they write curriculum. Class members better understood how the theme of "the evolution of consciousness" provided a means for unifying scholarly work in several fields of endeavor, for interpreting the course of history, and for recognizing the process of maturation of personality in a given individual.

DENOUEMENT: INTRODUCTION TO EDUCATION AND EDUCATIONAL PSYCHOLOGY

Upon leaving graduate school in 1975 and for ten of the subsequent twelve years, my curriculum work centered on the teaching of two sophomore foundational courses: Introduction to Education and Educational Psychology. The experiences described above provided a background for developing these initial core courses, which would be taken by nearly every preservice education student at Mount Union College during that decade, an average of 70 a year. Here my task included designing courses that fit within a small, closely knit department of five and that were intended to contribute to comprehensiveness in a stable program. Like courses at other college, these had to meet a number of state certification requirements, including awareness of human diversity, mainstreaming, school law, professional ethics, and so on. Clinical and field experiences were expected to be integral.

Each course contained a short, topical unit followed by four, three-week units. These major units were set within a historical framework: Classical, Romantic, Progressive, Contemporary. The courses might more accurately have been retitled "The History of Educational Philosophy" and "The History of Educational Psychology." Particularly in the latter case, this was a radical departure from the survey text approach. The courses were taken in sequence, and the parallel units were intended to heighten student awareness of the implicit evolution of the field of education. I made certain that both courses reflected a reliance on primary source material, an openness to phenomenological and depth psychological analyses, a focus on the process of individual development in a social context, and attention to holistic and affective views of education. (Janet Miller, in Chapter 6, recalls the personal tone of similar courses.)

Both courses had a number of structural features in common. Print material was complemented by field work, computer exercises, videotapes, and microteaching. In Introduction to Education the field experience was 60 hours of observation and assistance in an appropriate K–12 classroom, while in Educational Psychology students team taught a five-lesson weekly course in a local middle school. All students were evaluated by their peers on their microteaching, which also was videotaped for their individual review. As a further requirement, microteaching lessons were referenced to library resources. In each course students demonstrated competence with four software programs of varying levels of complexity. Also, to preserve class time students completed study guides in the educational media center while watching six supplemental videotapes for each course. This evaluation design satisfied student and college standards of fairness and comprehensiveness, but required a sizeable investment of time in monitoring student work.

Introduction to Education

The classical unit in Introduction to Education was built around Karl Jaspers' *Socrates, Buddha, Confucius, Jesus* (1962) and sought to capture the origins of education in oral traditions, religion, and the lives of "paradigmatic individuals." The purpose here was to reach anthropological and historical insights through biography and the history of ideas rather than through a textbook summary of education in ancient times. The messages of these individuals, their methods of communicating (or teaching), and the drama of their lives provided a curriculum rich in meaning and evocation. Although to Jaspers these archetypal personalities share a similar place in the history of philosophy, their messages diverge greatly. In the classroom these challenged students to position themselves among the four and in so doing develop their own points of view. The text is strong multicultural curriculum. It generally treats Jesus in the same objective, rationalistic manner as the others and fosters empathy on the part of Christian students for the feelings of non-Christians whose religious views are commonly treated in this unengaged way in the United States. Jaspers also offers a great deal on the topic of ethics in these excerpts from his two-volume history, *The Great Philosophers* (1962). The key moral principles espoused by each of the four provide a unique point of departure for later discussions of moral education and professional ethics.

Each unit's central reading was complemented by excerpts from contemporary theorists on similar themes. For example, during the romantic unit, which centered on Immanuel Kant's lectures *On Education* (1966), students also learned and applied Lawrence Kohlberg's "Stages of Moral Development" (1976) through analyses of familiar case studies. Kant's lectures emphasize his priority on personal discipline and his developed insights into ethics via the categorical imperative. Although an admirer of Rousseau, he argues against some of the values implicit in *Emile,* particularly with respect to the place of feeling. The text follows *Socrates, Buddha, Confucius, Jesus* effectively in the ongoing discussion of moral reasoning. *On Education* was, in turn, extended successfully by an introduction of depth psychological analyses on the same topic; for example, Esther Harding's (1973) argument for reworking the Golden Rule as "Do unto others as they would have you do unto them," a formulation that eludes the projective nature of the Biblical phrase. As an illustration of how these texts complement one another, it should be noted that students had earlier in the course studied Confucius' formulation, "Do not do to others what you would not have them do to you" (Jaspers, 1962, p. 51).

By organizing the progressive unit around *The School and Society* (Dewey, 1900/1966), the discussions of ethics, which had been relatively abstract up to this point, were convincingly set in the context of schools. John Dewey's thought was introduced with emphasis on five familiar characteristics: the interests of the child, the interplay of thinking and doing, the "miniature community," teacher as guide and coworker, and the metaphor of "growth." Pragmatism was defined and contrasted with idealism, among other schools of thought. Through the course's design, the stage had been set for the place of formal education in the transmission and reconstruction of society. Films, such as the *Education in America* series, which depict early forms of American schooling, showed the social values studied to this point in the course in institutionalized form.

The contemporary unit was organized around A. N. Whitehead's (1929/1957) *The Aims of Education.* Though originally published in 1929, this remains a standard reference in critiques of education because of its vision of how education in a broad sense should function. Whitehead is incisive and unorthodox in his discussion of curriculum and provides alternative schemas for organizing information in schools. His ideas on the "rhythm of education" and the stages of intellectual development direct students in Introduction to Education to further inquiry rather than create an inaccurate sense of finality about their study of pedagogy.

Educational Psychology

The four main units of Educational Psychology addressed the conventional subcategories of that discipline: learning, development, evaluation, and motivation. *Meno* provided a "classical" starting point for the course and a dramatization of the Socratic method and "reminiscence" as a learning theory. Mental discipline, Gestalt/inquiry, and behaviorist perspectives gave a comprehensive scope to the unit. In a supporting laboratory experience that met weekly during the course, the Wrenn Study Habits Inventory and the Classroom Environment Scale were administered and interpreted to illustrate learning preferences and habits of the students. (See Materials in the Annotated Resources at the back of the book for information on the diagnostic materials mentioned in this chapter.) As with each unit, the aforementioned out-of-class videotape viewings supported the current lesson.

The development unit began with *Emile* in which Rousseau introduced the concept of stage theory. With this historical foundation established, the curriculum moved to the study of the contemporary theories of Piaget and Erikson as examples of cognitive and social-emotional development, respectively. In the clinical laboratory, students self-administered the Mooney Problem Check List and discussed the nature and categories of problems faced by persons in the course of development. Demonstrations of Piagetian experiments also took place.

Evaluation was examined at the theoretical level through Dewey's *Experience and Education* (1938/1973), particularly its chapters on the nature of experience. Use of this text also extended the historical framework of the course by conveying key principles of progressivism. Closed reserve textbooks provided standard tests and measurement background. Laboratory curriculum explored different forms of evaluation through use of the Standard Score Converter, application of the Observational System for Instructional Analysis (Hough & Duncan, 1970), and administration of the California Phonics Survey. Simulations from the *Critical Moments in Teaching* Series of film vignettes and the computer software "School Transactions I, II" (Educulture, 1984) added another level of versimilitude to the study of evaluation.

The final unit, attentive to contemporary thought and the topic of motivation, employed C. G. Jung's *Psychological Reflections* (1973) as a central text. Motivation was discussed both from a behaviorist point of view and, more extensively, through Jung's self-realization analysis. His "structure and dynamics of the psyche" provided a vocabulary for discussing the human psyche, which was reinforced by laboratory administration of the Myers-Briggs Type Indicator (MBTI), a direct manifestation of Jung's *Psychological Types* (1921/1971) in a standardized instrument. The Bem Sex Role Inventory was administered for a supplemental and timely look at personality in a gender context.

Reconceptualist principles are evident in this educational psychology curriculum in several forms. There is extensive treatment of the affective aspects of personality and of the wide variations found in individuals. Political concerns are addressed in discussion of the abuses of standardized testing and the legitimacy of different learning styles and personality types, particularly with respect to gender stereotypes. Phenomenological and depth psychological perspectives run through the course, as does the traditional parallel between ontology and phylogeny. The underlying historical structure of the curriculum is particularly valuable in a course attempting to instruct about psychological development, because it can be used to offer a broad social metaphor for the process.

I refined Introduction to Education and Educational Psychology each term I taught them over a period of 10 years. Various laboratory and supplementary materials were altered, but the core structure and texts remained. Over the years their value was recognized by awards from the college and from the state organization of independent colleges as well as by support from the arts and sciences faculties of our liberal arts college. The courses appear to have conveyed the technical skills and professional curriculum expected of teacher education courses, while contributing to the liberal education of preservice teachers. As a test of reconceptualist theory, I strove through the courses to establish the claim that curriculum, even while serving a professional program, can address issues of profound personal meaning for students, heighten their motivation, and place education at the center of their field of interest. Using the characteristics described by Short (Chapter 12), it can be safely stated that the courses did not suffer from trivialization.

CONCLUSION:
PROBLEMS IN EDUCATION

In the winter of 1987, I was invited to serve as a visiting instructor at the University of Akron's Department of Educational Foundations and teach an evening section of Problems in Education, a senior capstone foundations course normally taught to students during the semester of their student teaching. This invitation afforded me an opportunity to step out of the articulated program in which I was serving and to test some ideas that were of interest to me. These included (1) using fiction to address multicultural teacher education, (2) steeping an entire course in the psychological-type theory of Jung and MBTI, and (3) employing educational foundations to explain the implicit modes of inquiry framework that gives structure to the students' general education program.

George Kneller's *Movements of Thought in Modern Education* (1984) lent structure to the 12 weeks of classes. Kneller organizes contemporary educational thought into eight formal philosophies or "movements" and the scholars most commonly associated with each. (The movements are: analysis, phenomenology, hermeneutics, structuralism, positivism, Marxism, romanticism, and conservatism.) Kneller follows his profile of each individual with a "Critique" and concludes each chapter with an "Appraisal" of the school's influence.

Selections from the text were used in juxtaposition with excerpts from film or literature and articles from *Annual Editions: Education 86/87* (Schultz, 1986), a volume in a series of compendia of scholarly articles organized along 40 disciplinary themes. One weekly lesson, "The Romantic Vision of the Humanities," for example, was illustrated through Kneller's treatment of Kohl, Kozol, and Illich; broadened to art and culture by excerpts from Kenneth Clark's film *The Romantic Rebellion;* personalized in readings from Richard Wright's *Black Boy* (1966); and related to everyday life in schools by articles like "A Long-Term View of School Desegregation: Some Recent Studies of Graduates as Adults" (Braddock, Crain, & McPartland, 1986). Multicultural sensitivity was emphasized through the priority assigned by Romantic writers to the value of the individual who differs from the norm. Finally, to serve a general education organizational role, Romanticism was discussed in the context of the university's curriculum by examining with students the courses and disciplines where they had found this point of view in evidence. Philip Phenix' *Realms of Meaning* (1964) provided a useful source in framing this material; like Kneller, he makes explicit the various movements of thought that shape the manner in which disciplines are taught.

"Normal Science and Positivism" was the title of one week's lesson in which Kneller's description of positivism (and behaviorism) was extended by the film *Theory,* which illustrates the role of theory in the sciences, and related to schools by articles like "What Do the SATs Mean?" (Morgan, 1986), "Disciplinary Strategies" (Talent & Busch, 1986), and "On Stir-and-Serve Recipes for Teaching" (Ohanian, 1986). Then, stepping back from their own experience of college, the preservice teachers analyzed the curriculum they had been exposed to, to determine in which courses and/or disciplines this philosophy had prevailed. For virtually all class members, these discussions of the modes of inquiry that were implicit in their education were unprecedented and, apparently, meaningful and revealing. (Schubert, in Chapter 13, notes similar benefits from such group inquiries.) Students have an instructional need for some set of organizing principles with which to rationalize the disparity of points of view in their general education.

I administered the MBTI to students early in the course and posted a chart indicating the results. Isabel Briggs Myers' *Introduction to Type* (1980) was assigned reading, while Jung's theory of the structure and dynamics of the psyche was introduced during the unit treating "structuralism." Scenes from the documentary *Matter of Heart* diversified the methods of instruction by showing the psychologist explaining type theory. The insight gained into their own learning styles through the MBTI enhanced the students' ability to understand the various modes of inquiry and their own respective affinities for some disciplines over others.

At the conclusion of the course it was recognized by the Evening Student Council of the university as the first winner of an outstanding teaching award in the Department of Educational Foundations. This recognition and the evaluations submitted by class members suggest that the course successfully achieved its reconceptualist aims in helping students better grasp the origins and diversity of educational problems and the hidden structures and potential purposes of their own education.

EPILOGUE

My purpose in this chapter was to share a curriculum theorist's experience in employing a reconceptualist framework to the development and instruction of a number of courses. This curriculum development work is about to extend to a college-wide level through a grant from the National Endowment for the Humanities to Slippery Rock University's College of Education and Human Service Professions. The purpose of the grant is to increase the humanities content of the teacher education curriculum in a manner guided by the principles that undergird this chapter.

• *Preservice teachers have the ability to comprehend challenging primary source material, but that ability is normally underestimated.* Assignments should be concise, directed by study questions, and quizzed before discussion to derive maximum benefit. In contrast to their blasé attitude toward survey textbooks, students achieve satisfaction from engagement with primary source authors. The standing of the discipline of education in the wider institutional setting is also enhanced by curriculum drawn from such sources as film, music, and so forth.

• *Phenomenological and depth psychological curriculum can motivate students to learn about the process of education while gaining insight about their own development.* Students' immediate needs for self-understanding normally have priority for them over their more distant need for professional competence. The most effective strategy for arousing and sustaining student interest is to relate the subject matter to student growth needs, while also meeting conventional teacher education aims.

• *If the college or university is not providing a rationale for the purpose and an explanation of the structure of general education, foundations of education courses should fill in the breach.* Of all professional persons in the community, teachers are the ones for whom it is most vital that the meaning of general education be grasped. Though teacher educators might prefer to deal more specifically with technical pedagogical issues, they must address this more pressing need if others have not done so.

• *Sound instruction in teacher education responds to diversity in preservice candidates' learning styles by providing curriculum through a variety of methodologies.* These include clinical and field experiences, computer-assisted instruction, film and videotape programs, and videotaped microteaching. Clinical experiences and other means of simulating applications of pedagogical knowledge may be the area of greatest promise for expansion and innovation. MBTI data indicate that teacher education students tend to value *praxis* more than their professor instructors, who tend to be centered on theory as a vehicle for preparation. This divergence in orientation has fostered much of the dissatisfaction associated with teacher education.

• *The individual path the instructor has found to learning about the process of education is a powerful source for planning teacher education curriculum.* Although teacher educators must recognize disciplinary, licensure, and accreditation structures, their own biographies and sources of intellectual inspiration are equally important in formulating curriculum that can be taught with effect and conviction. The importance of this is especially apparent in Chapter 15 by Kridel. In many cases the vital lesson taught to students is that the reflective life is uniquely rewarding and that the course of life does lend itself to rational inquiry.

In 1902 John Dewey (1902/1966) synopsized this curricular perspective in *The Child and the Curriculum* by contrasting the role of the scientist with that of the teacher.

> As a teacher he is not concerned with adding new facts to the science he teaches; in propounding new hypotheses or in verifying them. He is concerned with the subject-matter of the science as *representing a given stage and phase of the development of experience.* His problem is that of inducing a vital and personal experiencing. Hence, what concerns him, as a teacher, is the ways in which that subject may become a part of experience; what there is in the child's present that is usable with reference to it; how such elements are to be used; how his own knowledge of the subject-matter may assist in interpreting the child's needs and doings, and determine the medium in which the child should be placed in order that his growth may be properly directed. (p. 23)

Curriculum is by its nature a generalist pursuit, drawing on the range of disciplines to design an environment in which selected material can be taught well. Curriculum theory is a distinct endeavor that ultimately must define itself, not according to other models, but in light of its ability to effect intellectual growth in those who study and learn.

REFERENCES

Beyer, Landon, & Zeichner, Kenneth. (1982). Teacher training and educational foundations: A plea for discontent. *Journal of Teacher Education, 33* (3), 18–23.

Braddock, Jomills; Crain, Robert; & McPartland, James. (1986). A long-term view of school desegregation: Some recent studies of graduates as adults. In F. Schultz (Ed.), *Annual editions: Education 86/87* (pp. 144–149). Guilford, CT: Dushkin.

Bucke, Richard Maurice. (1969). *Cosmic consciousness.* New York: Dutton.

Dewey, John. (1900, 1902/1966). *The child and the curriculum* and *The school and society.* Chicago: University of Chicago Press. (Original publications 1900 and 1902, respectively.)

Dewey, John. (1938/1973). *Experience and education.* New York: Collier Books. (Original publication, 1938.)

Harding, M. Esther. (1973). *The "I" and the "not-I."* Princeton: Princeton-Bollingen.

Hough, John, & Duncan, J. Kelly. (1970). *Teaching: Description and analysis.* Reading, MA: Addison and Wesley.

Jaspers, Karl. (1962). *Socrates, Buddha, Confucius, Jesus.* New York: Harcourt, Brace & World.

Jaspers, Karl. (1962). *The great philosophers.* New York: Harcourt, Brace & World.

Jung, C. G. (1953/1973). *Psychological reflections.* Princeton: Princeton-Bollingen. (Original publication, 1953.)

Jung, C. G. (1921/1971). *Psychological types.* Princeton: Princeton-Bollingen. (Original publication, 1921.)

Kant, Immanuel. (1966). *On education.* Ann Arbor: University of Michigan Press.

Klohr, Paul. (1974). *Curriculum theory: The state of the field.* Paper presented before the Curriculum Theory Conference, Xavier University, Cincinnati.

Kneller, George. (1984). *Movements of thought in modern education.* New York: John Wiley.

Kohlberg, L. (1976). Moral stages and moralization: The cognitive developmental approach. In T. Lickona (Ed.), *Moral development and behavior: Theory, research and social issues* (pp. 31–53). New York: Holt, Rinehart & Winston.

Montessori, Maria. (1971). *The child in the family.* New York: Avon.

Mooney, Ross L. (1956). *The Mooney problem check list.* New York: The Psychological Corporation.

Morgan, Dan. (1986). What do the SATs mean? SATs are getting in the way of education. In F. Schultz (Ed.), *Annual editions: Education 86/87* (pp. 91–94). Guilford, CT: Dushkin.

Myers, Isabel B. (1980). *Introduction to type.* Palo Alto: Consulting Psychologists Press.

Ohanian, Susan. (1986). On stir-and-serve recipes for teaching. In F. Schultz (Ed.), *Annual editions: Education 86/87* (pp. 194–199). Guilford, CT: Dushkin.

Ouspensky, P. D. (1949). *In search of the miraculous.* New York: Harcourt, Brace & World.

Phenix, Philip. (1964). *Realms of meaning.* New York: McGraw-Hill.

Pinar, William. (1974). *Heightened consciousness, cultural revolution, and curriculum theory.* Berkeley, CA: McCutchan.

Pinar, William. (1975). *Curriculum theorizing: The reconceptualists.* Berkeley, CA: McCutchan.

Pinar, William. (1988). *Contemporary curriculum discourses.* Scottsdale, AZ: Gorsuch Scarisbrick.

Plato. (1956). *Great dialogues of Plato.* New York: The New American Library.

Poole, Roger. (1972). *Towards deep subjectivity.* New York: Harper & Row.

Rousseau, Jean-Jacques. (1762/1964). *Emile.* Woodbury, NY: Barron's Educational Series. (Original publication, 1762.)

Schultz, Fred (Ed.). (1986). *Annual editions: Education 86/87.* Guilford, CT: Dushkin.

Shaker, Paul. (1975). *A study of the evolution of consciousness: A foundational source for education.* Unpublished doctoral dissertation, Ohio State University.

Talent, Barbara, & Busch, Suzanne. (1986). Disciplinary strategies. In F. Schultz (Ed.), *Annual editions: Education 86/87* (pp. 139–141). Guilford, CT: Dushkin.

Whitehead, A. N. (1929/1957). *The aims of education.* New York: The Free Press. (Original publication, 1929.)

Wright, Richard. (1966). *Black boy.* New York: Harper & Row.

FILMS, SOFTWARE AND VIDEOTAPES

Art of the '60s. (1967). WCBS–TV, BFA.

The Blue Angel. (1930). Josef von Sternberg, Films Inc.

Civilisation XII. "The Fallacies of Hope." (1969). Kenneth Clark, BBC.

Critical Moments in Teaching Series. (1968). University of Missouri: Holt Rinehart & Winston.

Education in America. (1958). Coronet.

Fishing at the Stone Weir. (1969). Man: A Course of Study.

Huckleberry Finn and the American Experience. (1965). CTCH, Encyclopedia Britannica Educational Corp.

Life in the Thirties. (1959). NBC News, McGraw-Hill.

Matter of Heart. (1985). Jung Institute of Los Angeles, Kino International.

The Romantic Rebellion. (1973). Kenneth Clark, VPS, Pyramid.

School Transactions, I, II, (1984). Educulture.

Searching for Values. (1972). Learning Corporation of America.

Theory. (1979). Playback Associates, Phillips Pet.

15

Teaching Curriculum Through an Historical–Biographical Perspective

CRAIG KRIDEL
University of South Carolina

I was graduated from Ohio State University where I studied curriculum (secondary and higher education), foundations of education, and dance history. Presently, my primary field of study is curriculum of higher education.

My mentors are Paul R. Klohr and Paul Shaker. Shaker introduced me to the idea of the academic life, one which was totally unfamiliar and, for that reason, quite frightening. Paul Klohr embodied the progressive spirit of the university, the scholar-gentlemen—brilliance and dignity, excellence and equity, wit, and faith in the common man. Throughout my stay at Ohio State he introduced me to its tradition, "democracy as a way of life," as developed by Boyd H. Bode, furthered by his advisee, Harold Alberty, and carried further by his advisee, Klohr. My studies were enhanced quite significantly by a community of graduate students—Robert Bullough, Janet Miller, John Holton, Michael Olivas, and Nicolae Sacalis—and by professional friendships with Theodore Brameld, Maxine Greene, Harold Taylor, and Andrew Broekema.

The foundations of my pedagogical beliefs were laid previous to my entry into graduate school by two individuals outside of the field of education. Kenneth Wollitz (music) and Richard Klitch (athletics) displayed in ways I will never fully understand the ability to translate the most theoretical and esoteric ideas into understandable, tangible actions. Both displayed an entrancing pedagogical style and underscored the importance of a student's satisfaction coming not merely from understanding an idea but, instead, from initiating the idea into practice. Also, Wollitz and Klitch displayed how the learner's interpretations, with no concern toward validity and reliability, can become a legitimate and integral as-

pect of the pedagogical process. Theirs was a type of "involvement in learning" that escapes current national reports and, to a degree, eludes description. Yet, it is a phenomenon I have experienced and, no doubt, will devote the rest of my academic career trying to articulate.

Teaching a curriculum course is really a simple faculty assignment! In many, if not most, institutions, almost anyone can do it. If you do not believe this, examine current practices as I have. The field is not well defined, and no special training seems to be required. Moreover, the traditional content of curriculum courses is well laid-out. A bit of educational history serves as an introduction. The Tyler Rationale follows with a detailed examination of the Bloom taxonomy. (No matter if much of this is already the taken-for-granted content of other education courses.) Then comes the very heart of the typical curriculum course—how to use and/or develop teaching guides related to state courses of study. Much of that effort is centered on spelling out specific behavioral goals at various grade levels or identifying steps involved in implementing commercial curriculum packages. Also included are the instructor's perks, typically couched within a specific subject area and all related to an assortment of "students' interests," whatever those may be. This is simple stuff and, if succinctly presented (though it rarely is), would result in graduate curriculum courses being reduced to weekend workshops. I will be the first to agree that the essays in this book dispute this perspective; however, these contributions are by no means portrayals of traditional curriculum courses.

My statements above represent the trivialization of curriculum as identified in Chapter 12—in this case, the trivialization of the teaching of curriculum. I concur with Short that the tendency toward trivialization must be challenged; teaching curriculum is a complex, demanding matter that calls for thoughtful, imaginative presentations of the field. However noble this ideal seems, I am still confronted with an institutional situation not different from most. Many of my students, individuals returning for a master's level course while they pursue careers as teachers, aspiring administrators, or administrators, are quite strong, potentially good professionals. Yet, their expectations are such that curriculum teaching becomes even more simple— for when I attend to the "needs of my students," I find that they see no basic reason to learn about curriculum. If there is a recognition of the field, then what they wish to learn falls within the realm of curriculum development and practical strategies, lists, and steps to construct curriculum. In effect, they seek some entity more comprehensive than a collection of lesson plans, yet they realize their participation in curriculum development must not be important enough for it to be released from the bureaucratic control of their central administration. My impressions are not overly cynical. I sense that they are the common experience of curriculum professors. Pre-service teacher education programs rarely provide as sophisticated a view of the curriculum field as could be developed. Shaker displays such possibil-ities in Chapter 14. Students have not enlarged their initial views on their own by the time they come to me for graduate studies. The term *curricu-lum* is, indeed, mentioned during their preservice years, yet too often it occurs while students write individual teaching lessons. Or, commonly it is related only to a specific subject area. A comprehensive vision of the entire school program involving overall concerns with curriculum design is a rarity.

Each semester I am confronted with a large number of students who bemoan (never openly) the curriculum course requirement. They want, and to a certain degree "need," a systematic, effective process for developing and constructing specific curricula. The larger, foundational, and middle-range theoretical issues of curriculum, the "heart of the field" so well articulated by the authors of this text, are unknown to these students. If known, such material initially is viewed merely as "fugitive content" from a philosophy of education course—an area viewed as having little value in the real world of schooling.

This is my initial struggle, one that I anticipate and welcome, in part, because I know it is so easy to handle on its own terms if I choose to do so. I can attend to my students' wishes for knowledge of curriculum develop-ment and construction, an area wracked by protocol and emptiness. And I know I can satisfy all expectations, mine and theirs, within two to three class sessions supplemented by some outside reading. (These sessions, of course, never occur at the beginning of the course in a consecutive manner but are, instead, interwoven into the semester class meetings.) Having done this, I have an additional seven to eight class sessions to develop with them some insights into "the big picture" of curriculum. Since I am on a semester sys-tem of 16 class sessions, I am left with a considerable amount of class time for my perk, an historical-biographical perspective.

TOWARD AN ALTERNATIVE RATIONALE

My "idiosyncratic pedagogy" is more than a trick for "livening up" the class with a new twist on the traditional curriculum content. Indeed, I want to claim that it is an alternative rationale for viewing the curriculum field and making it come alive—an exciting journey both for me and the stu-dents. This chapter precludes an extensive exploration of the theoretical base underlying my teaching. I am currently in the process of explicating that base elsewhere. Yet, I sense my position approaches more nearly a 1990s extrapolation of much of what John Dewey was trying to say relative to the relationship between the individual and the social setting, that is, the concept of community (either the school setting or the larger community) as an "upward extension" of the individual. I view my efforts as a basic ingredient of what I call a redefinition of "collegiality." I am convinced that such a redefinition is basic to any approach to an understanding of curriculum theory and, in turn, curriculum teaching. This is the historical-biographical journey I wish to share.

Practically all students are interested in coming along for the journey. When they hear or read about the "big issues"—indoctrination, what knowledge is of most worth, curricular integration, political aspects of articulation, social injustice reflected in schooling, and the like—they begin to realize that this is what graduate studies should be about. We discuss the Tyler Rationale, and I assume they are already familiar with Bloom's taxonomy, as they always are. (Bloom's taxonomy is so integrated into all the South Carolina requirements that it must surely be taught to students in practically every course they take.) We examine the Progressive era in greater detail, discussing selections of Boyd Bode, George Counts, Harold Rugg, William H. Kilpatrick, Harold Alberty, W. W. Charters, and the Eight Year Study. The writings of Franklin Bobbitt, Hilda Taba, Broudy-Smith-Burnett, Philip Phenix, Harold Taylor, Maxine Greene, William Pinar, and Michael Apple emerge throughout the course. Students "take hold" of some (not all) of the ideas and leave the course with a sense of some of the big issues and a feeling for the ideas of certain individuals who have addressed these issues. They also have some sense of how to go about reconciling certain curricular dilemmas. Above all, there is an attitude toward scholarship, however conceived, that is recognized as being important. This heightened sensibility is somewhat unusual in comparison with the typical vocationally oriented education courses. Students realize they are beyond the days of learning new pedagogical tricks (or they accept the fact that they will learn new tricks in their districts' staff development programs).

This foundational material, so crucial to the curriculum field, can be presented in various ways. I develop what might be viewed as a personalized historical and biographical approach. This approach grows out of my evolving conception of the general education of teachers and its proven effectiveness as I have refined it over the past several years with groups of graduate students. I should clarify that I view the field of curriculum not as a unified body of knowledge with rigid discipline boundaries but rather as a group of hard-working individuals, not too terribly different from myself (with the exception of fame and intelligence) and my students, struggling to make sense out of the educational/social situations in which they work. While at this point I am uncertain of the impact of an historical-biographical approach to the teaching of curriculum, the method continues to bring new experiences and meaning to the study of curriculum, both to me and to my students as they engage in graduate studies.

JUSTIFYING THE HISTORICAL–BIOGRAPHICAL PERSPECTIVE

You can give humanistic value to almost anything by teaching it historically. Geology, economics, mechanics, are humanities when taught with
reference to the successive achievements of the geniuses to which these
sciences owe their being. Not taught thus, literature remains grammar, art
a catalogue, history a list of dates, and natural science a sheet of formulas
and weights and measures.   —William James

While the field of curriculum has received its criticisms for being ahis-torical, few would argue with the importance of historical material in an introductory curriculum course. Any review of current synoptic texts underscores this fact, for typically an obligatory chapter is devoted to the history of the field. After carefully reviewing an assortment of curriculum syllabi collected from institutions throughout South Carolina and the Southeast, I noticed that a few class sessions are commonly devoted to the works of the field's "patron saints" and one or two national curriculum projects from the 1960s and 1970s. Yet, rarely is the historical material integrated into further discussions of curriculum design and development. These uses illustrate flawed justifications of the importance of history.

Such uses of history represent an age-old belief that history is basic in that it comes first and is somehow "good for the student to know." This use of history is homage to curriculum's Grunderzeit, the time of the founders. We are supposed to know the names of our fathers, grandfathers, and earlier saints and sinners. This is "curriculum literacy à la Hirsh"—students should be able to identify Bobbitt, Tyler, 1918, scope, sequence, P.E.A., and 30 schools. Once such specific information has been satisfactorily displayed, students may get on with the "real task" of curriculum construction.

Yet another traditional rationale for an historical perspective in curriculum is the intent to portray the folly of past eras so we will not repeat the same mistakes. This attitude is reflected in Santayana's widely quoted statement, "Those who cannot remember the past are condemned to repeat it." Yet, the perspective is as flawed as this quote. Joseph Epstein (1988) points out that the original is, "Those who cannot remember the past are condemned to fulfill it."

Integrated into presentations of contemporary curriculum issues and practices, such a perspective is misleading in that it demonstrates a "neat" and "linear" conception of historical events and "progress." The difficulties of historical causality are overlooked in much the same way as they too often are in elementary social studies texts. As fourth graders are given the three reasons for the War Between the States, their teachers are told to avoid certain follies (all committed in times past) in order to obtain certain outcomes. The inadequacies of such a use of history are apparent and clearly fail as an effective mode of inquiry for understanding the field of curriculum.

Placed in good hands, these two conceptions of the use of history become a devotional to our patrons and, at best, are often inspirational. In bad hands, this use becomes merely a mockery of earlier eras. As Barry Franklin (1986) stated, "The age of Bobbitt-bashing is over." Similarly, there is no longer a need to discuss W. W. Charter's Commonwealth Study (1929) in order to laugh at the "teacher making a lampshade for superintendent's wife" competency (though it always did get a good laugh and provided a framework to begin questioning the 1970s CBTE/PBTE movement). When the points are made (or the textbook chapter is finished), history as survey, or history to avoid past mistakes, is over—little, if any, integration between an historical perspective and curriculum design or development results.

I draw on other justifications for an historical perspective in part because of the over-simplicity of contemporary curriculum construction and the naivete of well-meaning students. This must be countered by the "booming, buzzing confusion" of curriculum, education, and lived classroom experiences. While historical knowledge is important to establish a sense of the past, common learnings, and a "general education" for the field of curriculum, historical content must also be presented to demonstrate the richness of classroom life. While contemporary teaching may seem deceptively simple to my students, historical portraits of curriculum and classroom life, when studied as basic content of the curriculum field, become astonishingly complex. Practices, ideas, and issues seem quite contemporary, yet the "facts" do not fall neatly into place nor do ideological movements conveniently fit into perspective.

Since history is merely placing "limits on infinity," students begin to wonder about the similar complexity of their own workplaces and their emerging conception of curriculum. The material embodies a Deweyan conception of intelligence in which the function of the mind (in this case history) projects new and more complex ends. In effect, it frees experience from the routine and the capricious. History becomes messy and muddled, as so beautifully depicted in Frederick Rudolph's *Curriculum* (1977). Historical perspective, so conceived, tells numerous stories, tales with beginnings and endings, all intertwined with the passing of time. While these stories give no answers or predictions to contemporary trends, they do illustrate the fragility and temporality of the present. By studying the history of curriculum as a composite of dynamic forces, students witness their own discussions and experiences, voiced decades before—be it as Bode's anger at the progressive education conception of "needs," Phenix's call for imagination as an integral aspect of instruction, or the Progressive Education Association's 1930 criticism of secondary education—all as "arguments without end." My curriculum course becomes a time of "in medias res"—students are thrown into the thick of it, struggling to make sense of the past and wondering if, indeed, the present is equally complex.

These moments do not occur, however, in class discussions of sanitized excerpts from synoptic texts. In our course, saints and sinners speak for themselves in their own words. They are not reduced to ideological camps battling for high ground. These ideas came from people, some of whom drove fast, flew airplanes, published their own books and left them in conference hallways, played jazz, and followed baseball with a vengeance (Ralph Tyler, Harold Hand, Harold Benjamin, Harold Taylor, and Boyd Bode, respectively).

While the intellectual activity of studying curriculum becomes wonderfully rich and complex from my perspective, the experience typically is somewhat discomforting to those who return daily to the classroom. For those who are moved by this content, students who take an intellectual, thoughtful attitude to curricular issues, the return may often be somewhat lonely. As Martin Jay (1973) states, it is "commonplace in the modern world to regard the intellectual as estranged, maladjusted, and discontented" (p. xiii). While this tends to be an overstatement for a contemporary teacher, careful, thoughtful consideration of curriculum may well lead to a "lonely" educational life. I hold up biography not as therapy but as an opportunity to portray educational life and the ongoing intellectual struggle to make sense of conflicting ideas.

My description thus far of the use I make of history may seem less than fully innovative. It is the extension I make of this perspective that I want to claim as somewhat unique and a significant step in the teaching of curriculum. Geraldine Clifford (1975) has underscored the importance of "person-centered" history on academic grounds. My colleague Robert Bullough (1981) at the University of Utah has effectively demonstrated this person-centered approach in his excellent reconstruction of the ideas and life of Boyd Bode. My justification is more on pedagogical grounds—historical biography becomes a method of enhancing content, building collegiality, and establishing communicative action. Perhaps it is my determination of the question of worth as central to curriculum empowerment, as Schubert has underscored in Chapter 13.

CURRICULUM COMES ALIVE

My classroom effort to provide the setting for communicative action involves drawing on many resources. Initially, I do not expect students to go forth and locate such sources. I have taken the initial step and accumulated a comprehensive collection, all publicly available (as will be cited later). As I lay out in my course what I see as important ideas and works of selected curriculum leaders, we simultaneously examine biographical information. This investigation involves attention to birthplaces, locations where they worked, dates of their most prolific writing, times of their most important works, institutions where their careers may have overlapped with others, and common institutions of doctoral studies. We draw on Schubert and Posner's work (1980) in academic genealogy and look for similarities there.

Students do not attempt to determine the impact of formative experiences or to draw some unique connections from these historical data. Class members are just coming "to know" certain curriculum leaders. They are introduced with the thought that some will become friends and with the hope that one may become a best friend.

I continue the introductions by reading excerpts from any autobiographical or biographical accounts I have been able to find. Sometimes, these are formal books or essays; other times, it is personal correspondence that I have been able to locate. Once again, our intent is not to determine causality or some comprehensive scheme as Erikson (1958) found for young man Luther. But, knowing of Hilda Taba's childhood experiences in Russian-occupied Estonia and hearing her mention her after-school task of picking up the dead from skirmishes between the White and Red armies, in some way, brings her a little closer to the class members. The same feelings may emerge on learning of Harold Benjamin's distinguished and "unique" military career (after serving on the Mexican border with General "Blackjack" Pershing in the struggle against Pancho Villa, Benjamin became bored with normal military duty and went AWOL, riding a horse up to Oregon so he could re-enlist to serve with the WWI American forces in Europe). Similarly, knowledge of the books that most influenced William Van Til, Harry Broudy, Philip Phenix, Ralph Tyler, and Harold Shane may establish an intellectual rapport for those students new to the curriculum field. Knowledge of Alice Miel's professional work and career continues to be a source of inspiration for students struggling with the institutional sexism of the South Carolina educational system. One fact becomes clear—students recognize they are learning about people, many of whom have had the same types of experience as they, themselves. At this point the field of curriculum is no longer a set of steps, a collection of "isms," or a list of principles.

We continue this biographical immersion by looking at photographic portraits of our curriculum leaders, past and present. This was my introductory venture into historical biography begun 12 years ago with the establishment of the Curriculum Photo-Archives, then housed at Ohio State University. Unfortunately, no description of the impact of visual images on my students can be made without bordering on an abuse of clichés. Let me assure you the images are powerful, and the moment quite touching as I hear students whisper, "Ahh, just as I thought he [or she] would look." The study of curriculum has now taken on a human touch.

As powerful as the visual images are, in recent years I have been able to add yet another dimension—historical recordings drawn from the Museum of Education's Historical Recordings Project. It is a very special moment for me—my special gift to the class—when I bring in the tape recorder, and we actually hear George Counts. Being at a southern university, I need not identify the speaker to the class when we listen to the "white-haired gentleman from Georgia," Heard Kilpatrick (in his youth he was referred to as Heard). Being especially fond of Boyd Bode and Harold Alberty and their ideas, the moment they speak becomes a special, even sacred, event for me. It often does also for my students.

I have found that there is a significant difference between hearing new ideas or, indeed, direct accounts of old ones, and simply reading them. The speaker provides his or her unique emphases in ways impossible to communicate in print. Pauses and tonal changes create insights and increased understanding. While these interpretations could be viewed as random speculation with little historical validity, that is not the point. Students establish a sense of personal meaning and, more important, meaningfulness. The interpreted nuance may not be what the speaker intended, yet the interpretations create a personal bond bridging the present to the past. As long as students realize that their interpretations are "creative speculation," truth and accuracy are not compromised nor is historical fact transformed into fiction.

By this time in a curriculum course the class members need little convincing of the specialness of historical-biographical resources. They have become friends with a group of important educators and may have become especially attached to one or two. I ask them to seal this bond by obtaining a book (typically, out of print) written by their "friend." The initial reaction is always "yes, but how?" I remind them of the hordes of individuals who on weekends go "antiquing" throughout South Carolina. This is considered entertainment and a hobby for many. I maintain the same attitude can be taken toward finding out-of-print education books. One of my fondest moments as a graduate student was the day that Robert Bullough and I, armed with towels and flashlights, found an unopened room in a bookstore warehouse where, sitting on dust-covered shelving, were untouched, "new" textbooks assigned to classes by Bode, Charters, Sidney Pressey, and Hank Hullfish. Many students take my advice, and I have become adept at recognizing across a crowded classroom an excited facial expression as a student rushes to show me what used books have been found.

THAT PRIVATE COLLEGIAL GESTURE

I take one last step as teacher in helping students understand curriculum at what I am convinced is its deepest, most significant level. I ask them to "go home" with a curriculum friend and colleague. After a day filled with its normal complexities and vicissitudes, I ask that they return not to an evening of prime-time television but, instead, to a comforting moment with a curricular friend. It may mean, for me, just reading a passage from Bode. In doing this, I am reminded that I am not alone. My problems and concerns may be different from his, but we both struggled and, as friends, we struggle together.

This is the camaraderie I seek through the historical-biographical approach to the curriculum field. Of course, these fulfilling moments do not occur only after work; they may occur anytime throughout the day. Students come to this level of experiencing with or without my guidance. But I am convinced that what we undergo in the classroom is a crucial factor. Their intellectual life typically is quite lonely. However, they come to realize, in a very personal way, that they are part of a larger entity: members of a professional curriculum community. The moment can become as moving and inspirational as when one hears the second movement of Beethoven's Seventh Symphony. I usually ask students to identify a specific gesture that reminds them of their curriculum friend(s). Students cannot read Herb Kohl's 36 Children (1968) and then not feel something special when they make the commonplace gesture of closing the classroom door. The act of closing a door has taken on new meaning. My own gesture throughout the preparation of this chapter has been sharpening 20 pencils before each writing session, a mnemonic device that, according to Malcolm Cowley (1979), Hemingway completed before each day's writing task. I certainly have no illusions about being a Hemingway, but for a moment I know that Hemingway and I have had a shared experience—it is a good feeling. Similarly, when my preschool teachers learn of Philip Jackson's chapter on "real teaching" in The Practice of Teaching (1986, pp. 75–97), they will never bend at the knees to talk to a child in quite the same manner. In fact, some may smirk as they bend at the waist, like Jackson, who determined this was one way to distinguish himself from a real early childhood teacher. The feeling is special. Perhaps it is not as powerful as the myths Mircea Eliade (1963) describes, but the overall effect on one's consciousness of a personal/professional relationship between the historical past and the present lived-in experience is similar:

> Living a myth, then implies a genuinely "religious" experience, since it differs from the ordinary experience of everyday life. The "religiousness" of this experience is due to the fact that one re-enacts fabulous, exalting, significant events.... This also implies that one is no longer living in chronological time, but in the primordial Time, the Time when the event first took place. This is why we can use the term the "strong time" of myth; it is the prodigious, "sacred" time when something new, strong, and significant was manifested. (p. 19)

How significant these experiences are for students I will never know. Yet, I am convinced they are critical factors in the evolution of higher levels of insight and interpretation into the curriculum field.

To come full circle in the teaching process I am sketching here, I should make clear one of my efforts to use the kind of insights I have claimed are the hoped for, and frequently found, outcomes of my teaching. This is the relationship that I insist must be forged between the curriculum views of the historical "friends" we have made and the curriculum problems and issues of the 1980s. In part, evidence of a student's ability to identify and handle these relationships is a critical factor in his or her evaluation and serves as part of an overall evaluation of the course. The following questions are typical of the kind I pose:

1. You are taking a stroll with a curriculum leader (of your choice). What would be his (or her) criticisms of current educational practices in South Carolina (with specific emphasis on the state's Educational Improvement Act)? How would you try to defend the state's practices? What would be his (or her) compliments? What comments would you make to your friend to indicate that contemporary education, while struggling somewhat, is holding up "better than ever"?
2. You have just introduced your curriculum friend to members of the teaching staff and students from your school. Prepare a 12-minute (4–5 pages) transcript of the ensuing conversation. Comments by staff and students may be "fictional"; your friend's comments should be based on specific quotations (with minor modifications) from published works.

ADVENTURE AND EXPLORATION AS CURATOR/TEACHER

Lastly, I wish to describe my reasons for and experiences in actually pulling together resources. Such a description is essential in an essay underscoring the importance of an historical-biographical perspective. As director of an aesthetic education institute before arriving at the University of South Carolina, I was quite regularly placed in a position where I had to justify reasons for classroom teachers to enroll in the program. While there were many such reasons, one always seemed to resonate more than others: All educators must continue to learn; too often teachers, in their quest to control and coordinate the classroom setting in a most professional way, allow their instructional content to become static. I have never forgotten those discussions and swore that I would continue exploring for "introduction to curriculum" materials. I knew I must place myself in new learning situations of astonishment and confusion; I must never forget the bewilderment I felt when first trying to make sense out of the field.

This is one of the many reasons why I accepted the curatorship of the Museum of Education. I obtained closer access to a huge collection of materials, many of them pertaining to curriculum and attending specifically to my newfound interest in developing an historical-biographical perspective.

I have so enjoyed exploring the holdings of the museum—randomly pulling out books from the 6000+ textbook collection (dating back to 1799) and just snooping around in various other collections. So have my students. I encourage any teacher of curriculum to locate the nearest textbook collection and school museum, now made possible through surveys by ACRL and the Center for Rural Education (see Annotated Resources at the back of the book).

While establishing itself as an archival resource center, the Museum continues to fulfill its role as a museum through an extensive exhibition program. What has proven to be one of the more interesting displays for my students and me is the Margaret Willis Exhibition. Dr. Willis' teaching career spanned 35 years as a high school social studies teacher in one of the country's most experimental schools, the Ohio State University Laboratory School. The 1938 high school graduating class wrote a best-selling book, entitled *Were We Guinea Pigs?* (Class of 1938, 1938), describing their experiences in this progressive school (one of the 30 schools of the Eight Year Study). Dr. Willis, with assistance from Dr. Lou LaBrant, prepared a follow-up study, *The Guinea Pigs After Twenty Years* (Willis, 1961). Shortly after Dr. Willis' death, her entire professional education collection was donated to the Museum. We have reconstructed her library, complete with books, her writing chair, typewriter, and assorted photographs and momentoes. Students say it is as if they were looking through her window while she was out of the room. Her collection of books offers a glimpse of what a social studies teacher "on the cutting edge" was reading in the 1930s and 1940s (and implicitly makes a strong case for the general education of teachers). While I am not suggesting that others can establish museums (though it would be wonderful for each state to host a museum of education), similar innovative displays could be initiated in any college of education building.

Another exhibition at the Museum could be initiated by curriculum students in any setting that portrays a contemporary biographical perspective of curriculum and the schools. The Museum commissioned Dr. Alan Wieder, professor of educational sociology at the University of South Carolina, to prepare an exhibition of his choosing in the area of photographic sociology. The exhibition, "Possibilities, Lost Possibilities, No Possibilities: Images of Children and Adults," presents a compelling image of racial disharmony and growing class disparity in contemporary society. (The exhibition was one of our most successful, toured the United States, and was published in *The International Journal of Qualitative Studies in Education* [Wieder, 1988].) This type of photography can present an equally insightful vignette of contemporary curriculum and school life. I hope to include this as an option for students when they take their final examination stroll with a curriculum friend, that is, photographic representation of just what they see.

While I have mentioned the use of photographic portraits and audio recordings of curriculum leaders in my course, the Museum of Education is presently preparing the national dissemination of these materials. In 1989, the Museum of Education published *Images of the Curriculum Field,* a collection of photographs of prominent curriculum leaders taken from the Curriculum Photo-Archives. Coupled with each photograph will be a descriptive statement of the individual's contribution to the field of curriculum, biographical information, bibliographic material, and representative quotations from the individual's published works. Additionally, the Museum is completing its Historical Recording Project, in which it will prepare a series of three- to five-minute excerpts from 1940s audio recordings by Counts, Kilpatrick, Childs, Otto, Bode, Alberty, Thayer, Tyler, Dale, and others. The cassette will be accompanied by a monograph of biographical information and audio transcripts (see Annotated Resources at the back of the book).

Through good fortune, I have been able to take a more active role myself in the accumulation of biographical materials. As the former editor of *Teaching Education,* I included in each issue three or four biographical essays entitled "teaching profiles." In my class, I draw quite heavily on these profiles, which contain many unpublished anecdotes and insights. Publications have included profiles of Hollis Caswell, Harold Alberty, John Dewey, Ralph Tyler, Benjamin Bloom, Hilda Taba, George Counts, Boyd Bode, and William Kilpatrick (see Annotated Resources at the back of the book).

As an "outlander" in the South, I looked forward to learning about the curricular leaders of my state. I began the quest for materials at the local/regional levels. Once again, adventures abound. J. A. Rice (founder of Black

Mountain College and former resident of my city, Columbia) mentioned in his autobiography, *I Came Out of the Eighteenth Century* (1942), that many nineteenth-century male secondary school teachers were merely biding their time before careers in public office. The archival papers of many local and state politicians, housed in county and state archives, include personal letters and diary accounts of their teaching years.

When searching for local materials, I found county historical societies to be most accommodating; there always seems to be one member, typically a former teacher, who is a storehouse of local educational history. An invitation to visit my class has never been turned down.

If one is fortunate enough to uncover diary accounts of teaching, many interesting things can be done. In 1962, Curtis and Dorothy Hitchcock of Connecticut uncovered the letters of Miss Eliza Ann Summers (Hitchcock). Miss Summers taught the Freedmen and their children of Hilton Head, South Carolina, under the auspices of the American Missionary Association. The letters dated from 1867 and were written to her sister in Connecticut. The discovery led to the publication, *"Dear Sister": Letters Written on Hilton Head Island 1867* (Martin, 1977), and a beautiful portrayal of the educational practices of general culture of that time. The Museum of Education has commissioned a script for a 45-minute production falling within the genre of "living history." We plan to offer "Dear Sister" as part of the artist-in-the-schools program in South Carolina and believe the production will be as moving and informative for teachers as for students.

Another "rich and untapped" source of historical-biographical material is the local school district, college, and/or university. While higher education has a well-developed archives system, the "archives" of a school district may be a forgotten storage area waiting for decades to be cleaned out. Many possibilities are lying in wait, and the sense of exploration and adventure while stumbling through these closets is always entrancing. Biographical materials always seem to be found.

CONCLUDING REMARKS

My students leave class with the satisfaction that they know something about curriculum. There are always a few exceptions, but even they realize that they have been taught something about curriculum. All know the brass tacks of curriculum development—the original reason they came—and all know some of the big issues of the field. A few become entranced by the historical-biographical perspective and go out searching, tracking, and exploring. And all find the biographical dimension a nice touch to classroom discussions.

Garraty's (1957) statement is indeed true: "People are interested primarily in people. They have never had to be persuaded that 'the proper study of mankind is man.'" I don't expect my students to become biographers or historians of education. Actually, I have few expectations, for an historical-biographical perspective is not THE intent of the course. It is merely a touch. I do not present every bit of biographical material I have obtained. It is there when appropriate. And behind the scenes it is there constantly for me because as I continue tracking and exploring, new meaning is found in a course I teach year after year.

REFERENCES

Bullough, R. V., Jr. (1981). *Democracy in education—Boyd H. Bode.* Bayside, NY: General Hall.

Charters, W. W., with D. Waples. (1929). *The commonwealth teacher-training study.* Chicago: University of Chicago Press.

Class of 1938, University Laboratory School, Ohio State University. (1938). *Were we guinea pigs?* New York: Henry Holt.

Clifford, G. C. (1975). Saints, sinners, and people: A position paper of the historiography of American education. *History of Education Quarterly, 15*(3), 257–272.

Cowley, M. (1979). *—And I worked at the writer's trade: Chapters of literary history, 1918–1978.* New York: Penguin.

Eliade, M. (1963). *Myth and reality.* New York: Harper & Row.

Epstein, J. (1988). Quotatious. *The American Scholar, 57* (1), 7–16.

Erikson, E. (1958). *Young man Luther.* New York: Norton.

Franklin, B. (1986). Curriculum history through the monographic study. Paper presented at the Annual Meeting of the Society for the Study of Curriculum History, San Francisco.

Garraty, J. A. (1957). *The nature of biography.* New York: Alfred A. Knopf.

Jackson, P. W. (1986). *The practice of teaching.* New York: Teachers College Press.

Jay, M. (1973). *The dialectical imagination: A history of the Frankfurt school and the Institute of Social Research 1923–1950.* Boston: Little, Brown.

Kohl, H. (1968). *36 children.* New York: Signet.

Martin, J. W. (Ed.). (1977). *"Dear sister": Letters written on Hilton Head Island 1867.* Beaufort, SC: Beaufort Book Co.

Rice, J. A. (1942). *I came out of the eighteenth century.* New York: Harper & Brothers.

Rudolph, F. (1977). *Curriculum.* San Francisco: Jossey-Bass.

Schubert, W. H., & Posner, G. J. (1980). Origins of the curriculum field based on a study of mentor–student relationships. *The Journal of Curriculum Theorizing, 2* (2), 37–67.

Wieder, A. (1988). Possibilities, lost possibilities, no possibilities: Images of middle-class children and lower class adults. *The International Journal of Qualitative Studies in Education, 1* (3), 225–238.

Willis, M. (1961). *The guinea pigs after twenty years.* Columbus: Ohio State University Press.

Contestaire

WILLIAM F. PINAR
Louisiana State University

Impartiality and Comprehensiveness in the Teaching of Curriculum Theory

Perhaps the most serious problem in the United States in the teaching of curriculum theory is the neglect of many teachers of contemporary research and scholarship. (My impression is that this problem is smaller than it was, say, 10 years ago, but that it does persist to a dysfunctional extent.) This neglect seems to me to be of two types. The first has to do with ignorance, the second, with ideology. Too many professors and teachers of curriculum do not follow the major journals and thus are unfamiliar with contemporary scholarship. These individuals must be judged incompetent scholars and unprofessional teachers. There are as well those curriculum teachers who are aware of contemporary work but choose to ignore it. These are ideologues and pseudo-scholars. Both groups do irreparable harm to their students, by keeping them uninformed in the first instance, or indoctrinated in the second. They harm the field of curriculum as well. The consequences of these irresponsible teachers are slowed progress in the field, and students who have not acquired conceptual tools for their own empowerment. To illustrate one attempt to work with these issues, I will recall the curriculum of the 1987 version of a course I teach, Curriculum Theory.

A CURRICULUM THEORY CURRICULUM

In teaching Curriculum Theory in 1987 I employed Schubert's (1986) *Curriculum* for its impartiality and relative comprehensiveness, and also because it illustrates the long tradition of synoptic texts in our field. While it is an introductory text, I employ it in an advanced course because of a heterogeneous enrollment (which is typical of many curriculum theory courses, I suspect). In the 1987 version of Curriculum Theory, most were Ph.D. students, a few were M. A. students, but nearly everyone was an initiate to the field. (This profile is changing at LSU, as I will note below.) In effect, then, I was simultaneously teaching both an introductory and an advanced course in curriculum. The result was a long reading list, an unusual amount of work, and even then a sense that students had only begun to grasp the nature of the contemporary field.

I followed Schubert's introduction to the field with his bibliography (1980). This volume provides a comprehensive reference for students who wish to do further work in the field. Kridel's historical-biographical approach (Chapter 15) would be a welcomed addition to the course. Better yet, it could be included in a separate history of curriculum course. I look forward to the publication of *Curriculum History: Conference Presentations from the Society for the Study of Curriculum History* (Kridel, 1989), as this volume might augment the historical information I am able to present at this time.

From Schubert we moved to Kliebard's *The Struggle for the American Curriculum* (1986), whose impartial study constitutes essential but minimal historical knowledge for all graduate students in curriculum. Franklin's *Building the American Community* (1987) provides a provocative but particular version of curriculum history, and in so doing makes explicit the Marxist tradition in curriculum scholarship. The volume *Curriculum and Instruction: Alternatives in Education*, that Anthony Penna and I edited with Henry Giroux (1981) portrays the field in 1980, in "reconceptualization." We organized the essays according to curriculum, instruction, and evaluation, providing examples of "traditionalist," "conceptual-empiricist," and "reconceptualist" scholarship in each category. From 1980 in the United States the seminar moved to recent scholarship in Europe, as reported in Hameyer's *Curriculum Research in Europe* (1986). Then, in the eighth week of the semester, we were almost ready to study the North American field at the present time.

At this point I noted that "present time" is always something of a misnomer, as there is always a "lag"—a year or more passes after an essay is composed before it is published, and another year or longer before a "critical mass" of readers elevate a particular essay and/or idea to a status worthy of sustained treatment. "Empowerment" is a recent example of such an idea achieving terminological status, as was "hidden curriculum" 15 years ago. Such terms achieve conceptual or terminological status due to their complexity and usage. However, other notions are popularized ideas or slogans that will never achieve terminological status and are thus best ignored. These bogus ideas do not constitute an "organizing center" (Herrick's term; see Chapter 13) for a course, as, for instance, does the question of curricular "worth." As Schubert implies in Chapter 13, the question of worth—in common with other disciplinary questions—ought be treated as a historical as well as a contemporary and situated issue. Whatever concept is selected to serve as an "organizing center" (and I do not believe one is necessary for a sensible course design, as this commentary indicates), making explicit "lag" and the multifaceted and contested character of the field as well as one's theoretical position in it not only presents an accurate picture of curriculum theory but also helps to free the students to make their own judgments. Accuracy in representing the contemporary field and support for students' independent judgments are minimal requirements in teaching for "empowerment." To achieve this end, curriculum theory must be taught impartially and comprehensively. Otherwise, students remain uninformed and perhaps indoctrinated.

ANTECEDENT KNOWLEDGE

To begin to understand the major categories of work being done today, most students require "background" reading. *Feminist Theory* (Keohane, 1981, 1982) is a collection of essays that previously appeared in *Signs*, an interdisciplinary journal of feminist scholarship published by the University of Chicago. The work is sophisticated and allows the student an "inside" view of research in feminist scholarly communities. (For master's level students and groups without prior knowledge of feminist theory, a book like Hester Eisenstein's *Contemporary Feminist Thought*, 1983, is more accessible.) These books provide a disciplinary context for reading the work of Madeleine Grumet, Janet L. Miller, Leslie Roman, Patti Lather, and other feminist theorists in curriculum studies today. *Reason and Human Existence* (Miller, 1979) reviews the work of Marx, both "early" and "late"; Marxian theorists such as Gramsci, Lukcas, and Luxemberg; and phenomenologists such as Merleau-Ponty. While useful antecedent knowledge for reading the works of Apple, Giroux, and other Marxists and neo-Marxists, *Reason and Human Existence* also introduces the work of the phenomenologists, helpful in reading the work of Aoki (1988), Grumet (1988a,b), van

Manen (1988), and other phenomenological curriculum scholars. The phenomenological tradition is introduced from an aestheticist-historical point of view in Megill's study in *Prophets of Extremity* (1985). Megill begins with Nietzsche and moves to Heidegger, then to Foucault, and finally to Derrida, providing an introductory knowledge of existentialism and post-structuralism as well as of phenomenology. The last reading in the course is the 1988 volume I edited, *Contemporary Curriculum Discourses,* which is relatively comprehensive and impartially presents characteristic examples of work in each of the major categories of contemporary curriculum theory scholarship: the historical, studies of the field, political analyses, phenomenological and feminist studies, and aesthetic criticism. The introduction to the book provides a brief history of the "reconceptualization" of the curriculum field from its ahistorical, atheoretical, "moribund" past to the complex, vigorous, and multifaceted present.

TEACHING METHOD, STUDENT WORK

A majority of students become absorbed in curriculum theory. Some struggle with questions of theory and practice. These I encourage to reflect autobiographically on their practice through one or more of the "lenses" provided by contemporary curriculum theory. Other students utilize some aspect of curriculum theory to analyze an aspect of their specialization. Linkages between the curriculum theory literature they study and their specializations or their classroom practice are made in class and in their final paper. In class I use a version of group process, as various individuals and groups present commentaries on the assigned texts. These are two-part presentations: The first is a summary of the text, and the second is a critical analysis of it, punctuated by discussion. I grade on both the oral and written versions of these commentaries.

CONCLUSION

The aspiration of teaching curriculum theory must be to provide students with an impartial and comprehensive survey of contemporary scholarship, while emphasizing its historical and political character, as well as its links to classroom practice and other specializations in education. Work in antecedent areas, such as feminist theory, is advisable when students are naive. Through a version of group process, students can articulate both their understandings of curriculum theory and their (revised) understandings of their specializations and their teaching practice, empowering them to act in more profoundly educative ways.

REFERENCES

Aoki, T. (1988). Toward a dialectic between the conceptual world and the lived world: transcending instrumentalism in curriculum orientation. In W. F. Pinar (Ed.), *Contemporary curriculum discourses* (pp. 402–416). Scottsdale, AZ: Gorsuch, Scarisbrick.

Apple, M. (1968). The culture and commerce of the textbook. In W. F. Pinar (Ed.), *Contemporary curriculum discourses* (pp. 223–242). Scottsdale, AZ: Gorsuch Scarisbrick.

Apple, M. (1986). *Teachers and texts: A political economy of class and gender relations in education.* New York: Routledge & Kegan Paul.

Eisenstein, H. (1983). *Contemporary feminist thought.* Boston: G. K. Hall.

Franklin, B. (1986). *Building the American community.* London: Falmer Press.

Giroux, H. (1988). *The teacher as intellectual.* South Hadley, MA: Bergin & Garvey.

Giroux, H. (1988). Liberal arts,teaching, and critical literacy: Toward a definition of school as cultural politics. In W. F. Pinar (Ed.), *Contemporary curriculum discourses* (pp. 243–263). Scottsdale, AZ: Gorsuch Scarisbrick.

Giroux, H., et al. (Eds.). (1981). *Curriculum and instruction: Alternatives in education.* Berkeley, CA: McCutchan.

Grumet, M. (1988a). Bodyreading. In W. F. Pinar (Ed.), *Contemporary curriculum discourses* (pp. 453–473). Scottsdale, AZ: Gorsuch Scarisbrick.

Grumet, M. (1988b). *Bitter milk: Women and teaching.* Amherst: University of Massachusetts Press.

Hameyer, V., et al. (Eds.). (1986). *Curriculum research in Europe.* Berwyn and Lisse: Swets North America.

Keohane, N., et al. (Eds.). (1981, 1982). *Feminist theory.* Chicago: University of Chicago Press.

Kliebard, H. (1986). *The struggle for the American curriculum 1893–1958.* Boston: Routledge & Kegan Paul.

Kridel, Craig. (Ed.) (1989). *Curriculum history: Conference presentations from the Society for the Study of Curriculum History.* Lanham, MD: University Press of America.

Megill, A. (1985). *Prophets of extremity.* Berkeley, CA: University of California Press.

Miller, J. L. (1979). *Reason and human existence.* Berkeley, CA: University of California Press.

Miller, J. L. (1988). The resistance of women academics: An autobiographical account. In W. F. Pinar (Ed.), *Contemporary curriculum discourses* (pp. 486–494). Scottsdale, AZ: Gorsuch Scarisbrick.

Pinar, W. F. (Ed.). (1988). *Contemporary curriculum discourses.* Scottsdale, AZ: Gorsuch Scarisbrick.

Pinar, W. F., Reynolds, William, & Hwu, Wen-Song. (1989). *Understanding curriculum: A comprehensive introduction.* Scottsdale, AZ: Gorsuch Scarisbrick.

Roman, L., Christian-Smith, L., & Ellsworth, E. (Eds.). (1988). *Becoming feminine: The politics of popular culture.* London: Falmer Press.

Schubert, W. (1980). *Curriculum books: The first eighty years.* Lanham, MD: University Press of America.

Schubert, W. (1986). *Curriculum: Perspective, paradigm, and possibility.* New York: Macmillan.

van Manen, M. (1986). *The tone of teaching.* London: Heinemann.

van Manen, M. (1988). The relation between research and pedagogy. In W. F. Pinar (Ed.), *Contemporary curriculum discourses* (pp. 437–452). Scottsdale, AZ: Gorsuch Scarisbrick.

Whitson, J. (1988). Politics of "non-political" curriculum: Hetereoglossia and the discourse of "choice" and "effectiveness." In W. F. Pinar (Ed.), *Contemporary curriculum discourses* (pp. 279–330). Scottsdale, AZ: Gorsuch Scarisbrick.

Conversation parmi animateurs

O. L. DAVIS, JR.
University of Texas at Austin

PAUL KLOHR
Ohio State University

NORM OVERLY
Indiana University

KLOHR: Ed Short is right on target in his essay about the tremendous trivialization of the field. Schubert, Shaker, and Kridel address some ways in which we can get out of that trivialization. All four make the case that you need to attend to value questions. Those can't be avoided. These chapters, I think, document a real shift in the field of curriculum.

DAVIS: That there has been a shift in the field of curriculum during the past two or three decades is abundantly clear. These authors see themselves as related to what most of us have come to call the curriculum field. It does not, however, have to do with the enterprise of curriculum work in a school district, the outcomes of which are courses of study, development of individual courses, or revision of sequence. The curriculum field, as I came to know it as a student, was less self-consciously a field—that is to say, a community of scholars. In those days, the field of curriculum was an enterprise to get a job done. What is intriguing from the perspective of the field of study is that these persons are part of a larger community of scholars. In some respects, I believe that this self-conscious affiliation of individuals to the curriculum field, largely through graduate studies in the last 10 or 15 years, has created and made possible a group of people who understand themselves to be interested in and concerned with important curriculum questions.

OVERLY: I agree, O. L. The roots of the current discourse, however, are heavily grounded in the work of earlier generations of curriculum teachers. I think Jim Macdonald's work, among others, has demonstrated this. These authors are not discovering the world anew. But, these and other individuals have gone beyond those roots and are building on the changed context of social conditions, political patterns, and cultural forces. We went through a period of certainty during the 1940s and 1950s. Scholars, as well as national organizations, tended to lose sight of these big questions. These people became technicians, and their organizations became instrumental to technological ends.

KLOHR: But, I would argue that, in general, the current curriculum field, as I see it, represents a recurrence of the Bobbitt-Charters technological rationale. Actually, it has never been lost. In times of crisis, it reappears. We saw this, as you mentioned, Norm, in the post-Sputnik era and we are seeing it again today with concerns about technological and economic advancement, strong defense, and efficient and rigorous science and mathematics curricula—the sorts of things that lead to technological outcomes. And, throughout each of these eras normative statements were being made; they get lost when these crises arise—crises that find their proposed solutions in a technological curriculum. That is precisely the problem with curriculum reforms and the debate in the popular press today. We have two bestsellers, in the Bloom and Hirsch books, aimed at a fairly elitist view of education. There is no effort to ground these views in any value questions. There is no notion that you need to understand context. The major effort that is missing is the raising of value questions: "What does it mean to be a good person?" "What is a good society?" "What knowledge is of most worth?"

OVERLY: Maybe that's why I like the Schubert chapter so much. Actually, I am rather pleased with the kinds of curriculum discussions I am hearing these days. They're not just discussions among young people. There *is* some movement. I'm seeing a gradual reaction against the technocratic model. It may not reflect a very informed level of thought; maybe it's superficial. I think that we need to be concerned about how to keep these discussions from remaining superficial. And, I'd like still more emphasis on the growing realization that any curriculum teaching has to deal with concepts rather than "how to"—constantly asking the *why* questions rather than the *how*. This is not to say that you don't deal with the how: but, you don't deal with the how in set pieces that you can buy from publishing companies. It's the *how* you have to develop in context and individually.

DAVIS: I believe—as you talk about developing this *how* aspect of curriculum, Norm—that one way of doing this is through working with people in communities, which is one of the thrusts of this volume. But, instruction is not delivered in isolation. It must use content. It must be grounded in knowledge. Regardless of how we approach or understand what might be called "empowering pedagogy," it has, as its base, knowledge. In this case, that knowledge is the field of curriculum—however one might characterize it today.

KLOHR: What I think historically has happened is that the knowledge base that we use to undergird and generate both curriculum theory and practice has clearly become more diverse. This is good! To have people working in these different domains and feeding back into curriculum discourse is good, as contrasted with the work of people like George Beauchamp or Mauritz Johnson, who try to put all of curriculum in an empirical framework. The fact that we have interpretive and critical, as well as empirical, analyses in the field really gives the kind of richness that is needed for thinking and teaching about curriculum. That ought to be what individuals get into when they take a course in curriculum.

OVERLY: I think a distinction needs to be made here, Paul. The knowledge base of curriculum facts developed from *systematic research* hasn't changed much. However, I think the knowledge base, in terms of the way we look at things, has changed a good bit.

KLOHR: Well, history certainly supports your thesis, Norm. Jim Macdonald and Dwayne Huebner in the 1967 curriculum conference at Ohio State were invited to address questions about the field of curriculum posed 20 years earlier at the University of Chicago. They said some *very* different things then, which are clearly within the stream of thinking that characterizes these essays. And, several years later, Bill Pinar called a number of these people together in a small curriculum conference in 1973. Clearly their curriculum interests were in the direction of what Macdonald had labeled "theory development." But, we have to remember that these participants weren't way off to the side.

These were people who were curriculum teachers and who had come to realize that a theoretical and philosophical base for this field had to be broader and more diverse than it had historically been to that point. Whatever you would call this group, they were clearly working in the field with teachers and developing materials and teaching curriculum classes.

DAVIS: That's an excellent point, Paul. No one was any more active in curriculum work during our era than Jim. My hunch is that his career may be one of the strongest examples we have of this shift we're getting at. And, to the extent that my hunches have validity, I am convinced that curriculum has come to be understood as something very different from curriculum development. At the same time, I recognize that the current emphasis has close historical reference to Hollis Caswell's use of the term curriculum development. He asserted that individuals concerned with curriculum decisions and eventual teaching engagements with students must develop the *ideas behind* the course of study. It's this development of ideas by teachers, through their study and reflection, that is so interestingly highlighted in this collection of essays.

OVERLY: Yet, we still seem to have this image problem. As a field, these conferences convened in the 1960s and 1970s came out of a defensive kind of posture. We were responding to accusations of being moribund, which I think we were. Twenty years later, however, we still are concerned with respectability. We load up our writings with footnotes and references to European scholars, which can make the ideas to which we refer difficult for students and school practitioners to grasp.

KLOHR: You know, Norm, I remember worrying in the past about whether or not curriculum was indeed a field of study. I have come to think that that is a non-question. The question of whether a broader base for curriculum studies in any way diminishes the field is answered when you have substantial essays being written by scholars who are working and giving their professional careers to curriculum.

OVERLY: I agree, Paul, that we should not worry about or spend time trying to defend "the field." My concern is that we speak clearly to those with whom we wish to communicate—avoid jargon and obscure references, not avoid ideas from other sources. That is, if we use unfamiliar references, we should make clear the meaning in a language that will engage the uninitiated.

DAVIS: Well, this broader base has certainly created new problems for us. As a result of the emergence of the *field* of "curriculum" as distinguished from "curriculum development," we are seeing a further distancing between the teaching of curriculum and the world of curriculum practice. This was not the case years ago when, for example, university curriculum teachers, like Wells Foshay and Ken Wann, and school personnel worked together in Missouri identifying children's social values. There was work where the university professor was a collaborator with the local curriculum enterprise.

OVERLY: Times change, O. L. And with changing times come changing realities. If we have another war or something of that nature, as we did in the 1940s, that will have a profound influence on the curriculum field. Major social phenomena like that change the principles in the discussion, the people involved in the discussion, and the context of the discussion. I am hopeful that the eclectic, rather rich diversity represented in the curriculum field today will continue. In fact, maybe 20 years from now practitioners themselves may see the possibility of functioning within such diversity and engaging in such discourse.

REFLECTIONS

You And Me
and I And Thou

ARTHUR W. FOSHAY
Teachers College, Columbia University

Everyone knows that the world is full of mischief. So is the curriculum field. One kind of curriculum mischief may be called the great educational synecdoche—taking the container for the thing contained, or technique for substance. There are many examples of this: taking map reading for geography, spelling and grammar for writing and composition, computation for authentic mathematics, dates and events for history, and so on. There is a yet more invidious form of this mischief: taking a narrow view of what ought to be tested, and claiming that the test results represent more than they do—thus deceiving oneself, the students, and the public.

The authors of this book have pointed out an even more fundamental mischief. It consists of thinking of the curriculum impersonally, as if curriculum making could be reduced to a set of cold, "objective" techniques, or that all the curriculum maker had to do was to find "scientific" answers to Tyler's questions. Even Tyler doesn't believe that.

Not that cold, "objective" techniques aren't necessary. Of course they are. But to take them as sufficient to the task of curriculum making is to confuse what is necessary with what is sufficient—to take a part for the whole. Just now, there is a vogue for committing this mischief—taking "thinking" as the whole of the educational purpose, or taking SAT results as a sufficient evaluation of a school system. Any experienced educator could make a long list. To reduce curriculum making to a set of techniques, to ignore its personal meanings, is to do to it what a spider does to a fly—all the natural juices are removed, leaving only a shell. The shell looks like a curriculum, but it is dead.

I have chosen a strange title for these remarks in order to call attention to this kind of mischief. The situation in the curriculum field is like the problem faced by the translator of Martin Buber's remarkable book, which in German is called *Ich und Du.* That title was translated as *I and Thou,* a rendering that missed the meaning of the German *du,* which is the familiar form one uses in the family, toward children, and among close friends. There is no equivalent in English, since *thou* has become a term of formal address—a way of keeping the one addressed at arm's length. The translator who made that mistake changed something personal into something impersonal. That's what curriculum makers do when they take the form of the curriculum to be its substance. Curriculum makers who try to make the curriculum at arm's length kill the concept of learning as personal encounter, and only the shell is left. The curriculum becomes, as we say pejoratively, "merely academic," meaning that it has no real-world meaning.

The tendency for the curriculum to become a mere set of empty formalities was generally recognized about 400 years ago—as it happens, at about the same time that the English word *thou* lost its familiar meaning and became a term of formal address. The empty formalism we call "merely academic" was called "pedantry" then, and has been ridiculed by the thoughtful from that day to this.

The problem amounts to more than ridicule and name-calling. It corrupts the very meaning of formal education. The fact that students see little or no personal meaning in the curriculum leaves them to find another purpose for going to school, and they find it in the school's power to certify. For them, certification becomes the purpose of education, and grades are the coin of that realm. One does schoolwork, not because it has any intrinsic value, but to obtain good grades. Having obtained the grades and the certificate, the substance of the offering has no further value, and one quickly discards it as worthless baggage. How many adults, for example, have any use for knowing what a relative of mine once called the "participles of speech"?

The unrecognized irony is that we curriculum makers destroy the possibility of an excellent education in the course of seeking it. We play the game by the wrong rules, and thus distort things. We don't lose the game—we cast it aside.

What is required is that we recognize the curriculum as an array of personal encounters. Being personal, they are inward, in the main. One encounters the outside world in school, and uses the experiences as an instrument of self-discovery, or self-realization. It's an intimate affair. It isn't *I and Thou.* It's *You and Me.*

What are these encounters? They are with ideas and skills, with other people, with social institutions, and with oneself. Each of these encounters carries a risk. Each of them can, for example, be so seductive as to lead one to believe that it is the whole of education; thus, the curriculum is thrown out of balance. It takes competence in all these fields to make a satisfying and productive life possible.

The risk implicit in the pursuit of ideas and skills is, of course, that one will come to believe that the whole function of education is to develop the intellect, and that alone. This risks overspecialization for the student, which is as destructive for people as it has been for certain animal species. To *over*specialize in the love for ideas is to become a caricature of a person. To ignore ideas, of course, is to be an ignoramus.

The risk inherent in learning to work with other people and with social institutions is, again, that one can come to believe that that's all one needs to know. In so doing, one becomes "other-directed," as Riesman pointed out a generation ago. That is, one comes to depend on others to define oneself. In addition, effective social behavior conveys power. One can be so seduced by the power as to sacrifice one's integrity for it. That's what social climbers do, and unprincipled politicians and some executives. Caswell pointed out years ago that high school students sometimes become so entranced with their participation in projects intended to improve social conditions that they fail to prepare adequately, and thus not only make embarrassing mistakes but also deceive themselves. In studying a complex social problem like poverty in New York, for example, one group concluded that the whole problem could be solved through the distribution of free food.

The problem appears to be that to attack social problems intelligently, one must do some hard, often dull academic work before getting into the excitement of personal contact with the problem. That is the often unrecognized entrance requirement. There is also a value judgment to be made: Can a student have the experience of social action, and still have time to learn important academic knowledge in depth? When academic knowledge is pursued in depth, one learns *why* things happen, not only *how* they happen. Those who know *why* generally wind up in charge of those who only know *how*. It follows that one does not casually trade off understanding of an important concept, such as counterrevolution as illustrated by Shay's Rebellion in U.S. history, for a chance to do something immediate, such as reducing water pollution. Choices must be made.

The encounter with oneself, for growing young people especially, is the source of repeated joyful self-discovery as well as repeated frightening private crises. The joy often comes with the discovery of an unexpected talent, often in one of the academic fields. It's great to find that one can write well, or solve math problems well, or create a valid art work. Such discoveries can and should be celebrated publicly when possible. The private crises, however, are usually ignored by curriculum makers, who focus on building various competencies, leaving private crises to be handled by others, or not handled at all. For a high school student to perform well in public—as in athletics or a school play or musical event—is to discover something important about himself or herself. Being selected by one's peers for class or school office or other responsibility is a memory one carries throughout life. But equally important are the various failures one undergoes. Because most high school students are "other-directed," as discussed above, these marks of peer acceptance tend to be overvalued (remember the "big man on campus"?). The marks of peer rejection, or the private feelings of failure, are also overvalued. I mention these matters here because they are ordinarily ignored by those who make curricula. They need not be; certainly they ought not be.

The highly personal nature of the curriculum encounter places requirements on the curriculum maker. It is necessary for the curriculum to leave room for individual learning styles. The curriculum maker has to remember that each person in the educational endeavor *is* a person; that each has his or her own life to live, and his or her own way of confronting educational experience. The ways for teachers and other curriculum makers to do this are well known, if rarely employed. There is a literature on helping students learn how to learn; the needed classroom flexibility was described by Alice Miel and others in the literature on cooperative planning.

We tend to forget the individuality of students in the press of dealing with many people, making the institution of the school function as it ought to, attending to our own private needs, and, in general, dealing with the fact that it's complicated to be an adult. It's just as complicated to be a growing young person. Facing all this complexity, the simple thing to do is to deal with it on the surface—to be literally superficial. Since it's much easier to deal with a stereotype than with the person behind it, we stereotype students: "special needs," "reluctant learners," "gifted," and so on. We group them and group them again, but they remain individuals. Classification of students is a way of ignoring the personal quality of the curriculum for them. It is one of the most widespread forms of curriculum mischief.

Since the curriculum encounters are personal, let us consider what makes them valuable. It comes down to the kinds of interactions teachers and students bring about. The simplest human interaction is an imitation, or a reflection. If the student acts interested, the teacher will, too. If the teacher seems to care about a given student, the student is likely to return the caring. When teachers portray themselves as whole human beings, warmly and seriously engaged with their students as whole human beings, the interaction becomes personal in the best sense, and significant meaning emerges. When my seventh grade English teacher, Amelia Sellender, told me something of herself and also told me that she thought I could learn to write well, the English class came alive for me, and I treasure the memory of those days even now, many years later. When a professor of Elizabethan literature at Cal made his quest clear to us in a lecture, we joined in it, and brought that period of English lit to life. Later, when I became a guidance counselor in Oakland, I had a lesson powerfully taught to me by a grandmother whose grandchild had gotten into serious trouble at school. We talked about the child and her way of living her life. The family was black, and I, having little experience with blacks, attempted to deal with that portion of the problem relevant to the child's race. The lady, who had been born during the nineteenth century and had been through it all, interacted with me politely for a few minutes. Then she sat up, looked me in the eye, and said quietly, "Young man, you're washed, but you're not clean." I'll never forget that lesson. What made it powerful was that she let me into a little of her life, and powerfully entered mine.

Another aspect of the personal curriculum arises from the possibility of self-discovery in the substance of the encounter. Many of us have examined ourselves while being introduced to what is known about personality disorders in the field of psychology. We retrace our childhoods while studying child development. In the hands of some teachers, it is also possible to discover within oneself some of the elements of great historical figures like Lincoln or Louis XVI, or sense within oneself the thrill of discovery of some of the wonders of mathematical concepts like zero, proof, infinity, or abstraction itself.

A large portion of this book is devoted to answering for these times Counts' famous question of the 1930s: Dare the school build a new social order? The response that emerged during the succeeding decades seemed to be that the question should not have been asked. It distracted the schools from their main and proper business, which was to train the mind and prepare people for the work force. So Counts' question, and the consequences it had for the curriculum, were ignored by most educators and during the 1950s and since have been ridiculed repeatedly by a long succession of commentators on education.

But the question won't go away, as the authors of these chapters make evident. For these times, perhaps the question needs revision. Counts asked whether the school *dared.* Events since his time have shown that they *do,* whether or not they intend to. There is an example before us in the current concern for the environment. Here is the story.

Early in this century, Theodore Roosevelt captured the imagination of the young people with the concept of the conservation of natural resources and the preservation of natural beauty in the national parks. Some of these young people became teachers, and some of these teachers taught my generation these ideals. When my generation became teachers, we passed on the message as a given. When our students reached maturity, they joined the Sierra Club and other such groups, which had extended Teddy Roosevelt's idea to include the environment and the ecosystem we are part of. Many of these students had learned a little about social action in school; the massive environmental groups that have formed to exert political pressure are more than coincidental. In large measure, they are the product of three generations of schooling. The schools have changed the social order in this particular case.

The sensible response to Counts' question, therefore, appears to be this: Yes, the schools change the social order as well as reflect it. The important thing is for these changes to be done openly, consciously, and with clear intent and known purposes. In recognizing this, we in the schools must also recognize the obligations it places on us.

We speak much of "empowerment" these days. Empowering the ordinary citizen has always frightened those in charge, whether their names be Alexander Hamilton, or Jay Gould, or Stalin. It frightens certain businesspeople, who would take the schools from the public and give them to private institutions not strictly accountable to the public, but only to their immediate clients. In one sense or another, we're all afraid of the mob.

What is becoming more evident than it once was, especially after the emergence of project work by school children 60 years ago, is that empowerment requires that people be equipped with the relevant knowledge and skills, and especially the attitudes, that responsible public action demands. Ever since the 1920s, schoolchildren have been learning these things. It is not surprising, therefore, that teachers are taking a larger part in official curriculum making, that workers in large business organizations are increasingly drawn into what once were exclusively management concerns, and that there are now thousands of political action committees, or PACs. Many people have become civically competent.

We in education can be pleased at these developments. In pursuing them, we need only keep in mind the hazards that accompany them. People do not necessarily know how to handle power, once they have claimed it. I lived through the turmoil at Columbia University in 1968, and I had a good look at the turmoil at Berkeley, my alma mater, in 1964. In both cases, the students were intoxicated with their newfound power, and many of them destroyed large portions of their college educations, and in a few cases, themselves. There is no doubt that they were worse off for the experience. They didn't know enough to avoid hurting themselves. Without the perspective offered by the traditional liberal arts, students will flail about, doing damage and accomplishing little, as happened during the 1960s.

The rewards that come from acknowledging the personal nature of the curriculum are real and vivid, just as the risks are great. The authors of this book remind us of these risks and rewards.

We speak here of curriculum makers. In addition to the theoreticians, there are three groups of them: the official curriculum makers, who prepare courses of study and teaching materials; the teachers who make use of these materials; and the students. It is in the interaction of all three that one finds the actual curriculum. The apparently hierarchical arrangement of these groups can deceive us into believing that the curriculum is designed by one group, handed down to another, and received by the third. It was never so, and it isn't now. We need only recognize this to build the honesty and candor into our curriculum making that the authors of this book ask of us.

Toward a Continuing Dialogue

LOUISE M. BERMAN
University of Maryland

REFLECTIONS

Perched on a fulcrum between a host of curriculum-oriented persons who have left a legacy of rich and varied approaches to curriculum theory and development and a current group of enthusiastic and dynamic thinkers about the field, I find myself looking both backward and forward in time as I contemplate the contents of this book. As I reflect on the past I think of the involved individuals, including those of Teachers College, Columbia University, who introduced me to curriculum as a field of study—Hollis Caswell, Florence Stratemeyer, Alice Miel, Arno Bellack, Wells Foshay, Roma Gans, Dwayne Huebner, Margaret Lindsey, Gordon Mackenzie. I am aware that they, for the most part, were among early curriculum scholars, the field being a relatively new one. In fact during 1988, the Department of Curriculum and Teaching at Teachers College celebrated the fiftieth anniversary of its formation. It is the oldest of its kind in the country.

Although the roots of the field go back to classical writers, such as Aristotle, the genesis of curriculum as a formal field of study probably took place at the turn of the century. The influence of two trends, the scientific movement and the school as an agent of social reform, helped catapult the curriculum into a position of political and intellectual ferment, which has long characterized the field (Bobbitt, 1918, 1924; Charters, 1923; Dewey, 1902).

The 1920s through the 1940s saw rapid growth of this emerging and complex field. The first yearbook of the National Society for the Study of Education on curriculum appeared in 1926 (Whipple, 1926). The Association for Supervision and Curriculum Development was organized in the early 1940s (VanTil, 1986). Education has long been a topic of interest to philosophers and other thoughtful persons, but curriculum as a serious field of study may have emerged during the lifetimes of certain readers of this book.

As the field developed, numerous questions, orientations, and subspecialties appeared. For example, among the subspecialties frequently found in a department of curriculum are the study of teaching, teacher education, supervision, and the teaching of the various grade levels, such as elementary or secondary education. Indeed curriculum seemed to be an umbrella for what happened in school.

In reflecting upon *Teaching and Thinking About Curriculum,* certain other contextual elements complicate deliberations. First, several different philosophic lenses may be used in considering the field. Most commonly discussed are logical positivism, phenomenology, and critical theory. However, as the authors of this book and other thoughtful curricularists have dealt with curriculum issues, a number of permutations seem to be arising. Consider Grundy's recent book *Curriculum: Product or Praxis* (1987). The meanings of "the good," "empowerment," and "liberation" are being considered in a variety of quarters. In addition, as school-based persons use these terms in considering policy matters, they of necessity must take on more practical meanings. In other words, the discourse embedded in contemporary philosophical orientations to the curriculum invites practitioners to help shape curricular thought.

Second, the relationship of teaching and instruction to curriculum varies depending on one's philosophical persuasions. Phenomenological thought would place great emphasis on the enacted curriculum or the moment of now. Logical positivism might define curriculum as intent, with the teaching act considered separately.

A third contextual dilemma has to do with whether teaching is best considered as a generic act cutting across a variety of subjects or whether teaching acts are endemic to specific fields. How that dilemma plays itself out will partially determine whether teaching curriculum emerges as a new subspecialty within the curriculum field or whether research and thinking about teaching as a generic field then apply to curriculum.

The above discussion causes me to ask: When curriculum is considered, do certain ways of thinking and talking about curriculum necessitate a way of considering curriculum separate and distinct from ways of thinking about other subjects? Or does teaching curriculum have certain characteristics that suggest it should be studied separately from other fields. Perhaps one will never know until thoughtful and discerning attention is given to what it means to teach curriculum. After such attention, consideration may be given to ways in which teaching curriculum is like and unlike teaching other subjects. At present the seminal thinking of persons concerned about teaching curriculum is critical. For example, the journal *Teaching Education* is very useful at this point in the history of the curriculum field.

The authors of *Teaching and Thinking About Curriculum* cause several questions to emerge for me. First, what is the meaning of reflection in teaching? Reflection, a theme common to this volume, is also used in other fields, especially teacher education (Popkewitz, 1987; Schön, 1987). The above question warrants attention because it is antithetical to the predominant technical mode found in education, where observable behaviors are given more attention than inner work. The writers of this volume seem to believe that reflection results in more elegant judgments. Gaining access, therefore, to the inner lives of students is important. Miller (Chapter 6), Erdman (Chapter 11), and Doll (Chapter 3) are among those who recommend shared journal-writing as means of encouraging students to be increasingly penetrating in their self-analyses. Many questions are raised about reflection and its meaning to the teaching process; these questions are important to thoughtful teachers in various fields (Fulwiler, 1987).

Second, what does it mean to be a human being? Questions relative to the humanity of both students and teachers often surface in the previous chapters. Related questions frequently center around whether teachers and students are co-equal. If they are, which tasks should be common and which ones uncommon? Teachers and students share research in process, share their thoughts, and share poetry (Bowman and Haggerson, Chapter 4). If teachers and students share in a symmetrical rather than an asymmetrical relationship, then they are seen as fellow travelers, explorers, and inquirers. I wondered as I read about the role of the professor of curriculum whether the professor's professional inquiries were always of interest to students. When does the professor's research project become cumbersome to students, or when does the core of the professor's life seem incompatible with the feelings, pains, and priorities of students' lives? Does the professor have the responsibility to build the bridges that lead to co-equality, or can one assume that such will happen? How can all learn to accommodate to diversity, to uncover deepest predispositions and values? What is that core of humanity that may be common to all, and what differences may lead to asymmetrical rather than symmetrical relations among students and teachers? One can ask the question: Ought relationships between students and professor be symmetrical or asymmetrical? In what circumstances is each appropriate?

Third, what is the role of language in curricula that seek to uncover deeper meaning? Bowman and Haggerson (Chapter 4), Kantor (Chapter 5), Miller (Chapter 6), and Pink (Chapter 9) all refer to the use of metaphors and stories. Mytho-poetic language is discussed by Haggerson, who is also concerned about the inner language of being. According to Kantor, curriculum is a story to be unfolded. These authors illustrate, and also challenge the reader to uncover, deeper levels of meaning in the teaching process. The attention to affect, to feelings, and to dealing with the person at a fundamental level was reminiscent of certain earlier curricularists who placed major attention on the person. Today's curricularists have developed more telling ways of using language in teaching.

Fourth, what kind of social order should schools build? This question is treated by both those with a phenomenological and those with a critical theory perspective. The nature of empowerment and the building of community are themes running throughout the book. Yet authors differ in their meanings of social order. Wood is reminiscent of Miel and Brogan (1957), Stratemeyer (1957), and Smith, Stanley, and Shores (1957) in his discussion of five principles of democratic empowerment in Chapter 7.

The school should be a site where students, through experience, come to
1. Believe in the individual's right and responsibility to participate publicly
2. Have a sense of political efficacy, that is, the knowledge that one's contributions to community life are important
3. Value the principles of democratic life—equality, liberty, community
4. Know that alternative arrangements to the status quo exist and are worthwhile
5. Gain the requisite intellectual skills to participate in the public discourse

Wood differs in his consideration of the social order from certain of the other writers who do not necessarily lay out an agenda of values to be considered but rather advocate uncovering taken-for-granted assumptions (Pink, Chapter 9; Donmoyer, Chapter 10). Wood's values in many ways overlap the values of the critical theorists, which focus on justice and empowerment.

The book contains writings of both the phenomenologists and persons who have beliefs from other theoretical perspectives. The critical theorists in a sense have an agenda in terms of the values that concern them. The phenomenologists seek to uncover issues and values important in creating an agenda.

As educators attempt a move ahead, what are some possibilities?

POSSIBILITIES

Encounters with the authors of the preceding chapters suggest several places to explore. What are some possibilities as agendas are developed for future work in "thinking and teaching about curriculum"?

First, what possibilities exist in the preceding chapters for the public school curriculum developer or school principal? How do the principles, challenges, and good ideas of these chapters get translated into meaningful material for school-based personnel?

If movement from the predominant paradigm of schools, namely logical positivism, were to take place, what directions might the authors provide? Would they be in agreement on next steps?

The simplicity of logical positivism or similar paradigms coupled with greater ease in evaluative and accountability procedures continues to make the predominant paradigm the more compelling one among those charged with major curricular decisions. The authors have suggested certain components that might be considered in developing curriculum: values of justice, fairness, caring, and community; the person as reflective; content as nontrivial; and teachers as inquirers with students. In what kinds of forums might next steps be taken? What is the meaning of curriculum that invites practical consideration within a philosophical orientation empowering teachers and students? Toward what ends are teachers and students empowered?

The possibilities opened up by reflection on the above questions within a setting that values change, the richness of human diversity, and the meaning of an individual life are manifold. Those responsible for teaching curriculum might think with those responsible for developing curriculum about the translation of what is currently in curriculum texts into credible practice and plans for practice. Together teachers of curriculum and curriculum planners might search for fresh ways to create university–school partnerships dedicated to new ways of conceptualizing curriculum in real settings.

Second, what possibilities exist in terms of enlarging the audience of persons concerned about the issues raised in the preceding pages? Clearly college and university professors of curriculum have an interest in teaching curriculum. Yet a large number of persons outside academia think about curriculum. How do professors invite, entice, or even compel the larger public to examine assumptions underlying schooling, to be open to some alternative models, to encourage the inquiry process in curriculum, and to develop bold new visions of schooling? Indeed, does not the responsibility of the professor extend beyond university classes into the marketplace of ideas? And if the informed citizen becomes the marketplace for the exploration of the meaning of certain concepts explored in the preceding pages, how will such dialogue take place? In other words, what is the responsibility of those of us who teach curriculum to those distant from us in space and ideology?

Third, what possibilities are opened up when dialogue is encouraged between current authors and those who have previously shaped educational thought? Occasionally the curriculum field has been cited as "moribund," as devoid of exciting ideas and activity, yet since its inception as a formal field of study, the field has attracted many provocative thinkers. Embedding current thinking in the historical sweep of ideas strengthens the case for extending and enlarging recent curricular development.

Of over 300 bibliographical entries in the chapters I read, more than two-thirds (205) were from materials written after 1980. Only about 6 percent (17) entries were from the period between 1930 and 1960. In my review I made no attempt to cull out noncurriculum books, but several of the 6 percent were from fields other than curriculum. My point is that the field of curriculum and its subspecialties were in exciting stages of development during that period. Thinking about curriculum involves reflecting on one's current place in light of what has gone before, as well as envisioning what might be—possibilities. An agenda item might be to trace the origins of certain ideas so well explicated by many of the authors. Themes of control, empowerment, the person in community, and education within a democracy have been pervasive topics in curriculum. How has treatment of these themes changed through the years?

Finally, what possibilities emerge when the community of curriculum scholars in concert with concerned practitioners share a "common commitment to the good" (Bellah et al., 1985, p. 115)? What might be common elements on the agendas of those who teach and think about curriculum? Let me suggest a few items:

- The uncovering of hidden values and assumptions
- The critiquing of the origins of curricular knowledge
- The meanings of empowerment, liberation, justice, and caring to different persons in different times and places
- The utilization of the above meanings in thinking about and planning curriculum
- The search for alternatives to trivialization of the curriculum (Short, Chapter 12) as testing programs continue to emphasize discrete facts and skills
- The search for the starting points or bases for curriculum: the inner knowledge of students, the knowledge "out there," or some combination of the two
- The locus of responsibility for curricular decision making

The ageless question of living in a democracy persists. How can individual aspirations, longings, visions, and dreams be fulfilled within communities endowed with richness of a shared life? Curriculum has traditionally dealt with certain responses to this question. Yet, the authors have pointed the way to answering the question more powerfully and poignantly.

REFERENCES

Bellah, R. N. et al. (1985). *Habits of the heart: Individualism and commitment in American life.* Berkeley: University of California Press.

Bobbitt, F. (1918). *The curriculum.* Boston: Houghton-Mifflin.

Bobbitt, F. (1924). *How to make a curriculum.* Boston: Houghton-Mifflin.

Charters, W. W. (1923). *Curriculum construction:* New York: Macmillan.

Dewey, J. (1902). *The child and the curriculum.* Chicago: University of Chicago Press.

Fulwiler, T. (Ed.). (1987). *The journal book.* Portsmouth, NH: Heinemann.

Grundy, S. (1987). *Curriculum: Product or praxis.* New York: Falmer Press.

Kliebard, H. (1986). *The struggle for the American curriculum: 1893–1958.* Boston: Routledge & Kegan Paul.

Lewis, A., & Miel, A. (1972). *Supervision for improved instruction.* Belmont, CA: Wadsworth.

Miel, A., & Brogan, P. (1957). *More than social studies: A view of social learning in the elementary school.* Englewood Cliffs, NJ: Prentice-Hall.

Popkewitz, T. A. (Ed.). (1987). *Critical studies in teacher education: Its folklore, theory, and practice.* New York: Falmer Press.

Schön, D. A. (1987). *Educating the reflective practitioner.* San Francisco: Jossey-Bass.

Smith, B. O., Stanley, W. O., & Shores, H. J. (1957). *Fundamentals of curriculum development.* (Rev. Ed.). New York: Harcourt, Brace.

Stratemeyer, F. B. et al. (1957). *Developing a curriculum for modern living.* (2nd ed.). New York: Teachers College Press.

VanTil, W. (Ed.). (1986). *ASCD in retrospect.* Alexandria, VA: Association for Supervision and Curriculum Development.

Whipple, G. M. (Ed.). (1926). *The foundations and technique of curriculum construction. Part 1: Curriculum-making: Past and present.* The Twenty-Sixth Yearbook of the National Society for the Study of Education. Bloomington, IL: Public School Publishing.

Conversation parmi animateurs

O. L. DAVIS, JR.
University of Texas at Austin

PAUL KLOHR
Ohio State University

NORM OVERLY
Indiana University

DAVIS: What I would offer as a compliment to the contributors of this book is that the notion of empowerment is more than rhetoric; for them, empowerment is not simply a slogan. These curriculum teachers do not use concepts, such as control and resistance, as ideas to dress up college students for a children's crusade to overthrow the schools. Clearly, the contributors to this volume recognize that such ideas can generate meaningful attention to the teaching and thinking about curriculum. There is little here to put into a box of teaching recipes.

OVERLY: I would add another point. As curricularists, we have been talking to ourselves for years. Perhaps we are finally beginning to feel secure enough with our own ideas to talk—as those in this book do—with students, encouraging them to explore other areas and try other methods. Similarly, there are practitioners in curriculum who have become disillusioned with the quick curricular fixes of the technology-based reforms of the past decade. We now are at the point where a genuine dialogue among curriculum scholars and workers can occur. We are at a point to work with them, to be supportive, and to encourage them as they dream a little bit. These are tomorrow's practitioners of possibilities.

DAVIS: And these authors appear to be people who are serious about working with their students. They begin by asking, "What are we doing?" In Richard Niebuhr's terms, they are being personally responsible. They acknowledge that some knowledge and skills are more important than others, and that some are better done earlier than later. That's attention to sequence! Of course, they're not using familiar curriculum words like scope, sequence, and so forth. But, I think they should. These kinds of words are important as we communicate with school people. After all, this is the language of school people.

OVERLY: At some point, too, the question will be raised about why the more conventional aspects of curriculum, like scope and sequence, effective teaching, instructional leadership, and so forth, are missing from this collection of essays. But, those are already available in the synoptic texts and even more so in the many how-to books. For example, if you want to write objectives with a passion, look at Mager.

KLOHR: But questions such as those, Norm, seem to me to be an artifact of a mindset that focuses on the nuts and bolts of curriculum while ignoring its totality. In such a case, the components of curriculum are less than the sum. This inability to distinguish the tools of curriculum from curriculum itself is similar to the distinction often made between curriculum and instruction. Instruction, as we all know, went through such phases as the Flander's business, placing the whole field within a so-called "scientific framework." Jim Macdonald demonstrated years ago that these two domains clearly overlap. Every chapter in this book reflects such an overlap. If you had asked these authors to write about instruction, they would have had to address curriculum. Instruction, like curriculum, acknowledges the importance of self and the setting in which it takes place.

DAVIS: That overlapping of curriculum and instruction is something I particularly appreciated as I read this collection, Paul. I think if people read these essays carefully, as I hope many will do, they will also recognize a sense of change of emphasis over time—but probably not a change of underlying concern for other people. And, these authors reflect that personal concern. Some of these people I am very much like; others I am not like at all. At the same time, I am deeply aware that, in some sense, I am the way I am because people like Harold Drummond not only encouraged me to follow my own direction but insisted I be myself.

OVERLY: Well, I certainly see reflections of myself as curriculum teacher in this book. The crazy thing is, I don't think I personally was ever taught most of the curriculum stuff that is traditionally taught. I had to learn all of that on my own. All of these little categories that you are supposed to do or to know: curriculum guides, scope and sequence, and so forth. Any of the people I ever had in curriculum courses never bothered to talk about that stuff. I find that rather remarkable. That may be why I am not as passionate a critic of the field—because I haven't felt as personally constrained.

DAVIS: That is one of the beauties of curriculum as a field of study. It is, to borrow Janet Miller's (Chapter 6) metaphor, a prism into which each of us peers in gaining different insights and making unique contributions. One of the books that affected me tremendously was Harold Benjamin's little book, *The Cultivation of Idiosyncrasy*. Benjamin never wanted to replicate himself; he honored the individuality of the person and the result of it. He also insisted that he be accorded that same tolerance. Certainly curriculum workers like Caswell, Miel, Alexander, Klein, Berman, and Foshay are individuals who celebrate this individuality of personhood. The curriculum field will continue to grow as people are less Knights of the Round Table than they are disciples. The Knights of the Round Table are people who defended the honor and position of their king. The Biblical image of disciple is related to the notion of discipline, and in this sense disciples must build a community by carrying with them a set of ideas—but they build these ideas as well. The kingdom set on the hill did not have architectural renderings; the kingdom was to be constructed. It was to be, in fact, designed.

OVERLY: Within the field of curriculum, there do seem to be some younger scholars or curriculum students who search for certainty. It's rather ironic that this discourse in the curriculum field that we celebrate has grown out of risk taking and a kind of freethinking during the past two decades. Those who believe they have found the Holy Grail, in a way, aren't too different from those whom they criticize. They ask important questions, sometimes with passion—the kind of passion you get from new converts to an idea, or people who are beginning to see the possibility of education in a different form. I think that there isn't even as much risk taking as there may appear to be.

DAVIS: Good point! The curriculum field has been richest when it has not emphasized orthodoxy. I remember very well, during the curriculum explosion of the early 1960s, when Galen Saylor wrote an article entitled, "Don't Just Do Something, Stand There!"

KLOHR: When I began my work as curriculum director in the Columbus public schools, a more static understanding of the curriculum field, like the one Saylor probably preferred, was common. During subsequent decades, however, this understanding has broadened as those entering the field have become more diverse. They have not been people who have stood still. This expansion of the curriculum field makes me somewhat more sure, though I hope I've never been dogmatic, about ways to teach and think about curriculum.

OVERLY: I never found you dogmatic. But, over the years, I've become very suspicious of people who are set in their ways and look at curriculum from only one perspective. I don't think that scholars like Aoki, Apple, Greene, or Pinar look at curriculum from just one perspective. Now, they may focus in a particular article or series of articles on one perspective. But, the perspective does not define them or limit their vision.

DAVIS: Well, if the reader of these essays can find a singularity of intent or commonality of purpose among the contributors, I don't find that particularly objectionable. My objection is if these authors or the readers of this volume proclaim this collection of essays to be a representation of the entire curriculum field.

KLOHR: It's probably safe to say that no single book or group of persons has ever represented the field, O. L., although during its evolution there have been ups and downs. I think this collection of essays reflects a fresh impetus in the field that is far more diverse than what we've known in past years. New ideas from areas such as gender studies, critical social theory, literary theory, women's studies, and deconstructionism gives vitality to a field whose health can perhaps best be judged by its lack of definition!

Annotated Resources

ORGANIZATIONS

American Educational Research Association
1230 17th St., N.W.
Washington, DC 20036
This preeminent association of scholars in education has a section on curriculum studies, Division B. Membership of $45 a year (students $20) includes a subscription to *Educational Researcher* and a Division B newsletter.

Association for Supervision and Curriculum Development
125 N. West St.
Alexandria, VA 22314–2798
National organization of curriculum developers, teachers, and school district personnel. ASCD sponsors annual national and statewide conferences, and also conducts a variety of professional workshops. Membership dues of $53 a year include a subscription to *Educational Leadership* and four books.

Society for the Study of Curriculum History
c/o Dr. Craig Kridel
College of Education
University of South Carolina
Columbia, SC 29208
Organization for persons interested in discussing and documenting the history of curriculum. Newsletter and annual meeting held in conjunction with the American Educational Research Association. A forthcoming publication of the Society, *Curriculum History* (University Press of America), is a collection of its conference presentations from the first 10 annual meetings. Membership is $5 a year.

World Council for Curriculum and Instruction
c/o Dr. Maxine Dunfee, WCCI Secretariat
School of Education
Indiana University
Bloomington, IN 47405

A global network of educators who seek through contact and cooperation to discuss and collaborate on areas of mutual interest. Quarterly newsletter and journal; triennial world conference and yearly regional conferences. Dues $15 annually.

NETWORKS AND INSTITUTIONAL RESOURCES

Action Linkage Networker
5825 Telegraph Avenue, #5
Oakland, CA 94609

Futuristic network organized by Robert Theobald that focuses on social issues, including concerns for curriculum and empowerment. Monthly newsletter, audio recordings, and annual book. Dues $60 a year.

Institute for Democracy in Education
McCracken Hall
Ohio University
Athens, OH 45701

Brings together teachers, administrators, and parents who believe that school should prepare students as democratic citizens and explores methods of democratic teaching. Publications include monthly newsletter, quarterly journal, and occasional papers. Dues $20 a year (students, $12).

National Curriculum Teachers Network
c/o Marian Schoenheit, Secretary-Treasurer
College of Education, Rich Hall
State University of New York
Oswego, NY 13126

Three newsletters yearly, network directory, and special sessions on the teaching of curriculum sponsored at the annual conference of the Association for Supervision and Curriculum Development. Dues $10 yearly.

Regional Laboratory for Educational Improvement of the Northeast
c/o Susan Loucks-Horsley
290 South Main Street
Andover, MA 01810

One component of this laboratory's teacher education program is "teachers helping teachers" in staff development. Publishes thematic newsletter five times a year. No subscription fee.

Social Issues in Education Network
c/o Alex Molnar
College of Education
University of Wisconsin-Milwaukee
Milwaukee, WI 53401

An informal network of K–college educators committed to the integration of social issues in the curriculum. Publishes a semiannual newsletter and membership directory. Dues $5 a year.

MATERIALS

The Teachers' Press
3731 Madison Ave.
Brookfield, IL 60513

High school teachers who, with their students, have developed socially interactive units of study that include "How to Think about Social Issues," "Prejudice in Group Relations," and "Seeking Information."

Consulting Psychologists Press
577 College Avenue
Palo Alto, CA 94306

Source for the diagnostic materials cited in Chapter 14: Wrenn Study Habits Inventory; The Bem Sex Role Inventory; The Classroom Environment Scale; The California Phonics Survey; and The Myers-Briggs Type Indicator.

Dean Lois J. Lehman
Dean of Libraries
CBN University
Virgina Beach, VA 23463

Directory of historical elementary-secondary textbook collections in the United States prepared by the Association of College and Research Libraries.

Dr. William H. Drier
School of Education
University of Northern Iowa
Cedar Falls, IA 50614

Survey of school museums in the United States.

Museum of Education
University of South Carolina
Columbia, SC 29208

Curriculum leaders of the twentieth century archival materials, including photographic portraits and audio recordings of curriculum leaders, as well as the Margaret Willis Exhibition.

CURRICULUM JOURNALS
AND POST-SECONDARY TEACHING PUBLICATIONS

College Teaching
Dept 24–5
HELDREF Publications
4000 Albermarle St., N.W.
Washington, DC 20016

Quarterly interdisciplinary publication on issues related to teaching in higher education. Short articles focusing on educational outcomes and methods, and teacher concerns and roles. $38 a year.

Curriculum Inquiry
Subscription Department
John Wiley & Sons
605 Third Ave.
New York, NY 10158

Quarterly journal that features distinct and opposing ideas penned by curriculum specialists, evaluators, historians, psychologists, and anthropologists. $54 a year.

Curriculum Perspectives
Australian Curriculum Studies Association
c/o Russell Mathews
School of Education
Deakin University
Victoria 3217
Australia

Twice yearly journal specializing in case studies of curriculum in action and concept-based essays. Two newsletters are included in the annual subscription. $A35 a year.

Curriculum Review
Suite 1360
407 S. Dearborn St.
Chicago, IL 60605

Published nine times a year, with critical reviews of K–12 textbooks, supplements, multimedia, and software. $35 a year.

Feminist Teacher
Women's Studies Program
Memorial Hall East 131
Indiana University
Bloomington, IN 47405

Interdisciplinary essays and reviews targeted for K–college specialists interested in using women's studies and feminist pedagogy to combat sexism and other forms of oppression in the classroom. Published three times a year at a subscription rate of $20 annually.

Journal of Curriculum Studies
Tayor & Francis, Inc.
242 Cherry St
Philadelphia, PA 19106–1906
Bimonthly journal of the British Association of Curriculum Studies. Publishes scholarly essays on the theory and practice of curriculum and teaching. $112 a year.

Journal of Curriculum and Supervision
125 N. West St.
Alexandria, VA 22314–2798
A scholarly journal published in conjunction with the Association of Supervision and Curriculum Development. Places priority on articles that have a comprehensive, holistic, or interactive view of professional practice. $30 a year.

The Journal of Curriculum Theorizing
53 Falstaff Road
Rochester, NY 14609
An interdisciplinary quarterly journal of curriculum studies, including essays, political notes, book reviews, and poetry. $35 a year.

National Women's Studies Association Journal
Ablex Corporation
335 Chestnut St.
Norwood, NJ 07648
Quarterly publication that links feminist theory with teaching and activism. Publishes scholarly articles in women's studies, with a special emphasis on interdisciplinary and multicultural perspectives. $28.50 a year (NWSA members, $15).

Parabola
150 5th Avenue
New York, NY 10011
An interdisciplinary quarterly journal exploring myth and tradition. $18 a year.

Phenomenology + Pedagogy
Publication Services
4–116 Education North
University of Alberta
Edmonton, Alberta, Canada T6G2G5
A human science quarterly dedicated to interpretive and critical studies of a broad range of pedagogic relations and situations. $25 a year (students, $19).

Rethinking Schools
PO Box 93371
Milwaukee, WI 53202

A quarterly independent journal by local educators dedicated to helping parents, teachers, and students solve the many problems of schooling. $10 a year.

The Teacher's Journal
Education Department
Box 1938
Brown University
Providence, RI 02192

A new quarterly journal whose developers and contributors are classroom teachers. $5 a year.

Teaching Education
College of Education
University of South Carolina
Columbia, SC 29208

Twice yearly publication includes articles describing contemporary course descriptions at both the undergraduate and graduate levels, current texts, and resources effectively used by education professors. $15 a year.

The Teaching Professor
2718 Dryden Drive
Madison, WI 53704

Multidisciplinary monthly newsletter that combines practical techniques for improving classroom effectiveness with the more philosophical aspects of teaching. $39 a year.

ARTICLES AND BOOKS

Critical Teaching and Everyday Life (1987)
Ira Shor
Boston, MA: South End Press

Articulates a teaching theory coupled with political analysis of schooling rooted in a Freirean methodology.

Schubert, W., & Schubert, A. (1982). Teaching Curriculum Theory. *Journal of Curriculum Theory, 4* (2), 97–111

Provocative dialogue between two curriculum theorists exploring what conceptions of curriculum theorizing are implicit in one's classroom teaching.

Social Issues and the Curriculum (1987)
A. Molnar (Ed.)
Alexandria, VA: Association for Supervision and Curriculum Development

Ten essays challenging elementary, secondary, and college teachers to integrate a critical awareness of social issues into the curriculum.

Studies in Socialist Pedagogy (1978)
B. Ollman (Ed.)
New York: Monthly Review Press
Interdisciplinary collection of essays from leading socialist thinkers on approaches to teaching in higher education.

Teachers as Curriculum Planners (1988)
F. Michael Connelly & D. Jean Clandinin
New York: Teachers College Press
Guides teachers through the process of understanding their own personal thinking and practice in curriculum with a variety of illustrations from teachers' life histories on becoming and being a teacher.

The Teachers as Intellectual: Toward a Critical Pedagogy of Learning (1988)
H. A. Giroux
South Hadley, MA: Bergin & Garvey
Links educational reform efforts with teacher empowerment. Argues that the teacher's role is that of a transformative intellectual.

Eisner, E. (1988). Seeing the Forest and the Trees: Preparation of Curriculum Scholars in Research Universities. *Teaching Education, 2* (1), 87–90.
Outlines seven dimensions that ought to play a prominent role in the preparation of curriculum students who are grounded in both practice and curriculum scholarship.

Theory Into Practice
Over the years, this journal has provided insightful, well-balanced readings of the curriculum field. Three particularly relevant issues for teaching and thinking about curriculum are: Winter 1982, "Curriculum Theory"; Summer 1983, "Curriculum Change"; Winter 1986, "Beyond the Measured Curriculum."

Index

About the Editors

JAMES T. SEARS is an associate professor of curriculum in the Department of Educational Leadership and Policies at the University of South Carolina, and a research fellow at the South Carolina Educational Policy Center. Dr. Sears' areas of specialization are curriculum theory, teacher education, and gender studies. He earned graduate degrees from the University of Wisconsin–Madison and Indiana University. Dr. Sears is the editor of *Teaching Education,* has published in a variety of academic journals, and is the author of a book about growing up gay in the South.

J. DAN MARSHALL is an assistant professor in the Department of Curriculum and Instruction, and Associate Dean for Preservice Teacher Education at National College of Education in Evanston, Illinois. He received his Ph.D. in Curriculum and Instruction from the University of Texas at Austin, where he worked closely with selection and adoption, teachers' perceptions of curriculum, and teacher education reform efforts. His writings have been published in a variety of journals such as *Radical Teacher, Journal of Teacher Education, Changing Schools, Teacher Education,* and the *Journal of Curriculum Theorizing.*